To

_____

From

_____

Date

_____

"Each day proclaim the good news that he saves.
Publish his glorious deeds among the nations.
Tell everyone about the amazing things he does"
(Psalm 96:2-3 NLT).

Copyright © 2021 by Celebration Enterprises

All rights reserved. No portion of this book may be reproduced, stored in a retrieval system, or transmitted in any form or by any means—electronic, mechanical, photocopy, recording, scanning, or other—except for brief quotations in critical reviews or articles, without prior written permission of the author.

Scripture quotations marked KJV are taken from the King James Version of the Bible. Public domain.

Scripture quotations marked NIV are taken from the Holy Bible, New International Version®, NIV®. Copyright © 1973, 1978, 1984, 2011 by Biblica, Inc.™ Used by permission of Zondervan. All rights reserved worldwide. www.zondervan.com. The "NIV" and "New International Version" are trademarks registered in the United States Patent and Trademark Office by Biblica, Inc.™

Scripture quotations marked NKJV are taken from the New King James Version®. Copyright © 1982 by Thomas Nelson. Used by permission. All rights reserved.

Scripture quotations marked TLB are taken from The Living Bible copyright © 1971 by Tyndale House Foundation. Used by permission of Tyndale House Publishers Inc., Carol Stream, Illinois 60188. All rights reserved. The Living Bible, TLB, and The Living Bible logo are registered trademarks of Tyndale House Publishers.

Scripture quotations marked NLT are taken from the Holy Bible, New Living Translation, copyright © 1996, 2004, 2015 by Tyndale House Foundation. Used by permission of Tyndale House Publishers, Inc., Carol Stream, Illinois 60188. All rights reserved.

Scripture quotations marked MSG are taken from THE MESSAGE, copyright © 1993, 1994, 1995, 1996, 2000, 2001, 2002 by Eugene H. Peterson. Used by permission of NavPress. All rights reserved. Represented by Tyndale House Publishers, Inc.

New American Standard Bible®, Copyright © 1960, 1971, 1977, 1995, 2020 by The Lockman Foundation. All rights reserved. The "NASB," "NAS," "New American Standard Bible," and "New American Standard," are trademarks registered in the United States Patent and Trademark Office by The Lockman Foundation. Use of these trademarks requires the permission of The Lockman Foundation. For permission to use the NASB, please visit The Lockman Foundation website.

Scripture taken from the New Century Version® (NCV) Copyright © 2005 by Thomas Nelson. Used by permission. All rights reserved.

GOD'S WORD TRANSLATION (GW) Copyright © 1995, 2003, 2013, 2014, 2019, 2020 by God's Word to the Nations Mission Society. All rights reserved. No part of this publication may be reproduced, stored in a retrieval system, or transmitted in any form or by any means—for example, electronic, photocopy, recording—without prior written permission of the publisher.

Contemporary English Version® Copyright © 1995 American Bible Society. All rights reserved. Bible text from the Contemporary English Version (CEV) is not to be reproduced in copies or otherwise by any means except as permitted in writing by American Bible Society, 101 North Independence Mall East, FL 8, Philadelphia, PA 19106-2155 (www.americanbible.org).

The "Amplified" trademark (AMPC) is registered in the United States Patent and Trademark Office by The Lockman Foundation. Use of this trademark requires the permission of The Lockman Foundation. All rights reserved. For Permission to Quote information visit http://www.lockman.org/.

Scripture quotations from the New Revised Standard Version Bible (NRSV), copyright © 1989 the Division of Christian Education of the National Council of the Churches of Christ in the United States of America. Used by permission. All rights reserved.

For foreign and subsidiary rights, contact the author.

Cover design by Sara Young

ISBN: 978-1-957369-20-4   1 2 3 4 5 6 7 8 9 10

Printed in the United States of America

365 DAYS OF Faith, Hope & Courage

BROUGHT TO YOU BY
THE WORD FOR YOU TODAY

SCRIPTURE TRANSLATIONS AND PARAPHRASES

This book utilizes several different translations and paraphrases. Why? First, the Bible was originally written using 11,280 Hebrew, Aramaic, and Greek words, but the typical English translation uses only around 6,000 words. Obviously, nuances and shades of meaning can be missed, so it is always helpful to compare translations. Second, we often miss the full impact of familiar Bible verses, not because of poor translating, but simply because they have become so familiar! Therefore, we have deliberately used paraphrases in order to help you see God's truth in new, fresh ways.

ABBREVIATIONS USED:

AMPC   The Amplified Bible (Classic)
CEV   Contemporary English Version
GNT   Good News Translation in Today's English Version
NAS   New American Standard
NCV   New Century Version
NIV   New International Version
NKJV   New King James Version
NLT   New Living Translation
NRS   New Revised Standard Version
TLB   The Living Bible
TM   The Message

All unnoted references are from the King James Version.

New Year's Day - January 1

"Blessed are the poor in spirit."
Matthew 5:3 (NKJV)

THIS YEAR, LIVE BY THE BEATITUDES (1)

For the next few days, let's look at the Beatitudes (what our attitudes should be). Jesus said, "Blessed are the poor in spirit, for theirs is the kingdom of heaven." Now Jesus wasn't saying He's against you having money; He was saying He's against money having you. He will actually prosper you so that you can finance and fulfill His purposes on the earth. But He doesn't measure the size of your faith by the size of your bank balance. In one of His parables, Jesus called a wealthy man a "fool." That wasn't because the man was rich; it was because he wasn't "rich toward God" (Luke 12:21 NKJV). Old John D. Rockefeller once said, "I've made many millions, but they brought me no real happiness. I'd barter them all for the days I sat on an office stool in Cleveland and counted myself rich on three dollars a week." Having more money may give you social status, but serving God gives you kingdom-significance. Big difference! So keep your focus on what matters and live for what lasts. In Kemi, Finland, they built a sprawling ice castle that featured a theatre, a playground, an art gallery, and a chapel. The castle walls were 13 feet high and stretched for 1,650 feet. The chapel was a popular wedding venue, and the theatre could seat 3,000 people. In it, they held rock concerts, musicals, modern dance, and opera recitals. The problem was, its upkeep cost millions of dollars, and it all melted in the spring. Are you getting the idea? Focus on what lasts, not on what doesn't.

January 2

"Blessed are those who mourn."
Matthew 5:4 (NKJV)

THIS YEAR, LIVE BY THE BEATITUDES (2)

Jesus said, "Blessed are those who mourn, for they shall be comforted." Grief is the price we pay for love. One author writes: "We wonder when grief hits hard, 'Why did this happen? Was it to remind us of the brevity of life? Was it to deepen the faith of those who carry on?' It's hard to answer 'yes' when everything seems dark. The most important thing to us at that moment is to be relieved of the pain. But when we move through adversity rather than avoid it, we greet it differently. We become willing to let it teach us. Like Joseph, we see how God can use it for some larger end. Ultimately, mourning means facing what wounds us in the presence of the only One who can heal us." The Bible says, "Weeping may endure for a night, but joy cometh in the morning" (Psalm 30:5). Morning will come; God has promised it! Your grief will ease with time. The fact that you're willing to embrace the pain rather than try to escape it guarantees that. It's not that you'll forget; it's that you'll remember differently—with more gratitude and less grief. This beatitude answers two questions: (1) What happens to those who die in the Lord? "Let not your heart be troubled . . . In my Father's house are many mansions . . . I go to prepare a place for you . . . that where I am, there ye may be also" (John 14:1-3). (2) What about those of us who must go on living? "The . . . God of all comfort . . . comforts us . . . that we may be able to comfort those who are in any trouble" (2 Corinthians 1:3-4 NKJV).

January 3

"Blessed are the meek."
Matthew 5:5 (NKJV)

THIS YEAR, LIVE BY THE BEATITUDES (3)

In our macho world, meekness is often mistaken for weakness. But Jesus' definition of meekness pictures a powerful, majestic stallion that has been brought into submission. It hasn't lost any of its stamina. Whereas it once had a will of its own, it now yields to the will of another. The breaking process is complete; it now responds to the tug of the reins. Meekness involves three things: (1) Sensitivity to God's presence. In a good marriage, two people often understand each other's needs without a word having to be spoken. The time they've spent together makes them aware of the things that enrich and the things that offend, and their devotion to one another makes their marriage a top priority. And it's the same in your relationship with God. (2) Surrender to God's way. The key to breaking stubborn habits is not fighting them in your own strength. That only keeps your focus on the problem, intensifying its power. Changing your focus and submitting to God moment by moment is the key to winning, whether it's a problem or a hang-up. "Not that we are sufficient of ourselves to think of anything as being from ourselves, but our sufficiency is from God" (2 Corinthians 3:5 NKJV). (3) Submission to God's will. To understand the difference between submission and selfishness, you must ponder these words: "So they come to you as people do, they sit before you as My people, and they hear your words, but they do not do them; for with their mouth they show much love, but their hearts pursue their own gain" (Ezekiel 33:31 NKJV).

January 4

"Blessed are those who hunger and thirst for righteousness."
Matthew 5:6 (NKJV)

THIS YEAR, LIVE BY THE BEATITUDES (4)

This beatitude corrects two mistakes we make when it comes to our salvation. The first: that it's all about believing. The second: that it's all about behaving. Actually, it's about both! The new birth brings: (1) A position of righteousness. If you stacked up all your good works until they were as big as a mountain, you'd still come up short of the payment required to get into heaven. That's true before you become a Christian, and it's true after you become one. If you saw the movie *The Passion of the Christ* and thought, "Why did He have to die such a death?" here's the answer: "God made him who had no sin to be sin for us, so that in him we might become the righteousness of God" (2 Corinthians 5:21 NIV). The moment you accept Jesus as your Savior, you become "righteous" in God's eyes. Awesome! (2) A condition of righteousness. "Count yourselves dead to sin but alive to God" (Romans 6:11 NIV). Salvation is not just a position of righteousness you hold before God, but a condition of righteousness you live out before others every day. How do you do that? By valuing God's will more than your own (see Proverbs 3:5). By seeking to display the character qualities of Christ as described in Scripture: "Love, joy, peace, patience, kindness, goodness, faithfulness, gentleness [and] self-control" (Galatians 5:22-23 NAS). You say, "That's a tall order!" Yes, but we are not left to do it alone: "As the Spirit of the Lord works within us, we become more and more like him" (2 Corinthians 3:18 TLB).

January 5

"Blessed are the merciful, for they shall obtain mercy."
Matthew 5:7 (NKJV)

THIS YEAR, LIVE BY THE BEATITUDES (5)

Hurting an enemy puts you beneath them; taking revenge makes you even with them; forgiving sets you above them. The Bible says, "Never take revenge. Leave that to . . . God" (Romans 12:19 NLT). Revenge is not sweet; it leaves a bitter taste. It keeps you in such a constant stew that you're not able to enjoy God's blessing. Don't let that happen to you. Instead, choose to do these things: (1) Forgive and forget. Unforgiveness keeps you on the treadmill of resentment. Why is it so important to you to make others wrong and yourself right? If you're right but miserable, what good is it? Listen to Christ's words: "If you forgive men their trespasses, your heavenly Father will also forgive you" (Matthew 6:14 NKJV). Charles Spurgeon said, "When you bury a mad dog don't leave his tail above the ground." So forgive, bury it and move on. (2) Deal with the root of your anger. Sometimes the source of our anger is hidden from us; we are "acting out" the unresolved hurts within us. Exaggerated anger is often displaced anger. Instead of dealing with the person who hurt us, we vent our wrath on those closest to us. Ask God to show you where the real issue lies and help you to deal with it. (3) Take back your power. Mercy heals, but unforgiveness makes you a perpetual victim. Plus, while you're obsessing over the event and planning your payback, the other person is out enjoying life. God has promised you justice, so leave it in His hands. In fact, the only people you should consider getting even with are those who've helped you.

January 6

"Blessed are the pure in heart, for they shall see God."
Matthew 5:8 (NKJV)

THIS YEAR, LIVE BY THE BEATITUDES (6)

Make your heart "a controlled environment," because what happens there determines how you respond to life. When it comes to people, pastimes and pursuits, don't open yourself to anything that has the potential to take you captive or to make you cynical and cold-hearted. If you do, you'll shut yourself off from God's blessing. In his book, *Next Door Savior*, Max Lucado writes: "The countryside was flat and predictable, that's why the refinery stood out like a science-fiction city. The function of that maze of machinery is defined by its name. A refinery takes whatever comes in and purifies it so that it's ready to go out. It does for petroleum what your heart should do for you—remove the bad and utilize the good. Jesus said, 'A good man brings good things out of the good stored up in his heart (Luke 6:45 NIV). So here are some questions you need to ask yourself: 'When I'm criticized or ignored do I bite back or bite my tongue? When I'm on overload, do I blow my top or stay cool? When I hear gossip do I entertain it, silence it, or spread it? When somebody offends me, do I harbor a grudge or choose to forgive?' It all depends on the condition of your heart." When your heart has been purified, you'll begin to "see God" in people and situations you never noticed Him at work in before. Knowing first-hand the dangers of spiritual heart disease, the Psalmist wrote, "Create in me a clean heart, O God" (Psalm 51:10). If you need a spiritual catharsis, spend time in the presence of God.

January 7

"Blessed are the peacemakers."
Matthew 5:9 (NKJV)

THIS YEAR, LIVE BY THE BEATITUDES (7)

The story's told of two guys who were arguing about religion. One of them finally shouted, "Okay, you serve God your way, and I'll serve Him His way!" When we make our opinions a precondition for loving one another, we end up alienating one another. Much of what we fight about doesn't matter. Jesus said, "By this all will know that you are My disciples, if you have love for one another" (John 13:35 NKJV). It's not enough to love peace; you've got to become a peacemaker. When a fight erupted in the New Testament church over-eating certain foods, Paul stepped in: "Let us stop passing judgment on one another. Instead, make up your mind not to put any stumbling block or obstacle in the way of a brother or sister. I am convinced, being fully persuaded in the Lord Jesus, that nothing is unclean in itself. But if anyone regards something as unclean, then for that person it is unclean. If your brother or sister is distressed because of what you eat, you are no longer acting in love. Do not by your eating destroy someone for whom Christ died. Therefore do not let what you know is good be spoken of as evil. For the kingdom of God is not a matter of eating and drinking, but of righteousness, peace, and joy in the Holy Spirit, because anyone who serves Christ in this way is pleasing to God and receives human approval. Let us therefore make every effort to do what leads to peace and to mutual edification . . . So whatever you believe about these things keep between yourself and God" (Romans 14:13-22 NIV). So, be a peacemaker!

January 8

"Blessed are those who are persecuted for righteousness' sake."
Matthew 5:10 (NKJV)

THIS YEAR, LIVE BY THE BEATITUDES (8)

In Yellowstone National Park, there's an interesting tree called a Lodgepole Pine. Its cones can hang on for years before falling off. Even then, they remain tightly closed. They open only when they are in contact with intense heat. Whenever forest fires are raging, and all the trees are being destroyed, the heat opens these particular pinecones. As a result, they are the first to assist nature in repopulating the forest. Jesus said to His disciples, "Blessed are those who are persecuted for righteousness sake, for theirs is the kingdom of heaven." There's potential in each of us that's only released when we're under pressure or in a fiery trial. Job discovered this when God permitted Satan to test him. Job lost everything he had, including his children. And to add insult to injury, he was forced to endure the scorn of his wife and friends because of his unwavering faith. When it was over, Job, who got back twice as much as he lost, prayed, "I have heard of You by the hearing of the ear, but now my eye sees You" (Job 42:5 NKJV). It's one thing to hear how God works based on somebody else's experience. It's another to see it first-hand when you're wondering, "What did I do to deserve this?" or asking, "If God's really there, why am I here?" Why? (1) Because it's in the fire that you discover new aspects of God's care and character. (2) What turns worthless carbon into diamonds? Heat! Pressure! (3) In the fire, you discover that when others abandon you, God remains faithful.

January 9

"When I am afraid, I put my trust in you."
Psalm 56:3 (NIV)

SHRINK YOUR FEARS

Mary loved being a homemaker. She'd been married for thirty years to John, a successful businessman. Because John had always taken care of things, Mary had learned never to take risks. As a result, her biggest fear was that she'd be left alone one day. Sometimes she would tell her friends, "I hope I go before John because I don't think I could handle things by myself." But then John became ill, and Mary was placed in the position of caring for him, plus having to make all the decisions for them both. It was nerve-racking at first. But once she put her trust in God and decided to take charge, she made an interesting discovery: security doesn't lie in having things, but in handling them! She found that facing her fears was easy compared to the years she'd spent feeling inadequate, helpless, and dependent. Facing your fears is always easier than living with helplessness. In fact, when you let fear stop you, you end up living with feelings of dread and helplessness that are a hundred times worse than if you had just faced your fears and moved forward. The truth is, if you tell yourself often enough that you can't do something, you will be unable to do it—even though you have the talent, time, resources, strategy, and friends to accomplish it. Only those who say they can, do. Saying you believe in yourself and the God who lives within you may not guarantee your success, but saying you don't, will guarantee failure. So today, face your fears head-on and watch them shrink.

January 10

"Judge nothing before the appointed time."
1 Corinthians 4:5 (NIV)

HANDLING CRITICISM

Someone once quipped, "Every baseball team could use someone who knows how to play every position, never strikes out, and never makes an error. The only problem is, it's hard to make him set down his hotdog and come out of the spectator stands!" All of us need the advice and input of others. But you should only consider the advice of a critic when: (1) you know you are valued by the one who criticizes you; (2) the criticism is not tainted by his or her personal agenda; (3) the person is not naturally critical of everything; (4) the person will continue giving support after giving advice; (5) he or she has knowledge and success in the area of the criticism. What really hurts is the criticism of people who are important to you. It's hard to have your dream criticized by those you admire, love, and respect. But if you want to achieve your dream, you'll have to learn how to pay that price too. On the other hand, Stacy Allison, the first American woman to reach the summit of Mount Everest, points out that there are times in your life when it's okay not to listen to what other people are saying. "If I'd listened to other people, I wouldn't have climbed Mount Everest." If you have a God-given promise and purpose, and if your heart is right, then disregard unjustified criticism and stand on this Scripture: "Judge nothing before the appointed time; wait until the Lord comes. He will bring to light what is hidden in darkness and will expose the motives of the heart. At that time each will receive their praise from God."

January 11

"Teach me to do your will, for you are my God."
Psalm 143:10 (NIV)

LET IT GO

When God promises you something and it doesn't happen right away, it's easy to get impatient, start doubting Him, and think He needs you to go to work and make it happen. Abraham did that. God promised him children "as numerous as the stars" (Genesis 22:17 NIV). Tired of waiting, he took matters into his own hands and fathered Ishmael with his wife's maidservant, Hagar. And that's when his troubles began in earnest. Now, God loved Ishmael and had great plans for him, but Abraham had to let go of him in order to fulfill God's will. It was one of the most painful experiences of Abraham's life. (1) Refuse to let the enemy send anything into your life that will undermine what you have been waiting and praying for. (2) Be careful who you take advice from. Fathering Ishmael was a "good idea" Abraham's wife, Sarah, had. (3) Because you are willing to take responsibility for your actions doesn't mean there won't be consequences, long-lasting ones! Be careful where you lie down; getting up again may not be as easy as you think. (4) There are things you can give up effortlessly, and other things that will take every ounce of grace you've got. And it's especially hard to give up something you're attached to and see yourself reflected in, like a job you love, a house you're living in, or a relationship you're tied to. But when you've gone as far as you can with your "Ishmael" and you're ready to see God's promise fulfilled in your life, you must be willing to let it go.

January 12

"Mark . . . is profitable to me for the ministry."
2 Timothy 4:11 (KJV)

GIVE THEM ANOTHER CHANCE

Paul, who demanded 100 percent commitment from himself and those he worked with, was angry with Mark for wanting to take a break and go home and spend time with his family. But later, after reconsidering the whole thing, Paul gave Mark a second chance, saying, "He is profitable to me for the ministry." God sees potential in people, even flawed people, and we must too. When we believe in people and encourage them, they can move from the loss column to the profit column. Some years ago, in a manufacturing town in Scotland, a young lady gathered a class of street kids to teach them God's Word. To keep them coming back, the superintendent bought each of them a new suit. But after a few weeks, Bob, the most unpromising boy in the class, was missing. When she went looking for him, she found him with his clothes torn and dirty. So, the superintendent bought him another suit and invited him back again. After a few weeks, he dropped out of Sunday school once more. Disgusted, the teacher wanted to give up on him. But the superintendent said, "I'll buy him a third suit if he will promise to attend regularly." Bob did. He kept coming, committed his life to Christ, and studied for the ministry. That discouraged, forlorn, ragged, runaway boy was Robert Morrison, the great missionary to China who translated the Bible into the Chinese language and opened the kingdom of heaven to countless millions who live there. So, who are you thinking of giving up on? Don't do it! Give them, and God, another chance!

January 13

"These trials will show that your faith is genuine."
1 Peter 1:7 (NLT)

BUMPS

It is impossible to tell by looking at a person how much faith they have. Compare your faith to a bucket of water; you only discover how much is inside when somebody bumps it. Likewise, when life bumps you, you spill out what you are full of. Maybe you took a financial hit in the last few years: bump! What spilled out, fear or faith? Maybe you, or a loved one, received bad news from the doctor and you're going for tests: bump! What splashed over the side? Dreading the worst or trusting God for the best? People can't tell by looking at you how much faith you have, but they can tell by listening to you. In life, bumps are going to happen. You will be tested. And the purpose of the test is not just to reveal your faith, but to refine it. God doesn't test your faith in order to know how much you have. He already knows. No, He tests your faith so that you can know—and start strengthening it. Stop and consider the hardest thing that's going on in your life right now, then ask yourself, "Is this situation decreasing my faith or increasing it?" The Bible says: "These trials will show that your faith is genuine. It is being tested as fire tests and purifies gold—though your faith is far more precious than mere gold. When your faith remains strong through many trials, it will bring you much praise and glory and honor on the day when Jesus Christ is revealed to the whole world."

January 14

"Lord, 'Increase our faith.'"
Luke 17:5 (NKJV)

MOVING FROM DOUBT TO FAITH

Why do we experience so much doubt? (1) Because doubt satisfies our need for self-protection. We don't like to be wrong, to get hurt, or to fail, so our subconscious reasoning says, "It's easier not to trust, to lower my expectations so I won't be disappointed." But you are disappointed, aren't you? Why? Because of your doubt. (2) Because doubting comes easy. We don't wake up in the morning and say to ourselves, "Today I'm going to doubt God." No, doubt moves into a vacuum, it takes over when we don't do the right things. "Faith cometh by hearing, and hearing by the word of God" (Romans 10:17). If you don't keep your mind filled with God's Word, you'll be constantly assailed by doubts. (3) Because doubters are easy to find. Sometimes the people around us dwell on all the obstacles and difficulties, opening the door to doubt. And once that stream starts flowing you get carried along with it. (4) Because doubting is contagious. Doubt is easier to catch than the common cold, and its carriers are words. The Bible says, "You are trapped by your own words" (Proverbs 6:2 CEV). The words you speak (and listen to) will either build you up or tear you down, increase your faith or decrease it. For example, "What will I do?" versus, "In God's strength I can handle it." Or "It's awful" versus, "It's a learning experience." Or "I see no way out" versus "It's not too big for God." Words are powerful things. They determine your outlook and approach to life. So in order to move from doubt to faith, you must start eliminating unscriptural words from your life!

January 15

"Approved and acceptable and in right relationship with Him."
2 Corinthians 5:21 (AMPC)

WHY GOD ACCEPTS YOU (1)

God loves and accepts you as much on your bad days as He does on your good ones. In a performance-based society, that's easy to forget. But you mustn't! God's acceptance is based on your standing in Christ, not the state of your life at a given time. "For our sake He made Christ [virtually] to be sin Who knew no sin, so that in and through Him we might become [endued with, viewed as being in, and examples of] the righteousness of God [what we ought to be, approved and acceptable and in right relationship with Him, by His (not our) goodness]." Think of the cross as a trading post. There God took every sin you'd ever commit and laid it upon Jesus. And the moment you place your trust in Christ, God takes all of Christ's righteousness and wraps you up in it. From that point on, He sees you only one way—in Christ. How liberating! Liberating, because now you realize that your worth isn't based on what you do, but on who you are in relationship to Christ. God actually assigned value to you by allowing Jesus to die for you. "But I can't believe that God doesn't care about what I do." You're right! And your rewards in heaven will be based on your stewardship here on earth. God wants you to do good works, but He doesn't want you to depend on them; He wants you to do them out of love for Him. Once you understand your position and who you are in Christ, you begin doing the right things for the right reasons.

January 16

"Approved and acceptable and in right relationship with Him."
2 Corinthians 5:21 (AMPC)

WHY GOD ACCEPTS YOU (2)

The world tells us that our value is connected to our "doing." Growing up, we're constantly compared. When asked why we were not doing as well as our brother or sister, we felt we were doing our best, and we had no answer. So we determined to try harder, but no matter how hard we tried, somebody still wasn't satisfied with us. We were still getting the message, "Something's wrong with you." This leaves us burned out, confused, and turned off. It drives many of us into therapy when all we need is the assurance of God's unconditional love! Your wrong behaviors won't be changed until you know you're loved by God apart from what you do. And that's what Jesus made possible through the cross. Why is this important to believe? Because until you know who you are in Christ, you'll stumble along believing that your acceptance with God is performance-based. Your acceptance with God *is* based on performance, but not yours—Christ's! Jesus loves you unconditionally and is committed to working with you. And the best part is, He doesn't condemn you while He's doing it! He understands your temperament, your struggles, and even the faulty foundation upon which you've based your self-worth. He not only understands—He cares. Once you enter into a personal relationship with Christ, He begins a process of relieving your pain, revealing your true value, and releasing your gifts. Bit by bit, He restores everything Satan has stolen from you. And while all this is happening, you are positioned securely "in Christ." Therefore, you're always acceptable to Him.

January 17

"Breath came into them, and they lived, and stood upon their feet."
Ezekiel 37:10 (NKJV)

REJOICING IN TROUBLE

Your hopes may be dead, and your dreams buried, but God can breathe into them again. Ezekiel stood in a valley of dead, dry bones. That's about as bad as it gets! Right? Then something amazing happened. God said to the Prophet, "Prophesy . . . and say . . . 'Thus says the Lord God: "Come from the four winds, O breath, and breathe on these slain, that they may live."' "So I prophesied as He commanded me, and breath came into them, and they lived, and stood upon their feet, an exceedingly great army" (vv. 9-10 NKJV). Any time you see a man or woman enjoying great success in God's kingdom, there's a good chance they've been through the valley of devastation, hurt, and rejection. It was after he had been thrown out of the city, stoned and left for dead, that Paul spoke of being taken up into the third heaven and experiencing things too wonderful to speak of on earth (See 2 Corinthians 12:2-4). It was after John was exiled to a penal colony in Patmos that he penned the words, "I was in the Spirit, and I heard behind me a loud voice like a trumpet" (Revelation 1:10 NIV). As a result, he wrote the book of Revelation. The Psalmist said, "In the day of trouble . . . my head will be exalted above the enemies who surround me . . . I will sing . . . to the Lord" (Psalm 27:5-6 NIV). That's how you "glory in tribulation," then look back and be able to say, "Thank you for the experience, Lord. Without it I'd never have gotten to know You like I do today."

January 18

"God has... given us... a sound mind."
2 Timothy 1:7 (NKJV)

SOUND THINKING

The Bible says, "God has not given us a spirit of fear, but of power and of love and of a sound mind." In order to improve your life, you must change two things: (1) Your thought processes. Gordon MacDonald says: "People who are out of shape mentally fall victim to ideas and systems that are destructive to the human spirit. They've not been taught how to think, nor have they set themselves to the life-long pursuit of the growth of the mind, so they grow dependent upon the thoughts and opinions of others. Rather than deal with ideas and issues, they reduce themselves to lives filled with rules, regulations, and programs." The moment you think you know it all, you've merely stopped thinking. (2) Your expectations. The story is told of a man who went to a fortuneteller. She said to him, "You'll be poor and miserable until you're fifty." The man asked her, "What will happen then?" She replied, "Then you'll get used to it." Be honest; how many successful people do you know who are apathetic and negative? None! Faith produces excitement, commitment, energy—characteristics that help you achieve success. If you'd like to possess these qualities, then raise your expectation level and bring it into alignment with God's promises. "Whatever things you ask when you pray, believe that you receive them, and you will have them" (Mark 11:24 NKJV). Do you want to succeed where you've failed before? To become the person you always hoped to be? Don't start by changing your actions, start by changing your mind. Renew it daily with God's Word. Nothing else you do will have as great an impact.

January 19

"His compassions... are new every morning."
Lamentations 3:22-23 (NIV)

WHAT'S NEW?

Are you going through a hard time at the moment? You're not alone! Things were so bad in Israel that when Jeremiah wrote one of the books of the Bible, he called it Lamentations. In a positive-thinking, feel-good world, that's not exactly a best-selling title. Jeremiah describes God's people as a "widow" and a "slave," and says, "All her friends have dealt treacherously with her; they have become her enemies" (Lamentations 1:2 NKJV). As you move through the book verse by verse, things just keep going from bad to worse as God's people reap what they have sown. Then suddenly, in the middle of all his lamenting, when you think things can't get any worse, Jeremiah writes, "Because of the Lord's great love we are not consumed, for his compassions never fail. They are new every morning; great is your faithfulness" (Lamentations 3:22-23 NIV). Isn't that wonderful? God's love, compassion, and faithfulness have been placed in an account that cannot be overdrawn, that you don't have to contribute to, and that'll last as long as you live. In a world that doesn't seem to care, where only the fittest survive, that's good to know. Next time somebody says to you, "What's new?" tell them, "God's love, compassion, and faithfulness." The dictionary defines compassion as "tenderness of heart that disposes a person to overlook injuries or to treat an offender better than he or she deserves." So, when you wake up each day, be like the lady who prayed, "Lord, I'm glad Your mercies are new every morning, because I sure used up all of yesterdays."

January 20

"He heals the brokenhearted."
Psalm 147:3 (NIV)

HEALING FOR YOUR GRIEF

One of the most moving scenes in Scripture is Jesus weeping at the graveside of Lazarus. It's not that He was powerless to change the situation, which He did, but that He empathizes with us in our time of loss. "He heals the brokenhearted and binds up their wounds." The Lord didn't promise to protect us from pain and loss, but to bring us through it. Perhaps these suggestions will help: (1) Don't isolate. Expand your "family." "Better a nearby friend than a distant family" (Proverbs 27:10 MSG). If you don't have family nearby, reach out to caring people who are close at hand. As part of a group, you discover that you're not alone, that mourning isn't sickness or self-indulgence, and that sharing brings healing. (2) Don't deny your loss. "The memory of the just is blessed" (Proverbs 10:7). When you're around friends, don't hesitate to talk about your loss. When you do, you're saying it's okay for them to share their memories too. A burden shared is a burden lightened. (3) Don't try to do it all. "There is a time to cry" (Ecclesiastes 3:4 NCV). Because grief is draining, you'll need more rest than usual. So, while your ability to function is reduced, let others help with the everyday stuff like cooking, cleaning, and shopping until you feel stronger. (4) Don't neglect your legitimate needs. Respect your body by using the acronym DEER (drink, eat, exercise, rest) to help you stay focused and set healthy boundaries. Nobody knows how you feel better than you, so give yourself permission to say, "No thanks," or "I'll take a rain check," without feeling guilty.

January 21

"That is why a man leaves his father and mother."
Genesis 2:24 (NIV)

ROOTS AND WINGS (1)

You'll know you've succeeded as a parent when your children are able to leave you and go out and build a successful life on their own. You will never cut them off, but there comes a time when you must "cut the apron strings," and let them stand on their own two feet. Remember, the children you are raising right now belonged to God before they belonged to you. "The earth is the Lord's . . . and all who live in it" (Psalm 24:1 NIV). You are a teacher, not an owner, and your opportunity to teach them is amazingly brief. Your children were born to "leave," not stay. You can't control their ticking biological clock. Your job is to prepare them for leaving. For the next few days, let's talk about giving your child roots and wings. "Roots." Before fruit develops, roots must thrive. And healthy roots require healthy soil with the right elements for feeding and protecting plants. Roots also depend on attachment to the soil. There are two kinds of families. The first offers "insecure attachment." Their parent-child connection is ambiguous, ambivalent, indifferent or even neglectful, making kids feel emotionally unprotected, uncertain they're wanted and loved, though they desperately need both of these things. These children lack confidence, self-worth, emotional strength, and the courage to take risks. The second offers "secure attachment." Their parent-child connection is expressed and consistently reinforced. Even during necessary absences, their children feel safe and securely attached. Such kids become spiritually, socially, and emotionally capable, with the self-worth and courage required to face the challenges life puts in their path.

January 22

"That is why a man leaves his father and mother."
Genesis 2:24 (NIV)

ROOTS AND WINGS (2)

On the journey from adolescence to adulthood, your kids will experience insecurity, contradictions, and mood swings. They will send you conflicting signals: needing closeness, yet distance; connection, yet independence; all at the same time. They will pull you in with one hand and push you away with the other. You must understand that your kids still need to feel securely attached, even while they're distancing from you. When they push you away, you must show maturity, remembering that it's not personal; it's just how they test their ability to become independent adults. Minutes, hours, or days later, they are your child again, wanting to be up close. It's the "tug-o'-war" of parenting youngsters, and it will resolve itself the right way if you handle it with understanding. Above all, contain your hurt and anger. "Fathers (mothers), do not … provoke your children to anger [do not exasperate them to resentment]" (Ephesians 6:4 AMPC). The worst outcome of frequent run-ins with your kids is that it produces long-term discouragement in them. Long after the "mop-up," your child can "lose heart" (See Colossians 3:21 NASB) and have a "crushed spirit" (MSG). In some cases, they give up trying altogether. In western cultures, girls hold onto the parent-child "rope" longer than boys, generally distancing later, and with less finality. Boys tend toward earlier, longer-lasting distancing. When you deny your son or daughter the God-given need for gradual latitude, they'll disconnect farther and faster. Use wisdom, "let out the rope" gradually, and they'll learn adult skills and stay more closely connected.

January 23

"That is why a man leaves his father and mother."
Genesis 2:24 (NIV)

ROOTS AND WINGS (3)

The second gift you must give your child is "wings." They are born to fly, not stay in the nest. By becoming overly protective and stifling them in the name of responsible parenting, you'll end up losing them. Jesus said children are designed to leave and go out and build a home of their own. Their drive for freedom is God-given, not a sign of ingratitude, disrespect or rebellion. A good carpenter works with the grain, not against it. So what should you do? Before your child demands outright independence, teach them how to handle it wisely. Give them opportunities to prove their readiness, and as they demonstrate trustworthiness, increase their autonomy—and vice versa. Let them know that in life you don't inherit happiness, you earn it. Be flexible – but take charge. Let your child know they can't demand privileges like driving, dating, and spending money—they have to prove themselves worthy. Help them see how they can earn increased autonomy, or lose it, and how they can earn it back. Make them responsible for their own freedom by letting them know that it's not a right or a gift, but a reward for showing maturity. A mother bird doesn't push her baby out of the nest until she knows it's ready to start flying. The gift of freedom to an unprepared child isn't "wings," it's an invitation to catastrophe! Don't sign their "bill of rights" to autonomy until they've proven they can handle their agreed-upon responsibility.

January 24

"For this reason a man shall leave his father and mother."
Genesis 2:24 (NIV)

ROOTS AND WINGS (4)

You can't always prevent your child from getting hurt. "In this world you will have trouble" (John 16:33 NIV). Either they'll get hurt and learn to deal with reality, or suffocate in your cocoon, never becoming mature – a hurt much sadder and much more painful and debilitating. What's involved in giving your child wings? (1) Realize that without autonomy, they'll never become a healthy adult. This involves learning things like clear thinking, being responsible for their own decisions, learning from bad choices how to make better ones, being free to make mistakes and pay the price of learning, and experiencing what it means to grow up. (2) Don't treat their need for autonomy as evidence you're failing as a parent. Indeed, if they fail to distance, you should question your parenting style! Making them independent is biblical and effective parenting. (3) Don't mistake their distancing as a rejection of you. It's not abandonment of you; it's advancement for them. It's not proof of ingratitude or selfishness and rebellion; it's their real-world opportunity to demonstrate your success as a parent. When they don't want to attend Uncle Bert's family reunion, don't tighten your grip to "save the family from disintegrating." The family is meant to disengage, like cells splitting off and multiplying. The Bible says we are to "Be fruitful and increase in number and fill the earth" (Genesis 9:1 NIV). They can't stay in the nest and fulfill their destiny. Release them, then get a life of your own! That's your responsibility—not endless parenting. Let out the rope, trust God, and they'll be back to see their "very cool" parents.

January 25

"That is why a man leaves his father and mother."
Genesis 2:24 (NIV)

ROOTS AND WINGS (5)

Healthy parenting calls for finding the right mix of autonomy with each of your children. Some kids distance sooner, some later; some take small tentative steps, some leap confidently into the gap. There are no "good" or "bad" kids when it comes to this, just more or less challenging ones. As a parent, you discover by trial and error what works for you and your kids. Criticizing, controlling, threatening incarceration, preaching, shaming, etc., are futile, counterproductive, and a sign you have lost your grip. It will only increase their flight instinct, or make them feel insecure, as though no one is really at the helm. Pretending you have "got it together" as a parent is a well-intentioned but costly game. Don't be intimidated by the idea of being honest and transparent with your kids. It's less stressful for you both, and it's much more effective. Kids know that they are imperfect—and they know you are too. So don't be afraid to say, "I'm learning to parent growing kids, like you're learning to be one. I need your help to be good at it, to discover what works for us both, and to help you be good at it too. Are you willing to be on the team and learn together?" That kind of honesty draws a positive response. It's also good role-modeling, teaching them humility and cooperation. As coach and players united, focus on winning together and learning to improve, not on competing or dominating. Succeeding or failing as a family is all about learning and growing!

January 26

"By your patience possess your souls."
Luke 21:19 (NKJV)

GOD'S TIMETABLE

When God makes you wait for something longer than you want to, He's teaching you patience. Your emotions are like a wild horse—they need to be reined in. "Patient endurance is what you need now, so that you will continue to do God's will. Then you will receive all that he has promised" (Hebrews 10:36 NLT). Your impatience will just make you and everybody around you miserable, but it won't rush God. He works according to His own plan and timetable: "In due season we shall reap" (Galatians 6:9). "Due season" is God's season, not yours. You're in a hurry, He isn't. He takes time to do things right. You may not know what He's doing, but He does. And that'll have to be good enough for you. God's timing seems to be His own business. He's never late, but He usually isn't early either. He takes every opportunity to develop in you the fruit of patience. But other fruits are being developed in you as well. There are several things that must arrive at the finish line at the same time in order for you to win the race. Developed potential, without character, doesn't glorify God. If you were to become a huge success and yet be arrogant and harsh with people, that wouldn't be pleasing to the Lord. So when you get ahead of yourself in one area, He gently but firmly blocks your progress in that area until the others catch up. You don't appreciate any of this while it's happening, but later on, you realize what a mess you'd have made if things had been done on your timetable instead of God's.

January 27

"Anger resides in the lap of fools."
Ecclesiastes 7:9 (NIV)

DON'T LOSE CONTROL!

The word "anger" is just one letter short of the word "danger." When you lose control, you risk losing other things as well, like the respect of others or the chance to find a constructive solution. Anger toward human suffering is not only appropriate, it's the catalyst for change. Paul writes, "Be angry . . . but . . . don't stay angry" (Ephesians 4:26 MSG). The Chinese have a saying: "Anger is the wind that blows out the lamp of the mind." So: (1) Before you react, take a walk. It burns off excess adrenaline and it's more effective than stewing. It also helps you to think more clearly and handle things in a way you won't regret. "A quick-tempered person does foolish things" (Proverbs 14:17 NIV). (2) Recognize the things you can't control. You can't control other people's attitudes and actions, or unforeseen events such as cancelled flights and traffic jams. "What should I do?" you ask. Count your blessings, particularly the fact that you have God, salvation, your health, your family, your job, and a car to get to it, etc. (3) Be careful where you vent. It's one thing to be angry, it's another to "sound off" at the wrong time. "A fool uttereth all his mind: but a wise man keepeth it in till afterwards" (Proverbs 29:11). It's okay to share your feelings with those you trust and who are not the targets of your anger. But be careful, your words can come back and bite you! (4) Keep your distance from angry people. The Bible says, "Don't hang out with angry people" (Proverbs 22:24 MSG). Anger, like joy and gratitude, is contagious, so keep your distance.

January 28

"I consider everything a loss ... that I may gain Christ."
Philippians 3:8 (NIV)

THE COST OF A GOD-GIVEN DREAM (1)

Your dream will never be fulfilled unless you're willing to pay the price that comes with it. And that price is paid not once, but over a lifetime. First, there's the initial cost. You will have to make personal and sometimes painful sacrifices. You may have to walk away from attractive options and valued relationships because they don't fit into God's plan for your life. Leaving things that have given you your security and your identity will require grit and grace that only God can provide. Paul's résumé included being "of the tribe of Benjamin, a Hebrew of the Hebrews ... a Pharisee." Paul once had wealth and status. Scholars reckon that when he committed his life to Christ, as was customary, his friends and family would have held a funeral service and considered him "dead" to them from that point forward. Paul's calling was to cover Asia with the gospel and write half the New Testament. But great assignments call for great sacrifice. And Paul wasn't alone. "By faith Moses, when he had grown up, refused to be known as the son of Pharaoh's daughter. He chose to be mistreated along with the people of God rather than to enjoy the fleeting pleasures of sin. He regarded disgrace for the sake of Christ as of greater value than the treasures of Egypt, because he was looking ahead to his reward" (Hebrews 11:24-26 NIV). So the question is: has God given you a dream? Do you have the faith and fortitude to fulfill it? Have you counted the cost, and are you ready to pay it?

January 29

"I have worked ... been in prison ... been flogged."
2 Corinthians 11:23 (NIV)

THE COST OF A GOD-GIVEN DREAM (2)

Second, there's the ongoing cost. We all want what successful people have. The problem is, we don't want to pay the price they paid initially and continue to pay every day. Paul spells out the true story behind his success: "I have worked much harder, been in prison more frequently, been flogged more severely, and been exposed to death again and again. Five times I received from the Jews the forty lashes minus one. Three times I was beaten with rods, once I was [stoned], three times I was shipwrecked, I spent a night and a day in the open sea, I have been constantly on the move. I have been in danger from rivers, in danger from bandits, in danger from my fellow Jews, in danger from Gentiles; in danger in the city, in danger in the country, in danger at sea; and in danger from false believers. I have labored and toiled and have often gone without sleep; I have known hunger and thirst and have often gone without food; I have been cold and naked. Besides everything else, I face daily the pressure of my concern for all the churches" (2 Corinthians 11:23-28 NIV). Most of us have a vague notion that someday we'll have to make sacrifices, but the price will have to be paid sooner than we think. Not expecting that, many of us become discouraged. Some of us table our dreams, putting them on hold. Others have abandoned them entirely. The question you must answer is: "Twenty-five years from now, what will I wish I had done today?" That's the cost of a God-given dream.

January 30

"I have suffered the loss of all things."
Philippians 3:8 (NKJV)

THE COST OF A GOD-GIVEN DREAM (3)

Stop and listen carefully to what some of the people around you are saying. Many of them express regret because they backed off from their dream of earlier years: a career not pursued, an opportunity left unseized, or a relationship allowed to wither and die. Decades later they come back to it and think more about it. But for some, it's too late. They can't achieve their dream at any price. For others, the dream is possible, but the price is much higher. In his book, *Put Your Dream to the Test*, John Maxwell writes, "Going after a dream is like climbing a mountain. We will never make it to the summit if we are carrying too much weight. As we enter each new phase of the climb, we face a decision. Do we take on more things to carry, lay down things that won't help us climb, exchange what we have for something else, or stop climbing altogether? Most people try to take too many things with them . . . when successful people climb, they let go of things or start changing them in order to reach a higher level . . . The payments required for reaching a dream never stop. The journey continues only if you keep paying the price. The higher you want to go, the more you must give up. The greater the price you pay, the greater the joy you feel when you finally reach your dream." Someone said a task without a vision is drudgery. A vision without a task is daydreaming. But a task with a vision is the pathway to victory and achievement.

January 31

"My Presence will go with you, and I will give you rest."
Exodus 33:14 (NIV)

SECURE IN GOD'S PRESENCE

Unless you spend time in God's presence, you will always have an underlying sense of insecurity. There are certain people we draw security from just by being around them; their presence and approach to life make us feel better. Likewise, when you need to be lifted and strengthened, you must spend time with God. Being in His presence is like being in a room filled with perfume; you take the fragrance of it with you when you leave. Moses spent a great deal of time with God. He knew that without God's presence, he wasn't worth two cents. Can you imagine being responsible for the daily care of two million people, getting them out of one country and into another—on foot? It's mind-boggling. And as if that wasn't bad enough, the Israelites spent much of their time complaining about their lot in life and finding fault with Moses. When things went wrong, he was their favorite target. It was an ideal situation for losing your mind. But God told Moses, "My Presence will go with you, and I will give you rest." God can give you rest in the midst of trouble, and peace in the midst of conflict. That includes a difficult workplace or a home that's in constant turmoil. God's presence can help you to show love in the face of mistreatment, and patience in times of stress. It can help you to bring positive change without a lot of words and end up feeling good about the way you handled things. So, spend time in God's presence today.

February 1

"God, the source of hope, will fill you ... with ... peace."
Romans 15:13 (NLT)

DEALING WITH LAYOFFS

We often use the word "hope" when we want something to happen, but we're not sure it will. We hope fixing the car won't cost too much. We hope our kids graduate. We hope the medical test goes well. But our hope isn't wishful thinking; it's trusting God. So how do you keep hope alive when you're out of work? "God, the source of hope, will fill you ... with ... peace because you trust in him." Jon Gordon says: "The media-created frenzy of panic is negatively impacting [our] collective psychology ... people are more stressed than ever ... like a horror movie, what you fear starts to happen ... However, the economy isn't some abstract entity ... Our thoughts and behaviors create it. So how can we trust ... when everything we've trusted in is falling apart? My answer: we've put our faith in the wrong things ... and the cracks have been exposed. It's a wake-up call. Charles West says, 'We turn to God when our foundations are shaking, only to learn that it's God who's shaking them.' Security is an illusion. There's no power in a bank account ... no peace in an investment portfolio ... our true purpose isn't in a retirement plan ... We're meant to trust God ... true power exists not in what seems strong and secure, but in what is silent and unseen ... Instead of starting your morning watching TV, take a walk of prayer; instead of looking down at the newspaper, look up to heaven." Prayer: "Lord, sometimes my hopes are just wishes but hoping in You is different; You give me solid ground. Today my hope is based on Your faithfulness and Your promise to meet my every need. Thank You; I know You'll do it. Amen."

February 2

"I am your shield, your very great reward."
Genesis 15:1 (NIV)

DON'T BE AFRAID, GOD IS WITH YOU

When God sends you into a new situation or asks you to do something you've never done before, you'll experience uncertainty, fear, and have a lot of questions. God knows that; that's why the promise He gives you is always equal to the project He gives you. Imagine selling your house, packing up your belongings, putting your family in the car, and heading down the road without having a clue where you're going. Sound crazy? That's what God asked Abraham to do. But He told him, "Do not be afraid... I am your shield, your very great reward." The word "shield" means God will protect you, and the word "reward" means He will provide everything you need. Does that mean you won't experience fear? No, it means you must trust Him in spite of your fears! Dr. Bernard Vittone says: "As we age, we lose the ability to distinguish between the negative anxiety associated with work, stress, and tension, and the positive type that's a natural and exciting part of trying something new. As a result, we become more fearful and avoid anxiety-producing situations. When that happens, the desire for safety keeps us stuck in neutral. Trying to avoid risk is like trying to avoid living; without a goal to strive for, you stop growing altogether." If Abraham had refused to obey God because he feared the unknown and the untried, he'd have missed his "very great reward." So press through your fear today and claim the blessing God has promised you on the other side of it. Don't be afraid; God is with you!

February 3

"Benaiah ... went down into a pit on a snowy day and killed a lion."
2 Samuel 23:20 (NIV)

COURAGE WITH COLD FEET

Benaiah was one of King David's "mighty men." His résumé reads: "Benaiah ... a valiant fighter ... He ... went down into a pit on a snowy day and killed a lion." That's what is called "courage with cold feet." The greatest courage of all is showing courage in the face of fear. Someone said, "Courage is just fear that has said its prayers." When you know you have heard clearly from God, you are filled with faith in that moment. It puts steel in your spine. But then, as you move out in faith, you encounter the lions of fear. "What if this doesn't work? What if I fail? What will people say?" Suddenly, you're having an attack of the "what ifs." Mark Twain said, "Courage is resistance to fear, mastery of fear, not absence of fear." You have to decide whether you're going to become a warrior —or a worrier. There's no middle ground. When you're faced with a health crisis, or a family crisis, or a financial crisis, you either choose to stand on God's Word and fight or give in to worry. On this side of heaven, we will never fully understand why bad things happen to good people. But we know that God is good—all the time! So when bad things happen, you will either give in to fear and allow it to destroy your peace and well-being, or you will become a warrior armed with God's Word and rise up against it. When fear threatens to engulf your mind, stand up with the Psalmist and say, "Whenever I am afraid, I will trust in You" (Psalm 56:3 NKJV).

February 4

"Faith is the substance of things hoped for."
Hebrews 11:1 (KJV)

YOU NEED FAITH

You don't need faith unless you're hoping for something. Hope establishes the goal; faith is the bridge that gets you to it. There's no need to build a bridge if you're not going anywhere. But if you're going after something you can't reach on your own, you need the bridge of faith to get you there. "This is the victory that overcometh the world, even our faith" (1 John 5:4). Never has it been more essential to teach moral standards. But unless we also teach people how to stand in faith in God's Word, they'll end up using willpower and discipline to fight the Devil, and they'll lose. Jesus told Peter, "I have prayed for you, that your faith should not fail" (Luke 22:32 NKJV). When you're up to your neck in problems and don't know which way to turn, speak to yourself and say, "Faith, don't fail me now!" The Bible says, "Faith cometh by hearing, and hearing by the word of God" (Romans 10:17). It's in hearing yourself declare God's Word that your faith grows. And here's another Scripture: "But the word which they heard did not profit them, not being mixed with faith in those who heard it" (Hebrews 4:2 NKJV). You can have an expression of faith yet not enjoy the benefits of faith. You can get excited about a sermon in church, yet nothing changes in your life. You've got to get the "mix" right. You've got to take what you hear and mix it with what you think, say, and do. Faith is not an emotion; it's a decision to stand on God's Word.

February 5

"Let us hold tightly without wavering to the hope."
Hebrews 10:23 (NLT)

HOPE

Some of the people around you today are living without hope. Look at them; they smile, but their eyes are dead. They talk, but the music has left their voice. They're like mannequins: all dressed up and going nowhere because they feel hopeless. But as a follower of Christ, you don't have to live that way. "Let us hold tightly without wavering to the hope we affirm, for God can be trusted to keep his promise." Our hope isn't luck, like winning the lottery. No, it's confidence that God will do what He said. No one knew the truth of this better than David. He had every reason to lose hope. After Samuel anointed him to be Israel's next king, he had to wait for seven years while a paranoid ruler occupied the throne. He had to flee for his life and hide in caves surrounded by enemies. He saw Israel devastated, his friends killed, and his family taken captive. But he never wavered or threw in the towel. Faced with circumstances that would wipe many of us out, the Psalmist said, "My hope is in You" (Psalm 39:7 NKJV). "Weeping may endure for a night, but joy comes in the morning" (Psalm 30:5 NKJV). In other words, "It's going to get better!" You can't lose with an attitude like that. David became king because he never lost confidence in the promises of God. They kept him focused; they kept him on top of the circumstances; they kept him going! What has God promised you? Stand on His Word and declare, "If God promised it, I believe it, and that settles it!"

February 6

*"The boat was now in the middle of
the sea, tossed by the waves."*
Matthew 14:24 (NKJV)

WHEN YOU'RE IN A STORM

Talk about a person caught in a storm! Jeremiah could tell you the height of the waves and the speed of the wind. He realized how fast he was sinking, so he shifted his gaze. "But this I call to mind, and therefore I have hope: The steadfast love of the Lord never ceases, his mercies never come to an end; they are new every morning; great is thy faithfulness. 'The Lord is my portion,' says my soul, 'therefore I will hope in him'" (Lamentations 3:21-24 RSV). When Jeremiah turned his eyes away from the waves to look to God, he started to recite a quintet of promises: (1) "The steadfast love of the Lord never ceases." (2) "His mercies never come to an end." (3) "They are new every morning." (4) "Great is thy faithfulness." (5) "The Lord is my portion." The storm didn't cease, but Jeremiah's discouragement did. Paul talks about "speaking to one another in psalms and hymns and spiritual songs, singing and making melody in your heart to the Lord" (Ephesians 5:19 NKJV). Great hymns are a great help. They help you to get your eyes on the One who walks on the water and calms the storm. "Great is Thy faithfulness, O God my father; There is no shadow of turning with Thee; Thou changest not, Thy compassions, they fail not; As Thou hast been, Thou forever wilt be. Great is Thy faithfulness! Great is Thy faithfulness! Morning by morning new mercies I see. All I have needed Thy hand hath provided; Great is Thy faithfulness, Lord, unto me!"

February 7

"Do not complain."
James 5:9 (NCV)

GO ON A COMPLAINING FAST

Whatever you keep doing becomes a habit. That's why James says, "Do not complain." Author Jon Gordon writes, "A complaining fast won't just make everyone around you happier... you'll experience more joy, peace, success, and positive relationships." So instead of complaining when things go wrong: (1) Practice gratitude. Giving thanks for three blessings every day energizes you and makes you feel happier. It's impossible to be grateful and negative at the same time. (2) Encourage others. Instead of complaining about what people do wrong, focus on what they're doing right. "Encourage... people who are afraid. Help those who are weak. Be patient with everyone" (1 Thessalonians 5:14 NCV). It's OK to critique people's weaknesses as long as you balance your critique with three times more praise. (3) Focus on your success. Start a success journal. Every night before you go to bed, write down something great about your day. It could be an uplifting conversation or an accomplishment you're proud of. There's truth to the old saying, "Nothing succeeds like success." When you focus on success, you set the stage for more to follow. (4) Learn to let go. Instead of obsessing about what you can't change, focus on what you can influence. When you stop trying to control everything and place your life in God's hands, things have a way of working out. (5) Use the power of prayer. Paul says, "Pray... on all occasions with all kinds of prayers and requests" (Ephesians 6:18 NIV). Prayer reduces stress, boosts positive energy, and promotes health. When you're under pressure, instead of complaining, plug in to God's power and recharge your batteries.

February 8

"This I recall to my mind, therefore I have hope."
Lamentations 3:21 ((NAS) 1995)

THE IMPORTANCE OF YOUR SELF-TALK

Lamentations chapter three describes how despair engulfs us and how we can conquer it. Jeremiah's downward spiral starts in verse one: "I am the man who has seen affliction" (v. 1 NAS 1995) and morphs into an unhealthy preoccupation with his troubles. The fact is, when our circumstances deteriorate, our self-talk sounds a lot like Jeremiah's. He blamed God for his physical symptoms, his emotional anguish, and his sense of entrapment. He rehearsed God's failure to answer his prayers, and his fear that he'd been singled out as an object of public ridicule: all classic elements of depression. No wonder he felt powerless and hopeless! (See v. 18 NAS 1995). That kind of self-talk initiates and intensifies despair and depression and feeds our negative outlook. The turning point came when Jeremiah changed his self-talk: "This I recall to my mind, therefore I have hope." He changed his thought process by recalling God's goodness and mercy: "Because of the Lord's great love we are not consumed . . . his compassions never fail. They are new every morning; great is your faithfulness" (vv. 22-23 NIV). When you change your mind—you change your mood! It doesn't happen automatically; you have to deliberately refocus your thinking at the very time when you feel least like doing it. Notice: Jeremiah's circumstances didn't improve—his outlook did. A stream of encouraging thoughts triggered a change in his self-talk—and his depression lifted: "'The Lord is my portion,' says my soul, 'therefore I have hope in Him'" (v. 24 NAS 1995). That's how important your self-talk is!

February 9

"You ... have ... spoken words that ... encouraged those who were about to quit."
Job 4:3 (MSG)

TODAY, SPEAK WORDS THAT ENCOURAGE

The Bible says, "Help others with encouraging words" (Romans 14:19 MSG). When Job was in trouble, his friend Eliphaz reminded him how in the past, Job's words had "encouraged those who were about to quit." Words can hurt or heal, bless or blister, destroy or deliver, tear down or build up. "The tongue has the power of life and death" (Proverbs 18:21 NIV). Jon Walker writes: "You ... the one with Jesus in your heart—are capable of murder. And so am I. We have the power to speak death with our words, and ... the power to speak life. Perhaps you've been on the receiving end of a message meant to murder. 'You're not smart enough ... thin enough ... fast enough ... good enough ... a real Christian wouldn't think such things.' In a world where people are beaten up and put down, God gives you superhero power to punch through the negativity. You speak life when you say, 'You matter to me. I like you just the way you are ... Your life counts. You were created for a purpose. God loves you, and you're incredibly valuable to Him.' You can become the voice of God's grace in the lives of others, supporting, loving, helping and encouraging them with the words that flow from your mouth." God wants us to encourage each other, but that doesn't mean flattering or buttering people up. It means speaking words that help them to stay on their feet and keep going. What you say can give fresh hope to a friend, a relative, a neighbor, or a co-worker who's about to collapse. What a gift!

February 10

*"He who began a good work in you
will carry it on to completion."*
Philippians 1:6 (NIV)

DON'T LET FEAR STOP YOU

Has God called you to do something you don't feel capable of doing? Could you think of a dozen others better suited for the job? It doesn't matter what you think, God didn't choose somebody else! He chose you in spite of your limitations and insecurities. Your inadequacies don't surprise Him. In fact, His "power works best in weakness" (2 Corinthians 12:9 NLT). Jon Walker says: "You may . . . hide your weaknesses from others, but you can't hide them from God. He created you (do you think He made a mistake?). He created you with weaknesses to keep you on your knees . . . without them to push you back to God you'll get prideful . . . and He won't allow you to use them as an excuse for avoiding your mission or ignoring your purpose. If God is calling you to a monumental task, He will equip you to complete it—and that includes the Holy Spirit working from inside you. So focus on His strength, not yours. Don't think about how incapable you are for the task. Remember, God is bigger than anything you face, no matter how overwhelming it may appear." The Bible says we were "created in Christ . . . to do good works, which God prepared in advance for us to do" (Ephesians 2:10 NIV). God's plans are never an afterthought. He designed you for a specific purpose, and the One who "began a good work in you will carry it on to completion." So instead of letting fear stop you, let it motivate you to get up and get going!

February 11

"Grace be unto you, and peace, from God."
1 Corinthians 1:3 (KJV)

HOW TO EXPERIENCE GOD'S GRACE

Several of Paul's epistles open with the words, "Grace be unto you, and peace, from God." That's because you cannot experience God's peace unless you first know how to receive His grace and walk in it. There are three things about grace you need to understand: (a) it cannot be earned; (b) it is God doing for you what you cannot do for yourself; (c) it doesn't kick in until you stop struggling and trying to do it in your own strength. The Bible says, "God opposes the proud but shows favor to the humble" (James 4:6 NIV). The "humble" are those who admit their total inability to succeed without God's help, but the "proud" are always trying to take credit. They like to think it's their ability that gets the job done, so they've difficulty asking God for grace, and even more difficulty receiving it. Peter writes, "Grow in grace" (2 Peter 3:18). You only learn to trust God—by doing it! You grow in grace by taking God at His Word, counting on His gracious provision for each day, and His intervention in situations that are difficult or impossible for you. There will never be a day when you don't need God's grace. And if you are willing to acknowledge you need it and receive it by faith, there will be no shortage of it. "For out of His fullness (abundance) we have all received [all had a share and we were all supplied with] one grace after another and spiritual blessing upon spiritual blessing and even favor upon favor and gift [heaped] upon gift" (John 1:16 AMPC).

February 12

*"Riches do not endure forever, and a crown
is not secure for all generations."*
Proverbs 27:24 (NIV)

WHERE'S YOUR FINANCIAL SECURITY?

One mega-insurance company advertises itself as "The Rock," claiming to be the foundation of your financial security. Remember when we trusted such slogans? Not anymore – it's not the same world! Financial uncertainty characterizes today's world of failing banks, crumbling investment giants, shrinking multinational corporations, swelling lines of the under-employed and unemployed, plus an epidemic of fear plaguing the hearts of the presently employed. For the young, the joy of graduation has become the stress of college debts and a shrinking job market. Many older folks are trading in their retirement dreams for a new twenty-first century reality: "work till you drop." In such times, where can we turn? To politicians? To government? To the next get-rich-quick guru? The Bible says, "Riches do not endure forever, and a crown (human government) is not secure for all generations." What's the answer? Turn to the only reliable source of security: God! There's no financial crisis in His kingdom! Israel hungered and thirsted, and He sent them fresh manna and water from the rock. He assigned ravens to feed Elijah, multiplied oil and flour to sustain a destitute widow's family, fed thousands from a boy's lunch of five loaves and two fish. And He asks us: "Is anything too difficult for Me?" (Jeremiah 32:27 NAS). No! So: (1) trust God to provide for you; (2) do what He tells you to do; (3) believe that God "will." "The lambs will provide you with clothing, and the goats with the price of a field. You will have plenty . . . to feed your family" (Proverbs 27:26-27 NIV).

February 13

"Give us this day our daily bread."
Matthew 6:11 (NKJV)

HOW JESUS TAUGHT US TO PRAY

Jesus taught us to pray, "Give us this day our daily bread." Notice the word "daily." You can't fight today's battles on the strength of yesterday's bread; you must have a fresh supply. In the wilderness, God's people were only permitted to collect enough manna for one day; if they tried to collect more, it rotted. It's wonderful to talk about what God did yesterday and what He's going to do tomorrow, but all you've got is today. "Give us this day our daily bread." Only as you partake of what God's provided for you today will you be able to stand up to the challenges you face. This prayer is an expression of faith. The very fact that you ask means you believe God's got what you need and that He cares enough to provide for you. It says, "I don't need to go to anybody else but You, Lord." So hang up the phone, turn off the TV, shut the door, get down on your knees, approach God in faith and pray, "Give me what I need for this day." God knows what you need. You don't! As you partake of what He provides for you each day, you'll be able to handle whatever life throws at you. And one more thought. When people start getting on your nerves for no apparent reason, or you start having all sorts of mood swings, or you begin living by feelings instead of faith, it's probably because you're not eating right. If that's so, it's time to go back to your source and say, "Lord, I've come for my daily bread."

February 14

*"As one whom his mother comforts,
so I will comfort you."*
Isaiah 66:13 (NKJV)

THE GOD OF ALL COMFORT

When you're troubled, remember: (1) God's comfort is real. Do you recall being sad or afraid as a child? And do you also remember feeling the comfort of your mother's presence? God's comfort is even more real than your mother's. "As one whom his mother comforts, so I will comfort you." God's more concerned about you now than your mother was in your childhood. "Can a mother forget the baby at her breast . . . ? Though she may forget, I will not forget you! See, I have engraved you on the palms of my hands" (Isaiah 49:15-16 NIV). You can always count on God when you need comfort! (2) The Comforter lives in you. When we're suffering, God seems distant and inaccessible. But He's not. Jesus resolved that concern for His anxious disciples—then and now. "I will pray to the Father, and he shall give you another Comforter, that he may abide with you forever" (John 14:16). The Holy Spirit who forever abides in you is closer to you than the air you breathe. He's equipped, willing, and able to comfort you. He will sometimes do it by reminding you of the verse from a hymn, a line from a poem, a sermon you heard, etc. When He does, believe it. Say to yourself repeatedly: "The God of all comfort lives permanently in me!" (3) Scripture brings comfort. The apostle reminds us "that we through patience and comfort of the scriptures might have hope" (Romans 15:4). When you're down, you may not feel like reading the Bible. Do it anyhow. It'll bring you the comfort you long for.

February 15

"Your heavenly Father already knows all your needs."
Matthew 6:32 (NLT)

HOW TO OVERCOME ANXIETY

Here are two more steps to overcoming anxiety: (1) Ask for help. Paul wrote, "Outside were conflicts, inside were fears. Nevertheless God, who comforts the downcast, comforted us by the coming of Titus" (2 Corinthians 7:5-6 NKJV). You're not unique; others are facing the same fears too. By "telling" on your anxieties, they begin to lose their power. Remember: "Two are better than one . . . If either of them falls down, one can help the other up. But pity anyone who falls and has no one to help them up" (Ecclesiastes 4:9-10 NIV). Share your feelings with someone you trust and ask them to pray with you. People are more willing to help than you might imagine. Less worry on your part often means more happiness on theirs. (2) Focus on God, not yourself. Jesus concludes His call to calmness with this challenge: "Your heavenly Father already knows all your needs. Seek the Kingdom of God above all else, and live righteously, and he will give you everything you need" (Matthew 6:32-33 NLT). If you seek wealth, you'll worry about every dollar. If you seek health, you'll fear every blemish and bump. If you seek popularity, you'll obsess over every conflict. If you seek safety, you'll jump at every crack of the twig. But if you focus each day on God's kingdom, "He will give you everything you need." An unknown poet wrote: "Said the robin to the sparrow, 'I should really like to know, why these anxious human beings rush around and worry so.' Said the sparrow to the robin, 'Friend, I think that it must be, that they have no heavenly Father such as cares for you and me.'"

February 16

"Let all that I am praise the Lord."
Psalm 103:2 (NLT)

THERE'S NOBODY LIKE HIM!

The Bible equates God with light, and light with holiness. "God is light; in him there is no darkness at all" (1 John 1:5 NIV). Paul said that God dwells in "unapproachable light" (1 Timothy 6:16 NIV). Scripture refers to Christ "who is holy, blameless, pure, set apart from sinners" (Hebrews 7:26 NIV). So how should you approach such a God? As you would an auditor when your books don't balance? Or a dictator who holds the power of life and death? No, Jesus told us to pray, "Our Father which art in heaven, Hallowed be thy name" (Matthew 6:9). There's your answer! You must come to God as a father who loves you dearly and desires only what is best for you, while always regarding Him with profound reverence. As your awe of God expands, your fears in life will diminish. A big view of God translates into big courage; a small view of God generates no courage at all. A puny God can't help you when cancer strikes, your family is in trouble, or you've no way to pay your bills. A "do-me-a-favor" Jesus may look good stuck on your dashboard, but that image can do nothing for your fears. You need an awesome God, who, while diminishing your ego, enlarges your faith and blows your mind. David wrote: "Let all that I am praise the Lord; may I never forget the good things he does for me. He forgives all my sins and heals all my diseases. He redeems me from death and crowns me with love and tender mercies. He fills my life with good things" (Psalm 103:2-5 NLT).

February 17

"Only the things that cannot be shaken will remain."
Hebrews 12:27 (NCV)

WEATHERING THE FINANCIAL SHAKEUP

Writing about a recent conversation, Rick Hamlin says: "Another guy like me said, 'I dread going to work. All these layoffs are depressing. I keep thinking I'm going to be next. I've tons of work, and my clients appreciate what I'm doing, but I start worrying and there's no stopping.' Worrying is the worst of it, and the stories are piling up: friends, friends of friends, people from church, neighbors, parents of our kids' friends. An early retirement here, a downsizing there, a severance payment, a pink slip . . . all put faces on the statistics and . . . that gnawing fear can make every day an agony." The chances are, you may be feeling some shots of discouragement yourself—daily arrows of frustration that wear you down and steal your joy. Satan is like a terrorist specializing in guerilla warfare. He knows he'd lose big time if he went against the forces of heaven, so he singles out individual believers. The question is, how do you stand firm when "everything that . . . can be shaken" is shaking? Well, for starters, Isaiah says, "You will keep him in perfect peace, whose mind is stayed on You" (Isaiah 26:3 NKJV). If Moses had focused on his circumstances, he'd never have had peace standing between the Red Sea and the Egyptians. His peace came from knowing he was where God wanted him to be. Peace in and of itself isn't the goal; peace is a by-product of knowing: "How abundant are the good things that you have stored up for those who fear [honor] you, that you bestow in the sight of all, on those who take refuge in you" (Psalm 31:19 NIV).

February 18

"Each day is God's gift."
Ecclesiastes 9:9 (MSG)

ENJOY EACH DAY

Solomon writes: "Seize life! Eat bread with gusto . . . Oh yes—God takes pleasure in your pleasure! Dress festively every morning. Don't skimp on colors and scarves. Relish life with the spouse you love . . . every day of your precarious life. Each day is God's gift. It's all you get in exchange for the hard work of staying alive. Make the most of each one! Whatever turns up, grab it and do it. And heartily! This is your last and only chance . . . for there's neither work to do nor thoughts to think in the company of the dead, where you're most certainly headed" (vv. 7-10 MSG). So, what are you waiting for? To graduate? To get married? To have children? To retire? Life is about the journey, not the destination! Your life is here and now, your family is here and now, your marriage is here and now, your career is here and now. The journey takes place every day, and you can find meaning when you search for a greater purpose. You can find small joys every day if you have eyes of faith. Solomon recognized that ultimately we all end up at the same destination—the grave. The only difference lies in how much we enjoy the journey. Instead of obsessing over the things you can't control, focus on what you can control and leave the rest to God. Phil Cooke writes: "I have to believe that God's in control, and for me to always demand answers is to assume His role. I've decided to sit back and let Him be God and let me be me." That's a philosophy you would do well to adopt!

February 19

"I am the Lord, who heals you."
Exodus 15:26 (NIV)

BELIEVE GOD FOR YOUR HEALING

In the Bible, one of the names God chooses to be called by is "Jehovah Rapha," which means "I am the Lord who heals." Now, if God calls Himself the healer, then you have the right to believe what He says and expect that, given an opportunity, He will perform His role competently. After all, His credibility depends on living up to His name. The Psalmist said, "Your promises are backed by all the honor of your name" (Psalm 138:2 NLT). Has God changed? No, He says, "I am the Lord All-Powerful, and I never change" (Malachi 3:6 CEV). And Jesus, who is God, is "the same yesterday and today and forever" (Hebrews 13:8 NIV). What He was, He still is. What He did, He still does. So, when you or a loved one is sick, do these two things: (1) Pray, in faith, believing. A "good faith" deal requires that both parties trust each other's word. Their trust is a rational decision of their will, not their emotions. Faith is your will deciding that God will keep the promise He has made to you. It's refusing to be ambivalent by saying, "If only I felt more positive." No business could survive such ambiguity. Jesus spelled it out clearly: "All things for which you pray and ask, believe that you have received them, and they will be granted to you" (Mark 11:24 NAS). (2) Look for faith-partners who will pray with you. "Pray for each other so that you may be healed" (James 5:16 NLT). "If two of you agree . . . concerning anything you ask, my Father in heaven will do it for you" (Matthew 18:19 NLT).

February 20

"I will give them an undivided heart."
Ezekiel 11:19 (NIV)

DO WHAT YOU LOVE, LOVE WHAT YOU DO

Successful people allow their God-given passion and talent to guide them in life. They have a single focus and an undivided heart. God doesn't create you to be talented in an area, then ask you to give yourself to some unrelated area. There's always a potential alignment of talent and passion, if you have the courage to pursue your life's purpose and take risks. Po Bronson, author of *What Should I Do With My Life?* writes, "I'm convinced that business success in the future starts with the question, 'What should I do with my life?' Yes, that's right . . . people don't succeed by migrating to a 'hot' industry or by adopting a particular career-guiding mantra. They thrive by focusing on the question of who they really are—and connecting to work they truly love (and, in so doing, unleashing a productive and creative power they never imagined)." Carly Fiorina said, "Love what you do, or don't do it . . . Make the choice to do something because it engages your heart as well as your mind. Make the choice because it engages all of you." Don't become a slave to someone else's dream, because once you own a dream that dream will own you. Being a slave to someone else's dream quickly becomes a nightmare. Paul writes, "But they are only comparing themselves with each other . . . How ignorant . . . We will boast only about what has happened within the boundaries of the work God has given us" (2 Corinthians 10:12-13 NLT). If you are confused, out of focus, or going in circles, pray, "Lord, give me a clear vision and an undivided heart." That's a prayer God will answer.

February 21

"The God of all comfort."
2 Corinthians 1:3 (NIV)

GOD WILL BRING YOU THROUGH

God can bring you through situations you think you won't survive or feel you'll be stuck in forever. He can make you comfortable in the most uncomfortable places and give you peace in the midst of trauma. Before your life is over, you'll live, love, and experience loss. Losing some things will actually help you to appreciate the things you still have. It's the taste of failure that makes success sweet. You'll live each day not knowing what tomorrow holds, but confident that God has your tomorrows all planned out. They're not in the hands of your boss or your banker or your mate or anybody else. Nor are they in your own hands to manipulate and control. No, all your tomorrows are in God's hands. Just because you don't recognize the path you're on doesn't mean that God's not leading you. He promises, "I will lead them in paths they have not known. I will make darkness light before them, and crooked places straight. These things I will do for them, and not forsake them" (Isaiah 42:16 NKJV). So get to know God – you'll need Him. And He'll be there for you. He'll be there when everybody and everything else has failed you. He'll be there for you in the dark places. "Weeping may endure for a night, but joy comes in the morning" (Psalm 30:5 NKJV). However long the night, morning always comes, and with it His joy. As you look back, you'll realize that His grace protected you, provided for you, secured you, calmed you, comforted you, and brought you through. Times and seasons change, but not God. He's always "the God of all comfort."

February 22

"A cheerful heart is good medicine."
Proverbs 17:22 (NLT)

LEARN TO LAUGH

If you're constantly negative in your outlook, something's wrong. "There is . . . a time to laugh" (Ecclesiastes 3:1,4 NKJV). You say, "Right now I can't find anything to laugh about." Then observe how the Psalmist opens Psalm 124, 125, and 126: "If the Lord had not been on our side . . . they would have swallowed us alive" (Psalm 124:1–3 NIV). "Those who trust in the Lord are like Mount Zion, which cannot be shaken" (Psalm 125:1 NIV). "When the Lord restored the fortunes of Zion . . . Our mouths were filled with laughter . . . Then it was said among the nations, 'The Lord has done great things for them'" (Psalm 126:1–3 NIV). When you can rejoice in the midst of trouble, people want to know what your secret is. And you can always find a reason to rejoice when you remember Who is on your side. Doctors have confirmed what the Bible teaches. Laughter de-stresses you and strengthens your immune system: "A cheerful heart is good medicine." Plus, a positive attitude will bring you favor and cooperation. When you keep adding to the heat and confusion of a crisis, people lose respect for your ability to handle things under pressure. But if you stay cool and maintain your sense of humor when things are falling apart, they'll show their appreciation in better work and increased loyalty. Sure, some problems are serious, but you gain nothing by dwelling on the bleak side. Put the problem into God's hands and watch the results! Job said, "He will . . . fill your mouth with laughter, and your lips with shouts of joy" (Job 8:21 NRSVPs). Now, if he could say that, surely you can!

February 23

"This is the victory that has overcome the world, even our faith."
1 John 5:4 (NIV)

FAITH: THE POWER TO OVERCOME

When your health, your finances, or family are at risk, you suddenly realize how fragile life is. Today you may be living on the sunny side of the street, but if you live long enough, adversity will come knocking on your door. When it does, you'll discover that things like power, possessions, and popularity won't sustain you. If power could do it, Joseph Stalin wouldn't have been afraid to go to sleep at night or been so paranoid that he appointed a soldier to guard his very teabags. If possessions could do it, fear wouldn't have caused billionaire Howard Hughes to live like a hermit and die alone. If popularity could do it, John Lennon's biographers wouldn't have described him as a fearful man who slept with the lights on and was terrified of germs. Earthly supports can only sustain you for so long. Courage for living comes from a deep abiding trust in God, whose Word says, "This is the victory that has overcome the world, even our faith." But faith is only as valuable as the thing it's placed in, and our faith is in a God who never fails! David said, "Through you we push back our enemies; through your name we trample our foes" (Psalm 44:5 NIV). Jesus said, "I have given you authority to . . . overcome all the power of the enemy" (Luke 10:19 NIV). Paul said, "Who shall separate us from the love of Christ? Shall trouble or hardship or persecution or famine or nakedness or danger or sword? . . . No, in all these things we are more than conquerors through him who loved us" (Romans 8:35-37 NIV).

February 24

"He walked on the water... to Jesus."
Matthew 14:29 (NKJV)

WALKING ON WATER

When Peter was certain it was Jesus who was calling him, he left the security of the boat and entrusted himself to the power of God. So far, so good. "But when he looked around at the high waves, he was terrified and began to sink. 'Save me, Lord!' he shouted" (Matthew 14:30 TLB). (1) You must focus on the Lord, not the storm. We all know what it's like to "see the waves." You begin a new venture—a job, a relationship, an area of spiritual growth—full of hope. Then you encounter storms and setbacks. Jesus said, "Here on earth you will have many trials" (John 16:33 NLT). Expect it; it's part of the journey of faith! (2) You must feel the fear and do it regardless. Growth requires taking on new challenges. Each time you do, you'll experience fear because growth and fear go together. But each time you risk leaving the boat, it means you're more likely to do it again. And each time you step out on the water without drowning, you realize that fear no longer has the power over you. On the other hand, each time you resist God's voice and choose to stay in the boat, His voice becomes a little quieter until eventually, you don't hear it at all. Wouldn't it be worth any risk to avoid that? Furthermore, staying in the boat doesn't guarantee your safety; it only guarantees you'll eventually die from something else. The answer to fear is to get out of the boat a little more each day, until fear loses its hold on you.

February 25

"The word of our God stands forever."
Isaiah 40:8 (NKJV)

WORDS TO LIVE BY IN TROUBLED TIMES

Here are some more wonderful promises from the Bible that you can stand on when trouble comes: (1) "Because you have made the Lord . . . your dwelling place, no evil shall befall you, nor shall any plague come near your dwelling; for He shall give His angels charge over you, to keep you in all your ways" (Psalm 91:9-11 NKJV). (2) "The angel of the Lord encamps around those who fear him, and he delivers them" (Psalm 34:7 NIV). (3) "I will take refuge in the shadow of your wings until the disaster has passed" (Psalm 57:1 NIV). (4) "The Lord is close to the brokenhearted and saves those who are crushed in spirit" (Psalm 34:18 NIV). (5) "The eyes of the Lord are on the righteous and his ears are attentive to their prayer" (1 Peter 3:12 NIV). (6) "He reached down from on high and took hold of me; he drew me out of deep waters. He rescued me from my powerful enemy, from my foes, who were too strong for me . . . he rescued me because he delighted in me" (Psalm 18:16-19 NIV). (7) "Do not gloat over me, my enemy! Though I have fallen, I will rise. Though I sit in darkness, the Lord will be my light" (Micah 7:8 NIV). (8) "You will have courage because you will have hope. You will take your time and rest in safety. You will lie down unafraid, and many will look to you for help" (Job 11:18-19 TLB). (9) "Now to him who is able to do immeasurably more than all we ask or imagine, according to his power that is at work within us" (Ephesians 3:20 NIV).

February 26

"These three remain: faith, hope and love."
1 Corinthians 13:13 (NIV)

KEEP HOPE ALIVE

In 1914, Sir Ernest Shackleton attempted the first land crossing of Antarctica. But his ship, the Endurance, got stuck in icy waters and sank. Shackleton and his twenty-seven-member crew were stranded twelve hundred miles from civilization, drifting on ice floes with just three rickety lifeboats, a few tents, and limited provisions. Eventually, they reached a small island and waited while Shackleton and a handful of men took one of the lifeboats eight hundred miles over tumultuous seas to a whaling station. Shackleton returned with a rescue ship, and every man survived the eighteen-month ordeal. How did he keep everybody's hopes alive? First, he modeled optimism. Shackleton, who described optimism as "true moral courage," always believed that he and his crew would survive, and he spread that optimism to everyone around him. Second, he nurtured their sense of significance. He kept everyone involved by seeking their opinions and giving them tasks, which made them feel like they were part of the solution. Third, he encouraged them. He used humor and promoted a lighthearted atmosphere. Shackleton recognized that under extreme pressure, the ability to lighten the mood neutralizes fear and enables people to focus, re-energize, and prevail over daunting obstacles. Isn't it interesting that one of the few items Shackleton rescued from the sinking ship was a crewman's banjo? He did it so the group could have music. Shackleton was a prime example of how one person can keep hope alive. If you know someone who's in the middle of a difficult trial, your words of kindness and love, your confidence in them, and your ability to lighten their load can keep hope alive.

February 27

"I pray that the eyes of your heart may be enlightened."
Ephesians 1:18 (NIV)

SEEING GOD IN YOUR SITUATION

When you are in a crisis, it's easy to lose perspective. It happened to Jesus' disciples on the Emmaus Road. Discouraged about His death, they were "going over all these things that had happened. In the middle of their . . . questions, Jesus came up and walked along with them. But they were not able to recognize who he was" (Luke 24:15-16 MSG). When you take your eyes off Jesus, you begin to feel helpless about things. Dr. Michael Youssef says: "Facing a major crisis . . . I tend to be the kind of person whose vision becomes blurred . . . my perceptions are shot . . . my contemplations one-sided . . . and I often shut out the very people who can deliver me . . . just like these two disciples . . . Their vision was blurred about the very person who was walking with them and talking to them. The One whose death they were mourning was alive . . . but they didn't realize it because their focus was on the wrong thing." But everything changed the minute they recognized Him. "Within the hour they were on their way back to Jerusalem. There . . . the two . . . told . . . how Jesus had appeared to them as they were walking along the road, and how they had recognized him as he was breaking the bread" (Luke 24:33-35 NLT). Notice the words "within the hour." In an instant, they went from fear to courage, pain to joy, and despair to hope. No matter how bad things may appear to be, when you set your eyes on Jesus, He will fill you with hope. So Paul writes: "I pray also that the eyes of your heart may be enlightened."

February 28

"Love ... keeps going to the end."
1 Corinthians 13:4-7 (MSG)

STAYING WHEN YOU FEEL LIKE QUITTING

When Ed and Alice went for marriage counseling, the therapist asked Alice, "What first attracted you to Ed?" She replied, "His strong, silent temperament." The counselor continued, "So why do you want a divorce?" Alice answered, "His strong, silent temperament!" Sometimes what drew us together ends up a major irritant. In every relationship, there are times when it would be easier to quit than to hang in. But short of physical and emotional abuse, there are advantages to working through your issues. Here are a few: (1) Emotional benefits. Contrary to what Hollywood culture would have us believe, divorced people are more likely to feel depressed due to loneliness. In fact, many say although there were disagreements in the relationship, they miss having somebody to come home to. (2) Health benefits. Emotional stress leads to physical problems, and being in a relationship, especially a good marriage, can be beneficial for your health. It's like having your own nurse or therapist. (3) Community benefits. What your kids see influences their future choices. Staying in your marriage teaches them how to work through relationship challenges. Couples with strong marriages are helping to build a nation of loving, responsible parents who can guide their children onto the right track. "Love ... keeps going to the end." Author Christy Scannell says, "When [my husband and I] got married, we agreed it was for life ... Weeks before our wedding we made a pact to work out whatever problems came our way ... Yes, we fight. We accuse. We toss barbs ... but we won't be moving out or filing papers ... whatever happens we're staying."

March 1

"That my joy may be in you."
John 15:11 (NIV)

THE SECRET TO HAVING JOY (1)

Jesus said, "I have told you this so that my joy may be in you and that your joy may be complete." The joy Jesus is talking about is unique: "My joy." And it's fulfilling in a way that the world's happiness isn't: "That your joy may be complete." Being a faithful follower of Christ's teachings brings inner joy that's real and resilient regardless of economic indicators, interest rates, government deficits, and even disease or death. You can't be happy without being joyful, but you can be joyful without being happy! How's that possible? Jesus had previously told His disciples that we enjoy a love which transcends all others—the love of our heavenly Father that's unconditionally offered, and once accepted, is permanently experienced. Nothing can compare to the love of God. His love isn't based on looks, personality, wealth, or even moral goodness. It's offered without any preconditions. And it's neither fickle nor failing. You can't do anything to make God love you more, and you can do nothing to make Him love you less. Furthermore, divine love doesn't just give you "warm fuzzies." It's constantly at work to direct you toward making wise decisions, to protect you from making poor ones, and to correct you when you make bad ones. God's love guarantees His acceptance when all others have rejected you, His forgiveness when all others have judged you, and His mercy when all others have condemned you. When you bask in His love, you experience a wellspring of joy bubbling up in your heart. And since the world didn't give you this joy—the world can't take it away.

March 2

"A merry heart does good, like medicine."
Proverbs 17:22 (NKJV)

THE SECRET OF HAVING JOY (2)

The Bible says, "A merry heart does good, like medicine, but a broken spirit dries the bones." Do you know that laughter is such good medicine that it can relieve stress, cure headaches, fight infections, and alleviate hypertension? Doctors tell us laughing produces physical benefits similar to the benefits we get from vigorous physical exercise. When you throw your head back and laugh out loud, the muscles in the abdomen, chest, shoulders, and elsewhere in your body contract, while your heart rate and blood pressure increase. Just one burst of laughter can cause your pulse rate to double from 60 to 120, while your systolic blood pressure can shoot from a normal 120, to 200. Then once you stop laughing, your heartbeat and blood pressure dip below normal—signaling reduced stress. God created laughter because He knows it's good for your health. Don't, however, confuse happiness with merriment. Merriment comes from joy, not happiness, and understanding this is crucial to your emotional well-being. There are times when we can't and shouldn't be happy—when people are hurting, going through tragedy, or losing jobs and loved ones. In the face of injustice, happiness is inappropriate, if not impossible. Yet the joy that comes from knowing that you are unconditionally loved and accepted by God enables you to remain joyful. That's because: (1) Happiness is external; joy is internal. (2) Happiness depends on outward circumstances; joy depends on inward character. (3) Happiness depends on what happens to us; joy depends on who lives within us. (4) Happiness is based on chance; joy is based on choice. So today—choose joy!

March 3

"I press on."
Philippians 3:14 (NAS)

PRESS ON

When "the bottom falls out" what do you do? Blame others? That only makes you bitter. Wallow in self-pity? That only paralyzes you! When David returned from battle and found his home burned to the ground, and his family taken prisoner, he cried until he had no tears left. (It's healthy to grieve your losses, just don't get stuck there.) Next we read, "David strengthened himself in the Lord his God" (1 Samuel 30:6 NKJV). That's it! You've got to learn how to get alone and give yourself a good talking to! You've got to learn to pray for yourself and to quote God's promises to yourself! "Weeping may endure for a night, but joy cometh in the morning" (Psalm 30:5). Did you hear that? "Joy cometh!" Change is on the way! Learn how to rise up and say, "What does not destroy me will only make me stronger! No day lasts forever. This too shall pass. In the meantime, it will only drive me closer to God." Come on, start talking to yourself! Your weakness can be the discovery point for strengths you never even knew you had! When Joseph recalled the worst time of his life he said, "God turned into good what you meant for evil" (Genesis 50:20 TLB). Others don't control your destiny—God does—and He's not like others! You will come out of this stronger and wiser! Look beyond the pain, and you'll find perspective. The word for you today is regroup, renew, and reload—and whatever you do, keep pressing on!

March 4

"If the Lord is with us, why has . . . this happened?"
Judges 6:13 (NIV)

TRUSTING GOD IN THE DARK

A hundred years ago, Germany's exclusive textile mills had special rooms dedicated to spinning the world's finest lace. Each room was dark, except for the light falling from a small window onto the weaver's work. That's because lace is more beautiful when the weaver is in darkness and his work is in the light. Usually, God's purposes are revealed, and His power displayed in our darkest experiences when, like Gideon, you ask, "If the Lord is with [me], why has . . . this happened?" When there seems to be no rhyme or reason, God's promise is, "I will give you hidden treasures, riches stored in secret places, so that you may know that I am the Lord . . . who [calls] you by name" (Isaiah 45:3 NIV). Anybody can be faithful in good times but standing "by night in the house of the Lord" (Psalm 134:1 NIV) takes real commitment. Hymn writer George Matheson wrote: "Will I remain in God's house at night . . . love Him for who He is . . . know I desire not the gift but the Giver? When I can remain . . . during the darkness of night and worship . . . I've accepted Him for Himself alone." When the Israelites faced their greatest challenge, the Red Sea, the Bible says, "All that night the Lord drove the sea back" (Exodus 14:21 NIV). Be encouraged, God is working, even though you can't see Him.

March 5

"Do not be anxious about anything."
Philippians 4:6 (NIV)

WHEN YOU FEEL ANXIOUS (1)

Anxiety starts as a trickle, then creates a channel in our mind through which all our thoughts begin to flow. Most of our anxieties fall into three categories: (1) Anxiety about things we all face: like aging, disability, retirement, loneliness, financial uncertainty, accidents, illness, losing a loved one, and death. (2) Anxiety about things we need to do like making decisions, starting and ending relationships, losing weight, changing careers, making a mistake. (3) Anxiety reflecting our inner state of mind: These anxieties reveal how we feel about our ability to handle things. For example, fear of rejection can affect every relationship in your life. In order to avoid being hurt, you shut others out, your world grows smaller, and your opportunities for personal growth are more limited. Many of our anxieties can be reduced to one question, "What if I can't handle it?" Your mind is the battlefield where victory is won or lost. So ask yourself, "Would I still be anxious if I knew for certain I could handle anything that came up?" The answer is no. Anxiety can't immobilize you and steal your joy when you know you can handle whatever happens. You say, "That sounds too simple." Not when you bring God into the picture! Here are two great anxiety-eliminating Scriptures you can stand on when times are tough: (1) "I can do all things through Christ who strengthens me" (Philippians 4:13 NKJV). (2) "Do not be anxious about anything, but in every situation, by prayer and petition, with thanksgiving, present your requests to God. And the peace of God, which transcends all understanding, will guard your hearts and your minds" (Philippians 4:6-7 NIV).

March 6

"Do not be anxious about anything."
Philippians 4:6 (NIV)

WHEN YOU FEEL ANXIOUS (2)

We all face times when we must choose between faith and anxiety. A woman trapped in an abusive relationship must choose between getting help, getting out, or staying stuck. A young person being pressured to do drugs can choose to give in, or say, "no" and walk away. A person anxious about death can read God's Word, talk to a friend or counselor, or continue to be anxious. The Bible says: "The righteous are bold as a lion" (Proverbs 28:1). You say, "Right now, I don't feel too bold." Courage doesn't eliminate anxiety; it rises above it! David said, "Wait on the Lord: be of good courage, and he shall strengthen thine heart" (Psalm 27:14). When your cause is right and you're committed to God, He gives you the courage needed to act. But you must learn to face the thing you fear. This can mean standing up for what you believe, making a phone call you've been putting off, expressing your opinion, acknowledging some character flaw, and asking God to help you change. What you must remember is, doing always comes before the feeling of increased confidence. Each time you confront your anxieties, you take a step forward. But when you allow anxiety to control you, you retreat into your "safe zone" and start seeing yourself as somebody who can't handle life. Here's some great advice for living: analyze the situation fearlessly, figure out the worst that can happen. Once you've accepted that, you experience a release of energy and you can begin doing something about it, even if all you can do is – leave it in the capable and loving hands of God.

March 7

"Do not be anxious about anything."
Philippians 4:6 (NIV)

WHEN YOU FEEL ANXIOUS (3)

John writes: "I pray that . . . you may prosper and be in good health, just as your soul prospers" (3 John 2 NAS). Why would he say that? Because your physical body thrives in relationship to how well you're doing spiritually. Doctors say anxiety suppresses your immune system, elevates your blood pressure, and creates cholesterol that blocks your arteries. It creates the very condition you dread! Did you know that a percentage of all first-year medical students assume the very symptoms of whatever disease they're studying? Some even faint when first exposed to them. Job said, "The thing which I greatly fear comes upon me" (Job 3:25 AMPC). Anxiety is one of Satan's most effective weapons. Your ignorance of his anxiety-inducing schemes is what enables him to gain a foothold in your thinking and rob you of the blessings that are rightfully yours, including your health. Are you anxious about your health? Write these Scriptures down on a 3 x 5 card and carry it with you: (1) "Worship the Lord your God, and his blessing will be on your food and water. I will take away sickness from among you . . . I will give you a full life span" (Exodus 23:25-26 NIV). (2) "'I will restore you to health and heal your wounds,' declares the Lord" (Jeremiah 30:17 NIV). (3) "Turn your ear to my words. Do not let them out of your sight, keep them within your heart; for they are life to those who find them and health to one's whole body" (Proverbs 4:20-22 NIV). "Therefore I tell you, whatever you ask for in prayer, believe that you have received it, and it will be yours" (Mark 11:24 NIV).

March 8

"Do not be anxious about anything."
Philippians 4:6 (NIV)

WHEN YOU FEEL ANXIOUS (4)

Are you feeling anxious today? Program your mind with these promises. Better yet, carry them with you and read them regularly: (1) "Be strong and courageous. Be not afraid or dismayed … for there is … with us … our God to help us" (2 Chronicles 32:7-8 AMPC). (2) "'I will rescue you' … declares the Lord; 'you will not be given into the hands of those you fear'" (Jeremiah 39:17 NIV). (3) "Fear not … When you pass through the waters … they shall not overflow you. When you walk through the fire, you shall not be burned" (Isaiah 43:1-2 NKJV). (4) "Be not afraid or dismayed … for the battle is not yours, but God's" (2 Chronicles 20:15 AMPC). (5) "In the world you have … distress and frustration; but … [take courage; be confident, certain, undaunted] … I have … [deprived it of power to harm you and have conquered it for you]" (John 16:33 AMPC). (6) "I will lie down in peace and sleep, for though I am alone … Lord, you will keep me safe" (Psalm 4:8 TLB). (7) "The righteous cry out, and the Lord hears them; he delivers them from all their troubles" (Psalm 34:17 NIV). (8) "You will be secure, because there is hope; you will look about you and … rest in safety" (Job 11:18 NIV). (9) "They will fight against you, but … not prevail … for I am with you to save … and deliver you" (Jeremiah 15:20 NKJV). (10) "Our fears for today … worries about tomorrow … even the powers of hell … nothing in all creation will … separate us from the love of God" (Romans 8:38-39 NLT). (11) "Those who know your name trust in you, for you … have never forsaken those who seek you" (Psalm 9:10 NIV). (12) "The Lord … watches over you … stands beside you … keeps you from all harm … watches over your life … keeps watch … as you come and go" (Psalm 121:5-8 NLT).

March 9

*"Those who have learned to acclaim
you ... walk in ... your presence."*
Psalm 89:15 (NIV)

PRAISE YOUR WAY THROUGH

Prisons in Bible times were miserable places, devoid of even the most basic creature comforts. It was in such a place that "Paul and Silas were ... singing praises to God ... [when] ... a strong earthquake shook the jail.... The doors opened, and the chains fell from all the prisoners" (Acts 16:25-26 CEV). And it can happen for you too. If you want to shake things up, see doors open, and chains break, begin to praise God "in spite of." The secret to soaring above your circumstances is approaching God on the wings of praise. David said, "Those who have learned to acclaim [praise, applaud, honor, pay tribute to] you ... walk in ... your presence, Lord." Praise isn't simply a reaction to coming into God's presence; it creates a channel through which He enters to go to work on your problem. When you're down and depressed, there's no incentive for your natural mind to praise God. It'll actually encourage you to wallow in misery and feel sorry for yourself. But that's completely opposite to what you should be doing! God is "Looking for: those who are ... themselves ... in ... worship ... [who] do it out of their very being" (John 4:23-24 MSG). It's not a matter of emotion; it's a matter of faith. It's not something that comes naturally; it's something you choose to do. Whether you're in the wilderness or the Promised Land, when you "rejoice, and sing praises" (Psalm 98:4 NKJV), things start to happen; as your praises go up, God's blessings come down. Nehemiah says, "The joy of the Lord is your strength" (Nehemiah 8:10). Praise actually helps to heal your emotions and lift the weight of negativity you're living under. Try it!

March 10

"Having hope will give you courage."
Job 11:18 (NLT)

KEEP YOUR HOPE ALIVE

Hope is a powerful force. It arouses your mind to explore every possible angle. It enables you to overcome daunting obstacles. It's absolutely essential to the life God wants you to live. It's the fuel your heart runs on. It's the single biggest difference between those who persevere and those who give up. Hope is what makes couples say, "I do," without any guarantees, and later, after all the broken promises, pick up the pieces and try again, knowing it can get better. It's why composers agonize over a score and artists over a canvas, believing some glimmer of beauty will emerge from the struggle. As an old man, Henri Matisse was crippled with agonizing arthritis. When asked why he continued to wrap his swollen fingers around a brush every day, he replied, "The pain goes away; the beauty endures." Laboring to paint the ceiling of the Sistine Chapel, Michelangelo grew so discouraged that he wanted to quit. But every morning hope pushed him up the ladder to fulfill his magnificent vision. Hope is what made Abraham leave home without knowing where God was taking him. It made Paul challenge the powers of Rome. It's what fueled the Old Testament prophets to keep taking on City Hall! This is not blind optimism, but faith-focused and hope—in God. "You have been my hope . . . my confidence since my youth" (Psalm 71:5 NIV). You can survive the loss of many things, but not the loss of hope. Nobody experienced greater loss than Job, yet he wrote: "Having hope will give you courage." So keep your hope alive by trusting in God!

March 11

"I will bless the Lord at all times."
Psalm 34:1 (KJV)

A THANKFUL HEART

David said, "I will bless the Lord at all times: his praise shall continually be in my mouth." A thankful heart should be a way of life. But did you know it can save your life? When Jonah ended up inside the whale, he told God, "I will sacrifice to You with . . . thanksgiving" (Jonah 2:9 NKJV). And when he did, God made the fish spit him up on dry land. When you're down in the pits, and all hell's breaking loose around you – that's when you need to raise your voice and praise God. Nothing demonstrates real trust like thanking Him when you're in the throes of crisis. A thankful heart does two things: (1) Builds your faith. The reason we can walk by faith and not by sight (See 2 Corinthians 5:7), is because we know that regardless of the circumstances, God is working on our behalf. David said, "Magnify the Lord with me" (Psalm 34:3). Praise acts like a magnifying glass; it makes God bigger than your problem. What changes? Your focus changes! Instead of dwelling on the problem and getting discouraged, your faith is released, and you begin looking to God for solutions. And a believing heart will recognize and receive those solutions faster than a doubting one. (2) Restores life. Before raising Lazarus from the dead, Jesus looked up to heaven and said, "Father . . . thank You that You have heard Me" (John 11:41 NKJV). Something amazing happens when you start thanking God in advance for saving you, protecting you, and providing for you. Your faith begins to soar, and you gain the confidence to command those things in your life that you thought were dead to live again.

March 12

"Perfect love expels all fear."
1 John 4:18 (NLT)

GOD'S FORGIVENESS, MERCY, AND GRACE

God cares about you too much to leave you in any doubt about His love. The Bible says His "perfect love expels all fear." If God loved us with an imperfect love, we'd have cause to worry. Human love is flawed; it keeps a checklist of our sins and shortcomings—and consults it often. God keeps no such list. His love casts out our fear because it casts out our guilt. John writes, "If our heart condemn us, God is greater than our heart" (1John 3:20). When you feel unforgiven, question your feelings but don't question God. Go back to His Word; it outranks self-criticism and self-doubt. Nothing fosters confidence like a clear grasp of God's grace, and nothing fosters fear like ignorance of it. The fact is, if you haven't accepted God's grace, you're doomed to live in fear. No pill, pep talk, psychiatrist, or earthly possession can put your mind at ease. Those things may help numb your fear, but they can't eradicate it. Only God's grace can do that. Have you accepted Christ's forgiveness? If not, get down on your knees and do it now. The Bible says, "If we confess our sins, he is faithful and just to forgive us . . . and to cleanse us from all unrighteousness" (1 John 1:9). The place of confession is also the place of cleansing and restored confidence toward God. Your prayer can be as simple as this: "Lord, I admit I've turned away from You. Please forgive me. I place my soul in Your hands and my trust in Your grace. In Jesus' name, I pray. Amen." Now, having received God's forgiveness, mercy, and grace—live like it!

March 13

"Your heavenly Father feeds them."
Matthew 6:26 (NKJV)

SPARROWS

A needy sparrow. Jesus said: "Look at the birds. They don't plant or harvest or store food in barns, for your heavenly Father feeds them. And aren't you far more valuable to him than they are? Can all your worries add a single moment to your life? And why worry about your clothing? Look at the lilies of the field and how they grow. They don't work or make their clothing, yet Solomon, in all his glory, was not dressed as beautifully as they are. And if God cares so wonderfully for wildflowers that are here today and thrown into the fire tomorrow, he will certainly care for you. Why do you have so little faith? . . . These things dominate the thoughts of unbelievers, but your heavenly Father already knows all your needs. Seek the Kingdom of God above all else, and live righteously, and he will give you everything you need" (vv. 26-33 NLT). If you need some more scriptural promises to stand on, here they are: "Fear the Lord, you his godly people, for those who fear him will have all they need" (Psalm 34:9 NLT). "Blessed is the man who fears the Lord, who delights greatly in His commandments. His descendants will be mighty on the earth; the generation of the upright will be blessed. Wealth and riches will be in his house . . . He will not be afraid of evil tidings; his heart is steadfast, trusting in the Lord" (Psalm 112:1-7 NKJV). God recorded these promises in His Word so that you could read them over and over, and in reading them, rise above worry and live your life with joy and confidence.

March 14

"Tribulation worketh patience."
Romans 5:3 (KJV)

DEVELOPING PATIENCE

How do you develop patience? Through tribulation! When your honesty seems to go unnoticed, when your hard work seems to go unrewarded, when your kindness is rendered without thanks, when your helping hand is offered and ignored, when even love is refused—that's when patience shines in all its beauty. Paul writes, "Tribulation worketh patience." You've seen this principle at work in the development of children. One child, overly shielded and protected, grows up into a weakling without ambition and courage, destined to failure. Another left to fight their own battles, to struggle, to learn through trial and error, grows into near-perfect maturity. The same principle applies to the Christian life when you realize that each storm brings its blessings, and each trial produces its rewards. Let's look at three practical benefits of patience: First, patience brings hope. "Such things were written in the Scriptures long ago to teach us. And the Scriptures give us hope and encouragement as we wait patiently for God's promises to be fulfilled" (Romans 15:4 NLT). Second, patience produces spiritual fruit. "And the seeds that fell on the good soil represent honest, good-hearted people who hear God's word, cling to it, and patiently produce a huge harvest" (Luke 8:15 NLT). Third, through patience you receive what God has promised. "Then you will not become spiritually dull and indifferent. Instead, you will follow the example of those who are going to inherit God's promises because of their faith and endurance" (Hebrews 6:12 NLT).

March 15

"Be kind . . . forgiving each other."
Ephesians 4:32 (NIV)

POWER OF FORGIVENESS

Here are four things you need to know about forgiveness: (1) Forgiveness doesn't make what happened to you right. It means you've made a decision not to let it control your life. By forgiving and attempting to restore the relationship, you reclaim your peace of mind. If the other person refuses to acknowledge what happened or that it was wrong, the offense can and should still be forgiven. Forgiveness doesn't depend on the other person; it depends on you. (2) Forgiveness matters, even when the offending party refuses to admit guilt. When you wait for someone to admit he or she was wrong, you're placing your future in that person's hands. Forgiveness is first and foremost for your own benefit, not the benefit of others. By forgiving, you're letting the pain and hurt go and moving forward. (3) Your willingness to forgive can move the other person to seek forgiveness. Perhaps the person who hurt you doesn't feel they deserve to be forgiven. Or they may know what they did was wrong but lack the courage to step forward and ask for forgiveness. When you make the first move, it opens the door and allows them to reach out and find mercy and understanding. (4) Forgiveness is easier when you accept that we all need it. When you refuse to forgive because you think someone's offenses are greater than your own, that's pride. And "God opposes the proud but gives grace to the humble" (1 Peter 5:5 NLT). The Bible says, "Be kind and compassionate to one another, forgiving each other, just as in Christ God forgave you." Once you realize the depth of God's grace toward you, it's easier to extend grace to others.

March 16

"Be still, and know that I am God."
Psalm 46:10 (NIV)

WHEN FATIGUE THREATENS YOU

When you're running on fumes, instead of berating yourself for failed attempts at "spirituality," one writer says it's time to "tie a tourniquet on the wound of busyness . . . [or] we'll bleed a spiritual death. Doing more, and doing it faster, isn't taking us to a place of peace. The distraction is nothing more than a momentary escape. Sooner or later, we have to stop . . . Psalm 46:10 says, 'Be still, and know that I am God.' When we're forced to be still the magnitude of the weight we carry becomes enormous, the loneliness unbearable. We think momentum keeps us from thinking . . . from feeling . . . from knowing sooner or later we have to stop." When you need to be spiritually restored, go to the throne, not the phone! No matter how good your friends are, they can't meet your need like God can. Jesus said, "Come to me . . . and I will give you rest" (Matthew 11:28 NIV). Consider it His personal RSVP to talk to Him and tell Him how you feel, like a child talks to a loving parent who can help them. Designate a special place to be alone with God, and discipline yourself to go there often. And don't just tell Him what you need; listen for what He's trying to tell you. Don't be in a hurry to get back into the rat race; stay in God's presence until you understand that the burdens you're carrying were never meant to be shouldered alone. Bottom line: we find time for what we consider important, so get your priorities straight and "seek first his kingdom" (Matthew 6:33 NIV). When you "come near to God . . . he will come near to you" (James 4:8 NIV).

March 17

"O Lord; point out the road for me to follow."
Psalm 25:4 (NLT)

DECISIONS, DECISIONS, DECISIONS!

Even simple decisions can be stressful. Ever watch a child struggle to choose between chocolate or strawberry ice cream? And the bigger decisions, like whom to marry, which career to choose, whether to buy a house or to undergo high-risk surgery, etc., can be nerve-racking! But you can reduce your stress level by following these biblical principles: (1) Do the research. "Anyone who answers without listening is foolish and confused" (Proverbs 18:13 NCV). Get all the facts and avoid making decisions you'll regret. Knowledge has never been more accessible; through the Internet, helpful books, and especially God's Word: "Your commands . . . are my constant guide" (Psalm 119:98 NLT). (2) Talk to God. "Show me the right path, O Lord; point out the road for me to follow." Consulting God helps prevent premature decisions, clarifies your priorities, and prepares you to hear His counsel. Is God interested in your decisions? Yes. "The Lord directs the steps of the godly. He delights in every detail of their lives" (Psalm 37:23 NLT). (3) Be open to new ideas. Don't get trapped in old mindsets. "Wise men and women are always learning, always listening for fresh insights" (Proverbs 18:15 MSG). Clinging to the familiar can be crippling. God may choose to lead you along a new path of fresh insight. So breathe deeply, seek His wisdom, and open up your heart to receive it. (4) Get advice from trusted friends. "It's a hard road that's walked alone," says an old Celtic proverb. So follow Solomon's counsel: "A fool thinks he needs no advice, but a wise man listens to others" (Proverbs 12:15 TLB).

March 18

"[God] has delivered us from the power of darkness."
Colossians 1:13 (NKJV)

THE BLESSINGS OF THE BLOOD (1)

History's crowning moment occurred when "Christ died for the ungodly" (Romans 5:6). He didn't just die for His friends and supporters, He died for people who despised Him. It was no quid-pro-quo deal where Jesus said: "I'll accept you if you accept me." No, it was a selfless, one-sided act of love. No conditions, nothing demanded in return. As a result, God "delivered us from the power of darkness and conveyed us into the kingdom of the Son of His love." Selah! Stop and meditate on the advantages you enjoy through Jesus' blood: (1) You've been delivered. The Greek word Paul used means to literally rescue by drawing us to Himself. Your deliverance was a deeply personal event to Jesus. By His shed blood, He drew you to Himself. The distance sin had put between you and God was reversed, and you were "accepted in the beloved" (Ephesians 1:6). (2) You've been freed from the power of darkness. That "power" is Satan's tyranny over those living under his control. Christ's blood liberated you from the darkness, ignorance, and blindness Satan uses to deceive and manipulate you. (3) You've been translated into the kingdom of God's son. The word "translated" implies being transferred from one place to another. In Paul's day, superpowers like Rome would annex other nations and make them part of Roman territory. Often the conquered were better off under Rome, enjoying such privileges as safety, food, mail service, travel protection, etc. Christ's blood transferred you into His kingdom to enjoy these advantages: guaranteed protection, abundant provision for all your needs, full status of sonship, and unlimited access to His throne.

March 19

"He has reconciled you to himself through the death of Christ."
Colossians 1:22 (NLT)

THE BLESSINGS OF THE BLOOD (2)

Observe: (1) You have been reconciled to God. God wants unbroken, intimate friendship with us, as with Adam in Eden. But sin made us enemies of God. "You who were once far away from God . . . enemies, separated from him by your evil thoughts and actions" (v. 21 NLT). Yet He never stopped pursuing that relationship, sending Jesus to restore it. He "made peace . . . by means of Christ's blood on the cross" (v. 20 NLT), resulting in your reconciliation to God. The Greek word for "reconciliation" means "to be friends as we once were." Now you can walk and talk with God as Adam did. Now God sees you as "holy and blameless . . . without a single fault!" (v. 22 NLT). (2) You are the Lord's redeemed. At the Jordan River, John saw Jesus and said, "Look, the Lamb of God, who takes away the sin of the world!" (John 1:29 NIV)—Jesus, "In whom we have redemption through his blood" (Colossians 1:14). The word "redemption" means "liberation from captivity by a ransom paid." Not only are you purchased at the cost of Christ's life, you are also adopted by blood into God's family. (3) You are forgiven of all sins. "In whom (Jesus) we have . . . the forgiveness of sins." How did He accomplish the total removal of all our sins? "Having canceled the charge of our legal indebtedness, which stood against us . . . he has taken it away, nailing it to the cross" (Colossians 2:14 NIV). He wrote in His blood, "paid in full" across your outstanding bill of indebtedness to God, nailing your "canceled debt notice" to His cross. You are forgiven. You owe nothing!

March 20

"Jesus... showed them his hands."
John 20:19-20 (NCV)

HE SHOWED THEM HIS HANDS

Dr. Paul Brand, a brilliant surgeon who worked at the Christian Medical College in Vellore, India, writes: "I work with the marvels of the hand nearly every day... But one time of the year holds special meaning for me... When the world observes Passion Week... I reflect on the hands of Jesus... those hands that had done so much good were taken, one at a time, and pierced through with a thick spike... Roman executioners drove their spikes through the wrist, through the carpal tunnel that houses finger-controlling tendons and the median nerve... maiming the hand into a claw shape, and Jesus had no anesthetic... Later his weight hung from them, tearing more tissue, releasing more blood. Has there ever been a more helpless image? The disciples, who'd hoped he was the Messiah, cowered in the darkness or drifted away." But that's not the last time we see Jesus' hands. The Bible says: "When it was evening on the first day of the week, Jesus' followers were together. The doors were locked because they were afraid of the elders. Then Jesus came and stood... in the middle of them and said, 'Peace be with you.' After... this, he showed them his hands... His followers were thrilled when they saw the Lord." Dr. Brand adds: "For the remainder of his time here, Jesus chose [to minister through] scars in each hand. That's why I believe God hears and understands our pain... he kept those scars as a lasting image of wounded humanity. He knows what life on earth is like because he has been there. His hands prove it." So bring your wounds to Jesus today and let Him make you whole—body, mind, and soul.

March 21

"Are you in health, my brother?"
2 Samuel 20:9 (NKJV)

VITAMINS FOR SPIRITUAL HEALTH (1)

The principles of God's Word work like spiritual vitamins. For the next few days, let's look at some: Never excuse in yourself what you accuse in others. King David did that. In confronting him over his sin with Bathsheba, Nathan the prophet told David a story about two men. One had many cattle; the other had only one lamb. When a guest came to the rich man's house for dinner, he took the poor man's lamb. "David's anger was greatly aroused against the man, and he said . . . 'the man who has done this shall surely die! And he shall restore fourfold for the lamb . . . because he had no pity.' Then Nathan said to David, 'You are the man!'" (2 Samuel 12:5-7 NKJV). Nathan continued: "Thus says the Lord God of Israel . . . I gave you your master's house and your master's wives . . . And if that had been too little, I also would have given you much more! . . . You have killed Uriah [Bathsheba's husband] . . . with the sword; you have taken his wife to be your wife . . . Now therefore, the sword shall never depart from your house'" (vv. 7-10 NKJV). David didn't know it, but he pronounced his punishment with his own lips: "He shall restore fourfold." And David did. First, the child he fathered with Bathsheba died. Second, his son raped his daughter, and he didn't have the moral authority to deal with it. Third, Absalom, the beloved son destined to inherit his throne, fomented war and died at the hands of his own people. Fourth, civil war broke out in Israel, and thousands of people died as a result. The lesson is clear: never accuse in another what you excuse in yourself.

March 22

"Are you in health, my brother?"
2 Samuel 20:9 (NKJV)

VITAMINS FOR SPIRITUAL HEALTH (2)

Never take God for granted. Don't become overly familiar with spiritual things. Samson did that, and he paid dearly. After discovering the secret of his strength: "[Delilah] lulled him to sleep on her knees, and called for a man and had him shave off the seven locks of his head . . . and his strength left him. And she said, 'The Philistines are upon you, Samson!' So he awoke from his sleep and said, 'I will go out as before, at other times, and shake myself free!' But he did not know that the Lord had departed from him. Then the Philistines took him" (Judges 16:19-21 NKJV). It's a story of tragedy. Samson was born to lead Israel to victory. But instead, he gave in to his lowest impulses, consorted with the enemy, and thought he could get away with it. Listen to him: "I will go out as before, at other times." But this was one time too many. His disobedience hadn't robbed him of his supernatural strength before, but it did this time. He crossed a line and ended up losing his sight, his strength, his liberty, his credibility, and his usefulness. Eventually, he died a prisoner of the Philistines. You say, "Today's devotion sounds a bit harsh." No, it's protective! The Bible says, "The fear of the Lord is the beginning of wisdom" (Proverbs 9:10). When you persist in disobeying what you know God has told you to do and think you can escape the consequences, you're headed for trouble. Repent, get right with God and get back on track while you still can.

March 23

"Are you in health, my brother?"
2 Samuel 20:9 (NKJV)

VITAMINS FOR SPIRITUAL HEALTH (3)

Never allow life's disappointments to make you cynical. If you live long enough, people will disappoint you, including your family. Even spiritual leaders will let you down! Paul wrote: "We wanted to come to you—even I, Paul, time and again—but Satan hindered us" (1 Thessalonians 2:18 NKJV). Did you think Satan was going to send you a congratulatory telegram because you decided to serve the Lord? Not a chance! The walk of faith is one of delight—and difficulty. When you signed on for the first, you signed on for the second. Paul was on a sixteen-month missionary journey—one of miracles and church building. But he ended up in prison on trumped-up charges and was left to rot there. How did he respond? "Rejoice in the Lord always. Again I will say, rejoice!" (Philippians 4:4 NKJV). You say, "How can somebody rejoice in prison?" When you see your disappointment as God's appointment, you start to understand its purpose. Paul had books to write that would change the world, so God needed to get him "off the road." Listen to what he wrote from prison: "I want you to know . . . that everything that has happened to me here has helped to spread the Good News. For everyone here, including the whole palace guard, knows that I am in chains because of Christ. And because of my imprisonment, most of the believers here have gained confidence and boldly speak God's message without fear" (Philippians 1:12-14 NLT). Hidden in some of your biggest disappointments, you will find treasures of truth that literally transform your life and your future.

March 24

"Are you in health, my brother?"
2 Samuel 20:9 (NKJV)

VITAMINS FOR SPIRITUAL HEALTH (4)

Never forget the law of sowing and reaping. God set in motion certain laws, and they never change. One is the law of gravity. Another is the law of sowing and reaping. "While the earth remains, seedtime and harvest . . . shall not cease" (Genesis 8:22 NKJV). This law works both negatively and positively. If you sow good things, you will reap good things; if you sow bad things, you will reap bad things. Consider parenting. Eli, the high priest, was not only called to be a role model to the nation but also to his two sons. Now, he may have been a great success in ministry, but he failed badly on the home front. His sons, who were also priests, enriched themselves by taking bribes. They even slept with women in the temple courts. Pretty shocking, eh? So what did God say? "I will judge his house . . . for the iniquity which he knows, because his sons made themselves vile, and he did not restrain them" (1 Samuel 3:13 NKJV). As a result, Eli's sons were killed at the hands of their enemies, and when the news of it reached Eli he dropped dead. That's the harvest law working negatively. But thank God it also works positively. Paul writes about it: "Knowing that whatever good anyone does, he will receive the same from the Lord" (Ephesians 6:8 NKJV). You say, "What does that mean?" It means that whatever good you make happen for others – God will make happen for you. So whether it's a smile, a prayer, a gift, or a helping hand, start sowing good seeds, and you will reap harvests of blessing.

March 25

"Are you in health, my brother?"
2 Samuel 20:9 (NKJV)

VITAMINS FOR SPIRITUAL HEALTH (5)

Never withhold because times are hard. The Bible teaches that those who set their mind on "getting" always lose, whereas those who set their mind on "giving" always win. The story's told of a dog walking across a bridge with a bone in his mouth. When he looked down into the river and saw his reflection, he thought it was another dog with a bigger bone. So he jumped in to get it—and drowned. Paul dedicates two entire chapters in the Bible to the subject of money. Perhaps that's a good answer to those who say, "All the church ever talks about is money." Since money is congealed sweat, coined time, coined talent, negotiable you, it's one way in which you can give yourself to God. It's not the only way, but it's a very important way. So Paul writes: "Remember this—a farmer who plants only a few seeds will get a small crop. But the one who plants generously will get a generous crop. You must each decide in your heart how much to give. And don't give reluctantly or in response to pressure. 'For God loves a person who gives cheerfully.' And God will generously provide all you need. Then you will always have everything you need and plenty left over to share with others . . . Yes, you will be enriched in every way so that you can always be generous" (2 Corinthians 9:6-11 NLT). Unless you practice generosity, there's no point asking God for more money. He doesn't pour His blessing into pots, but into pipes; not into reservoirs, but into rivers that let it flow out. Getting the idea?

March 26

"Are you in health, my brother?"
2 Samuel 20:9 (NKJV)

VITAMINS FOR SPIRITUAL HEALTH (6)

Never forget, you're not home yet. The story's told of an old steamship that pulled into Southampton harbor and the passengers got off. Helium-filled balloons rose into the air and the crowd went wild as a young Hollywood starlet walked down the gangplank to be greeted by her family and friends. The last person off the ship was an elderly man who had spent more than fifty years of his life as a missionary in India. All his earthly possessions were in a tattered suitcase he carried by his side. After getting to his room in a cheap boarding house, he knelt by his bed and prayed: "Lord, I've served you all my life. I've sacrificed everything to tell others the good news of the gospel and brought many to you. Yet there was no one to celebrate my arrival or welcome me home." As he knelt there, the voice of God spoke to him softly and said, "Son, you're not home yet!" And redeemed child of God, neither are you! If God has blessed you with a nice house, thank Him and enjoy it. But don't get too settled. At best, it's only temporary accommodation. Paul often thought of heaven: "For I am hard-pressed between the two, having a desire to depart and be with Christ, which is far better. Nevertheless, to remain in the flesh is more needful for you" (Philippians 1:23-24 NKJV). God has something "far better" in mind for you. A great preacher once said: "It is our main business in this world to secure an interest in the next one."

March 27

*"Come, follow me," Jesus said, "and I will
send you out to fish for people."*
Mark 1:17 (NIV)

COURAGE (1)

If you want to experience God's blessing in a new way, get ready to leave your comfort zone. When Jesus called His disciples they were on familiar turf, doing what they knew best: fishing. But they couldn't stay there and follow Him. Neither can you. The Bible records: "As Jesus walked beside the Sea of Galilee, he saw Simon and his brother Andrew casting a net . . . for they were fishermen. 'Come, follow me,' Jesus said, 'and I will send you out to fish for people.' At once they left their nets and followed him" (vv. 16-18 NIV). Notice, they had to leave the security of the familiar in order to fulfill their destiny. And in case you think you are too old to try something new, Abraham was seventy-five when he left the comforts of home to go out and establish a new nation. Your age is not the issue; your faith is. Understand this: today, you are just one step of obedience away from the next truth God wants you to learn about Him, so you can't afford to stay where you are. We all have a tendency to cling to the "tried and true." The trouble with that is, when you are no longer being stretched, you begin to shrink, you become complacent, you think you can handle things on your own, and you stop growing. That's a dangerous place to be. If you feel restless at heart today and believe that God has more for you than you've been settling for, then it's time to confront your fears, walk through them and launch out into a new experience with Him.

March 28

*"Rise up; this matter is in your hands . . .
take courage and do it."*
Ezra 10:4 (NIV)

COURAGE (2)

Pastor Andy Stanley writes: "I keep a little card in my desk that reads: 'Dream no small dreams, for they stir not the hearts of men.' More than once that simple statement has kept me from retreating from my dreams. I know from experience that it's impossible to lead without a dream. When leaders are no longer willing to dream, it's only a short time before followers are unwilling to follow. So dream! Dream big. Dream often. Somewhere in those random ideas that flood your mind, is one that will capture your heart and imagination. And that seemingly random idea may very well evolve into a vision for your life." Every great accomplishment begins as a dream in someone's heart. All things are created twice: first in your mind, and then in your life. Dreamers allow their minds to wander outside the boundaries of what is, creating a mental picture of what can be. They are not always the most talented or best-educated—just the ones who refuse to put brackets around their thinking or limit themselves to what others have done. Doing this requires courage, lots of it! On the heels of every dream, there's a demon of doubt. No sooner is your dream conceived than your mind is suddenly filled with all the reasons why it may not work. And there will be folks around you who'll be quick to confirm those fears. In spite of that, you must forge ahead and dream; otherwise, you'll spend the rest of your life fulfilling the dreams of others. "Rise up; this matter is in your hands . . . take courage and do it."

March 29

"There is a greater power with us than with him."
2 Chronicles 32:7 (NIV)

COURAGE (3)

David was bringing food to his brothers at the battlefront when he saw Goliath. He wasn't thinking of becoming a hero; he just seized an opportunity other soldiers only dream about. Opportunities will catch you by surprise, and if you're not alert and ready, you'll miss them. What others discovered in David that day—had been there all along! If you're a leader, you already possess the talent necessary to lead. But courage is what will establish you as a leader before others. The people we revere most demonstrate courage—courage on the battlefield and in the boardroom, courage to defend the defenseless, or simply to attempt what nobody else thought possible. You say, "But I don't have the money." Don't worry, capital follows courage. *What* always precedes *how*. Don't be intimidated by the numbers. God is not moved by spreadsheets and market conditions – He's moved by faith. Don't let the how intimidate you. It's because how is so challenging that it provides you with great opportunity. If the pathway to success were well lit, it would already be crowded. If how wasn't a problem, someone else would already have figured it out. All progress begins with one question: "What needs to be done?" And somebody needs to be asking that question—why not you? The future belongs to those who have the courage to ask that question and the faith to hang on until they discover the answer. When the obstacles look too big, and opposition seems too strong, stand on this Scripture: "Do not be afraid or discouraged . . . for there is a greater power with us than with him."

March 30

"Blessed is the one who perseveres under trial."
James 1:12 (NIV)

ARE YOU BEING TEMPTED?

You'll never be exempt from temptation. Each season of life just brings temptation in a different form. When you're young, you'll struggle with the need for companionship and sexual fulfillment. In business, you'll be tempted to distort the truth, cheat, and pocket the money. When you become successful, if you're not careful, you'll become ego-driven, controlling, and opinionated. The truth is you never become so spiritual as to be exempt from temptation. After forty days of prayer and fasting, Satan tempted Jesus. So you are as vulnerable to attack after a great spiritual experience as you are in your lowest moments. Satan understood Jesus' assignment, and he was out to stop Him from accomplishing it. And he is out to stop you too! The battle you're in is not over the past. It's over the future. In the face of repeated temptation, Jesus defeated Satan by using the Word of God, and you must too. Without it you have no defense. In what specific areas do you struggle? What's your strategy for victory? What percentage of the time are you successful? What Scriptures have you memorized to help you conquer the tempter when he comes against you? Look at Samson, God's champion: blinded, chained, grinding corn like an ox in a Philistine dungeon. Sin has a blinding effect, a binding effect, and a grinding effect. Graveyards and prisons are filled with people who were too weak to stand up against Satan. Dreams crash daily on the rocks of temptation. Move the ship of your life away from those rocks while you still can.

March 31

"I prayed for this child."
1 Samuel 1:27 (NCV)

RAISING SECURE KIDS IN AN INSECURE WORLD

Protectiveness is part of parenting. But unless you're careful, you can shield your kids from the very things they need to mature. Sheila Wray Gregoire says we should Surrender them to God. We think we control their futures, but most of the time, they turn out differently than we planned. Samuel's mother, Hannah, said: "I prayed for this child . . . Now I give him back to the Lord" (vv. 27-28 NCV). Whether He chooses to send them to the jungles of Africa, the inner city, or a house around the corner, God knows best. Live with hope, not wishful thinking. Trust God to use them and guide them through life, even if He never reveals how or why. From this perspective, it's easier to accept that circumstances don't determine the final outcome; they're just the tools God uses to shape character. Encourage responsibility. Letting kids experience consequences shows them what works and what doesn't. For example, a tumble off the swing set teaches them not to be reckless and that failure to study results in poor grades. "It is good for people to endure burdens when they're young" (Lamentations 3:27 GW). Kids who learn responsibility and independence early are better equipped to succeed. Pray often and with purpose. Instead of praying for his "spiritual children" to be spared persecution, Paul said: "My prayer [is] that your love . . . abound more and more in knowledge and depth of insight, so . . . you may be able to discern what is best and . . . be pure and blameless for the day of Christ" (Philippians 1:9-10 NIV). Being a Christian doesn't mean life is always easy. But when you, the parent, demonstrate faith in God, your kids learn to trust Him too.

April 1

"He struck three times, and stopped."
2 Kings 13:18 (NKJV)

JUST KEEP CHEWING!

When threatened by the Assyrian army, Israel's king turned to the prophet Elisha for help. Elisha told him to take some arrows and keep striking them on the ground. But the king did it only three times and stopped. So Elisha was angry with him and said, "You should have struck five or six times; then you would have struck Syria till you had destroyed it! But now you will strike Syria only three times" (v. 19 NKJV). It's a story of partial victory, of what might have been if the king had put more into it. You see, it's not just the opportunity—it's the attitude that meets the opportunity that determines the outcome. God will give you chances to win, but it's your commitment that determines the size of your victory. Paul writes, "Serve wholeheartedly, as if you were serving the Lord, not people" (Ephesians 6:7 NIV). The clock meant nothing to Paul because he was on a mission. "I consider my life worth nothing to me; my only aim is to . . . complete the task the Lord Jesus has given me" (Acts 20:24 NIV). People of impact live with that mindset. So here's the question: "Is your heart in what you're doing? Are you giving it your all?" When Paul Hogan, who portrayed the movie character Crocodile Dundee, was asked how he became successful, he answered, "The secret of my success is that I bit off more than I could chew and chewed as fast as I could." Visions don't come cheap or easy. The bigger your vision, the bigger the price tag. The secret to fulfilling your vision is—just keep chewing!

April 2

"Walk in wisdom . . . redeeming the time."
Colossians 4:5 (NKJV)

TAKE CONTROL OF YOUR TIME (1)

Nothing is more costly than wasted time. Every minute lost is gone forever. Today we have more time-saving devices than any other generation, yet we seem to have less time. To get control of your life, you must first get control of your time. That means redirecting each lost minute toward a worthy purpose. We all have things we want to do, plan to do, and feel bad about not doing. Understand this: the difference in who you are right now and the person you'll be ten years from now will largely be determined by your relationships and your reading habits. And the first book you should read is your Bible, the world's greatest wisdom manual. Here's a suggestion that will help you: instead of having an "all or nothing" attitude to Bible reading, seize your "in-between time." You'll be amazed how the wasted minutes in each day and week add up to hours of productive time. J. Oswald Sanders gives us three great insights: (1) Stop leaks. Let us not consider our day only in terms of hours, but in smaller areas of time. If we look after the minutes, the hours will look after themselves. (2) Set priorities. Much time is spent on things of only secondary importance. We give such undue attention to petty details that matters of major importance are squeezed out. This is especially so where spiritual things are concerned. (3) Start planning. Without a plan, we all tend to drift. So in the attitude of prayer, ask, "How can I best plan today?" Buy up the spare minutes as eagerly as a miser hoards money.

April 3

"Teach us to realize the brevity of life."
Psalm 90:12 (NLT)

TAKE CONTROL OF YOUR TIME (2)

Gordon MacDonald gives us some of the traits of a disorganized life. See if you recognize any: "(1) Appointments/messages/deadlines missed. I know I'm disorganized when there are a series of forgotten appointments, telephone messages to which I have failed to respond, and deadlines which I have begun to miss. The day becomes filled with broken commitments and lame excuses. (2) Unproductive tasks. If I am disorganized I tend to invest my energies in unproductive tasks . . . There is a tendency toward daydreaming, and avoidance of decisions that have to be made, and procrastination. (3) Lack of intimacy with God. Disorganized Christians rarely enjoy intimacy with God. No one has to tell them that time must be set aside for the purpose of Bible study and reflection, for intercession, for worship. They know all of that. They simply are not doing it. They excuse themselves, saying there is no time. But they know it is more a matter of organization and personal will than anything else. (4) Shallow personal relationships. Days pass without a significant conversation with my son or daughter. My wife and I will be in contact, but our conversations may be shallow. I may become irritable, resenting any attempt on her part to call attention to things I have left undone or people I appear to have let down. (5) Lack of self-esteem. When we are disorganized in our control of time we just don't like ourselves, our jobs, or much else about our worlds. And it is difficult to break the destructive pattern that settles in. This terrible habit pattern of disorganization must be broken, or our private worlds will quickly fall into total disorder."

April 4

"I must work... while it is day."
John 9:4 (NKJV)

TAKE CONTROL OF YOUR TIME (3)

Time is like money; it must be budgeted. That means determining the difference between the fixed—what you must do—and the discretionary—what you would like to do. What caused Jesus to be such an organized person? (1) He understood His mission. During His final walk toward Jerusalem where He would be crucified, His ears picked up the voice of a blind man and He stopped, much to the consternation of His friends. They were irritated that Jesus did not appreciate that Jerusalem was still six or seven hours away and that they would like to get there to achieve their purpose, the celebration of the Passover (See Luke 18:35-42). From where they were standing, it appeared that Jesus was misusing His time. But from where Jesus was standing, the time was well spent for it fitted the criteria of His mission. (2) He understood His limits. He knew what we so often forget: that time must be properly budgeted for gathering inner strength and resolve in order to compensate for one's weaknesses when spiritual warfare begins. Knowing His limits, such private moments were a fixed item on Jesus' time budget. And it was hard for even those closest to Him to fully appreciate this. (3) He had His eye on the future. Jesus spent the lion's share of His time training twelve men. He said, "I will build My church" (Matthew 16:18 NKJV). How did He plan to build it? Through others. So, the way to maximize your time—is to keep your life's purpose before you at all times and evaluate each decision in the light of it.

April 5

"Trust in the Lord."
Proverbs 3:5 (NKJV)

WHEN YOU CAN'T UNDERSTAND, TRUST GOD

The Bible says, "Trust in the Lord with all your heart, and lean not on your own understanding; in all your ways acknowledge Him, and He shall direct your paths" (vv. 5-6 NKJV). But what if your path leads through pain, pressure, and problems? John the Baptist's did. He didn't deserve imprisonment. After all, he was the forerunner of Christ and the voice of God in the community. Plus, he was Jesus' cousin. So he sent Jesus a message asking, "Are you really the Messiah, or should we keep looking?" (See Matthew 11:3; Luke 7:19) "Lord, if I'm in your will, how come I'm in this situation?" It's a question motivated by unfulfilled expectations. We think, "Lord, I've obeyed you; how come things aren't working out for me?" And it feels worse when you've faithfully served Him. Writing about her daughter's death, Meg Woodson says, "I'll never forget those shrill, piercing screams; that the God who could have helped, looked down on this young woman who was devoted to Him . . . and decided to sit on His hands and let her death top the horror charts." Talk about unmet expectations! Jesus could have saved John, but He didn't. Instead, He sent back word: "Don't worry, everything's on target, the kingdom is being built. You did your job well" (See Matthew 11:4-5). It probably wasn't the answer John hoped for. He was looking for solutions to temporal problems while Jesus was busy establishing an eternal kingdom. So next time God doesn't seem to meet your expectations, it's not that He doesn't care; it's that He sees the big picture and He's handling issues you can't even begin to comprehend. So trust Him!

April 6

"My life is worth nothing ... unless I use it for finishing the work assigned me by the Lord."
Acts 20:24 (NLT)

PURPOSE

There's an old saying: "If you love your job, you'll never work a day in your life." That's not quite true. Most people work hard. But even when they love their job, they still have to do things they don't like to do. They give effort above and beyond what's comfortable. It's probably more accurate to say that if you're doing something you believe in, the hard work you do will bring you deep satisfaction. Novelist Ursula K. Le Guin stated, "It is good to have an end to journey toward, but it is the journey that matters in the end." Some folks suffer from "destination disease." They think that arriving at a certain place in life will bring them happiness. What a shame. Because the reality is that many times when we arrive, we discover that it wasn't what we expected. If you become fixated on a destination, you can miss the great things that happen along the way. You miss the joy of today. If you're convinced that "someday" is going to be your best day, you won't put enough into today—or get enough out of it. If you're not doing something significant with your life, it doesn't matter how long it is. It's not enough just to survive, you need a reason to live. This is where Christ comes in: He will give you A new life and add purpose to your life—plus the power to fulfill that purpose. D. L. Moody once said, "Let God have your life; He can do more with it than you can."

April 7

"I will pour out my ... blessing on your children."
Isaiah 44:3 (NLT)

HOW TO PRAY FOR YOUR CHILDREN

You must pray, claiming God's promises over your children. Are such prayers effective? Yes. God says, "I am ready to perform My word" (Jeremiah 1:12 NKJV). We serve a promise-making, promise-keeping God! "So shall My word be that goes forth from My mouth; it shall not return to Me void, but it shall accomplish what I please, and it shall prosper in the thing for which I sent it" (Isaiah 55:11 NKJV). So pray for your children each day and stand on these promises: "I will pour My Spirit on your descendants, and My blessing on your offspring" (Isaiah 44:3 NKJV). "'And this is my covenant with them,' says the Lord. 'My Spirit will not leave them, and neither will these words I have given you. They will be on your lips and on the lips of your children and your children's children forever. I, the Lord, have spoken!'" (Isaiah 59:21 NLT). "Now this is what the Lord says: 'Do not weep any longer, for I will reward you,' says the Lord. 'Your children will come back to you from the distant land of the enemy. There is hope for your future,' says the Lord. 'Your children will come again to their own land'" (Jeremiah 31:16-17 NLT). "The posterity of the righteous will be delivered" (Proverbs 11:21 NKJV). "Blessed are those who fear the Lord, who find great delight in his commands. Their children will be mighty in the land; the generation of the upright will be blessed" (Psalm 112:1-2 NIV). "Believe on the Lord Jesus Christ, and you will be saved, you and your household" (Acts 16:31 NKJV).

April 8

"Husbands, love your wives."
Ephesians 5:25 (NKJV)

HOW'S YOUR COMMUNICATION?

One of the biggest challenges in marriage is communication. Here's an example: in the past, husbands went to work, and wives stayed home to raise the children. Now, someone has estimated that the average man speaks about twenty-nine thousand words a day and the average woman speaks about thirty-three thousand words a day. That may not be accurate, but let's use it as an illustration. He's been out in the workplace all day, and by the time he gets home, he's used up twenty-six thousand of his words, leaving only three thousand he feels no need to say. But she's been locked up all day with the dishes, the diapers, and the drudgery. She has talked to her mother, friends, and neighbors and used up about eight thousand words. So when he gets home, she has twenty-five thousand words waiting for him. After a silent supper, he spends the evening watching TV, then they go to bed. As he's about to fall asleep, a voice says, "Are you awake?" If you are wise, you will be! If not, tomorrow night, there will be fifty thousand words lying beside you. Do the math; in ten years, there will be enough words to fill the central library. But maybe not; maybe there will be no words. A frequent reason given in divorce is: "We just got to where we had nothing to say to one another anymore." The Bible says, "Husbands, love your wives." Love listens when we have nothing particularly interesting to say. It listens because only when we have been heard and validated do we feel cherished. So, "How's your communication?"

April 9

"When it prospers, you will ... prosper."
Jeremiah 29:7 (GW)

MAKE THE MOST OF IT

Are you at a place in your life and you'd rather not be there? Well, God has a word for you, but it may not be one you want to hear. It's the same word Jeremiah brought to his people when they were slaves in Babylon, far from everything near and dear: "You're not going home anytime soon, so change your attitude, dig in and make the best of it. Buy homes, plant gardens, let your children get married ... and in addition, pray for the peace and prosperity of the city where you're living because when it prospers, you will prosper" (See Jeremiah 29: 5-7). The Israelites were in exile because God had allowed them to be taken captive. So, could it be that you are where you are today because God placed you there to bless those around you? Instead of putting your life on hold waiting for circumstances to change, start sowing into other people's lives what you want to come back as a harvest in your own. Why? Because when they are blessed, you'll be blessed too! How do we know? Because Jesus said, "Give, and it will be given to you ... the measure you use ... will be measured to you" (Luke 6:38 NIV). Martha Washington said, "I'm determined to be cheerful and happy in whatever situation I may be. I've learned that the greater part of happiness or misery depends upon our dispositions, and not upon our circumstances." That sounds just like Paul: "I have learned [to be] content in ... every situation" (Philippians 4:12 NIV). If you want to go from surviving to thriving, make the most of where God has placed you.

April 10

"In Him we have . . . the forgiveness of sins."
Ephesians 1:7 (NKJV)

YOU'RE FORGIVEN (1)

When God forgives you, but you refuse to forgive yourself, you're spurning His grace and choosing to be miserable. When you do that: (1) Your loved ones are at risk. It's not just about you. When you wallow in guilt, you tend to be more withdrawn and critical and less open and affectionate. So your spouse, children, parents, coworkers, friends, and even your pets suffer along with you. (2) Your health is at risk. Your mind affects your body. Doctors say bitterness generates chemicals that affect your vital organs. They increase your heart rate, raise your blood pressure, disrupt your digestion, tense your muscles, dump cholesterol into your bloodstream, and reduce your ability to think clearly. Each time you rehearse the past, those bad feelings deliver more corrosive chemicals. Science is now confirming what God has said: namely, that those who don't forgive themselves, and others, are more prone to heart attacks, depression, hypertension, and other serious illnesses. (3) Your future is at risk. The Bible says, "You will again have compassion on us; you will . . . hurl all our iniquities into the depths of the sea" (Micah 7:19 NIV). Stop dredging up what God has buried. Start looking ahead; otherwise, you'll get mired in a bog of your own making. The Bible says, "He is so rich in kindness and grace that he purchased our freedom with the blood of his Son and forgave our sins. He has showered his kindness on us, along with all wisdom and understanding" (Ephesians 1:7-8 NLT). With God's forgiveness comes the wisdom and understanding to not only survive your past but grow stronger as a result of it.

April 11

"Bless the Lord ... who forgives all your [sins]."
Psalm 103:2-3 (NKJV)

YOU'RE FORGIVEN (2)

We tend to forgive others more easily than we forgive ourselves. This is especially so when we fail in a major area like a marriage or career, or our actions have hurt others, or our habits have hurt us, or we know we are not doing what we should. So what should you do? (1) Acknowledge it. Don't be afraid to confess what you've done. You're not unique. You're not the first, and you won't be the last to fail. Once you've obtained God's forgiveness, get the support of a trusted friend. "Confess your trespasses to one another, and pray for one another, that you may be healed. The effective, fervent prayer of a righteous man avails much" (James 5:16 NKJV). (2) Delete it. Often it's not the offense itself but the guilt and stress associated with remembering our actions that make us feel bad. Our reaction is the problem! Continually revisiting our failures doesn't help at all, and it disappoints God. So catch yourself doing it—and hit the delete button! Focus on the fact that God has forgiven you, then put it behind you. "In Him we have ... the forgiveness of sins" (Ephesians 1:7 NKJV). (3) Replace it. Instead of guilt, choose gratitude. That's not hard to do; just begin to reflect on God's goodness. That's what David did: "Bless the Lord, O my soul, and forget not all His benefits: who forgives all your iniquities, who heals all your diseases, who redeems your life from destruction, who crowns you with lovingkindness and tender mercies" (Psalm 103:2-4 NKJV). When you start to look for them, you'll find lots of things to thank God for.

April 12

"Conquer evil by doing good."
Romans 12:21 (TLB)

A MEMO FROM HEAVEN

It's easy to forget why God saved you, what He's called you to do, and how you're supposed to live. So here's a memo from heaven: "Don't just pretend that you love others: really love them. Hate what is wrong. Stand on the side of the good. Love each other with brotherly affection and take delight in honoring each other. Never be lazy in your work, serve the Lord enthusiastically. Be glad for all God is planning for you. Be patient in trouble, and prayerful always. When God's children are in need, you be the one to help them out . . . If someone mistreats you . . . pray that God will bless him. When others are happy, be happy with them. If they are sad, share their sorrow. Work happily together. Don't try to act big. Don't try to get into the good graces of important people, enjoy the company of ordinary folks. And don't think you know it all! Never pay back evil for evil. Do things in such a way that everyone can see you are honest clear through. Don't quarrel with anyone. Be at peace with everyone, just as much as possible . . . never avenge yourselves. Leave that to God, for he has said that he will repay those who deserve it . . . Instead, feed your enemy if he is hungry. If he is thirsty give him something to drink and you will be 'heaping coals of fire on his head.' In other words, he will feel ashamed of himself for what he has done to you. Don't let evil get the upper hand, but conquer evil by doing good" (vv. 9-21 TLB).

April 13

"It is not good that man should be alone."
Genesis 2:18 (NKJV)

BUILDING LASTING RELATIONSHIPS

God's plan for your life always requires building relationships with the right people. To succeed, you must be able to recognize these people and work with them. Remember Jonathan, who loved David even at the cost of his own life? Or Ruth, who loved her widowed mother-in-law Naomi and gave her a reason to live again? Or Paul, who wrote, "I have no man like Timothy. For all men seek their own" (See Philippians 2:19-21). God wouldn't say, "It's not good that man should be alone," then tell you to do it all by yourself. But there may be areas in your life that need to be healed before you can enter these relationships and enjoy them. There's a world of difference between "using" relationships and "heart-ties." Blood-ties don't wear as well as heart-ties. So allow God to work on you. When you are ready, He will make the necessary introductions. In the meantime, get to know Him better. Make His opinion the source of your self-worth. If your last relationship stripped you of worth and drained you spiritually, use this time to get back on your feet. You may never have this opportunity again. And one more thought: begin to love as God loves. He sees your imperfection, handles your rejection and loves you regardless. That should help you not to throw someone away because they made a mistake. You wouldn't discard your car over a faulty part, right? If God forgave you as you forgive others, what shape would you be in? Come on, let God teach you how to build lasting relationships.

April 14

"What you say can mean life or death."
Proverbs 18:21 (NCV)

THE RIGHT WORD AT THE RIGHT TIME

To honor her students, a teacher gave each a ribbon that stated, "Who I am makes a difference," and asked them to pass it along to someone who'd made a difference in their lives. One kid gave his to a young executive who helped him plan his career. He, in turn, gave it to his boss, who was hard to get along with. He told him how much he'd been influenced by his creativity and asked him to give the ribbon to somebody he admired. That night the boss told his fourteen-year-old son, "I've thought about who I want to honor—and it's you. My days are hectic, and I'm always complaining about your grades and your messy bedroom. Tonight, I want to let you know the difference you've made in my life. Besides your mother, you're the most important person I know, and I love you." Fighting back tears, the boy replied, "Earlier today, I wrote a letter explaining why I'd taken my life and asking you to forgive me. I was going to do it when everybody was asleep. I didn't think you'd care. I guess I won't need the letter now." Upstairs in his son's room, the father found the anguish-filled note beside a loaded gun. God can help you to "speak a word in season to him who is weary" (Isaiah 50:4 NKJV). Words change lives: "What you say can mean life or death." So go out of your way today to speak words of encouragement to somebody you don't normally think about. "A word spoken at the right moment—how good it is!" (Proverbs 15:23 AMPC).

April 15

"[He] redeems your life from destruction."
Psalm 103:4 (NKJV)

LOOK BACK AND REMEMBER

Dr. Ann Shorb writes: "The key to being able to rejoice in the past is not found in counting the number of good things that have happened, but in remembering that God remembers! He never forgets His plan, and He never forsakes His promises. Even when life is tough, and things don't make sense, He's in control, and He's working out His plan." The Bible says, "The word of the Lord came to [Jeremiah]: 'What do you see?'... 'I see the branch of an almond tree,' I replied. The Lord said... 'You have seen correctly, for I am watching to see that my word is fulfilled'" (Jeremiah 1:11-12 NIV). Almonds blossoming; it's springtime! The change of seasons is a reminder of God's faithfulness. It gives you hope that the winter season you are in right now will soon give way to springtime and new life. How can you be sure? Because the Bible says that God keeps "his agreement forever" (Psalm 105:8 NCV). In life, every investment comes with the possibility of loss. But there's a big difference between losing and being wiped out. The truth is, God has too much invested in you to let His plans for your life be destroyed. The damage others can do to you is limited by the shield of God's divine purpose. Even when you are not aware of it, "[He] redeems your life from destruction." Stop and think back on some of the doors He closed that didn't make sense to you at the time. Now you realize that without His guidance and protection, the enemy waiting behind some of those doors would surely have destroyed you, right?

April 16

"You are precious to me."
Isaiah 43:4 (NLT)

HOW GOD FEELS ABOUT YOU

If you are struggling with feelings of unworthiness, praying longer, working harder, and vowing to do better won't necessarily change how you feel. Like remodeling an old house with a cracked foundation, you can redecorate every room, but the floors and ceilings will just keep sagging until eventually, it collapses. You've got to address the foundation! To do that, you must begin seeing yourself as God sees you; only then will you experience the stability and security you seek. Have you any idea how God feels about you? He sees you as: (1) Loveable. "You are precious to me. You are honored, and I love you. Do not be afraid, for I am with you" (vv. 4-5 NLT). What assurance! The Bible says, "The one the Lord loves rests between his shoulders" (Deuteronomy 33:12 NIV). What a secure position to be in! (2) Valuable. If you grew up feeling unwanted, you got the wrong message. God established your worth at the cross. "The Son of God, who loved [you], and gave himself for [you]" (Galatians 2:20). The slogan on Hallmark cards says, "When you care enough to send the very best." That's what God did for you at the cross. (3) Capable. Without a supportive environment to grow up in, you can end up with a diminished sense of ability. It's why we compensate by overachieving. But God knows that you are capable because He's "given . . . you . . . special abilities" (1 Peter 4:10 TLB). Furthermore, He has "set [you] down in . . . company with Jesus" (Ephesians 2:6 MSG). So stay in your seat and don't let anybody tell you that your life doesn't matter. It does because God says so!

April 17

"My grace is all you need. My power works best in weakness."
2 Corinthians 12:9 (NLT)

WHAT'S YOUR GREATEST WEAKNESS?

Self-help gurus assure us that we can overcome any weakness, so it must be true, right? Look around you! The evidence doesn't show it. What we have seen, however, are people who, with God's help, have changed their lives by building on time-tested scriptural principles. Trying to "cure" your weaknesses just wastes valuable time and energy that could be redirected toward healthier pursuits. For example, when an addict stays clean, does that mean they are no longer vulnerable in that area? No, it just means they have filled the vacuum with something better. Paul writes: "The temptations in your life are no different from what others experience. And God is faithful. He will not allow the temptation to be more than you can stand. When you are tempted, he will show you a way out so that you can endure" (1 Corinthians 10:13 NLT). But what about all those socially acceptable weaknesses that masquerade as strengths, like perfectionism, materialism, judgmentalism, and status-seeking? Many who would be ashamed to admit they are an alcoholic are proud to be a workaholic. Driven by fear and obsessed with time, they are totally focused on doing instead of being. That is, until their obsession with not having enough and being enough lands them in cardiac rehab, bargaining with God for another chance. Constantly dwelling on a weakness just reinforces it, whereas applying the scriptural solution brings results. And the good news is, you don't have to do it alone. God is available to help you. He told Paul, "My grace is all you need. My power works best in weakness."

April 18

"Jesus made the disciples get into the boat and go."
Matthew 14:22 (NIV)

WALKING ON WATER (1)

When you find yourself in trouble, do you sometimes think, "I must have done something wrong? Perhaps I've missed God's will, and He's punishing me"? No. Trouble is multi-sourced and frequently unrelated to our wrongdoing or God's punishment. The disciples weren't in the storm by disobeying, but by obeying Jesus; not by rejecting God's will, but by embracing it. The Bible says, "Jesus made the disciples get into the boat and go," and they obeyed. At times you'll find yourself in troubled waters because you did what was right rather than what was popular, easy, or selfish. When that happens, here are some helpful lessons from the disciples' experience: (1) Obedience doesn't guarantee there will be no storms. The disciples had just seen Jesus feed five thousand people with five bread rolls and two fish and end up with more food than He started with. Shouldn't their faith have been strengthened? Yet they forgot it completely when fear came knocking. Jesus had told them He'd meet them on the other shore, yet they forgot His miracle-working power and His promise and gave in to anxiety. Understand this: When God doesn't solve your problem, He will show up in the middle of it and cause you to come out with your faith fortified. (2) Fear doesn't mean you're a failure. It's just a reminder that you're human, and, like the disciples, you've forgotten Who has the power and Who's in charge. And these are lessons that transform your trial into triumph.

April 19

"The boat was ... buffeted by the waves because the wind was against it."
Matthew 14:24 (NIV)

WALKING ON WATER (2)

Notice: (1) Trouble doesn't mean God has abandoned you. The disciples learned that Jesus may be out of sight, but He's never out of touch. To "walk by faith, not by sight" (2 Corinthians 5:7 NKJV) means sometimes you'll walk in darkness without visible cues. Someone put it this way: "When you can't trace His hand, you can trust His heart." When the disciples were being tossed like a cork on the waves, Jesus was up on a mountain praying for them! He was aware of the problem and He was working on the solution. He was their mediator and their need-meeter, just as He has one hand on your need and the other on your answer. "He always lives to intercede for [you]" (Hebrews 7:25 NIV). Can you imagine Jesus praying to the Father for His fear-filled disciples? And can you imagine the Father refusing to answer His prayers? Never! "The Spirit himself intercedes for us" (Romans 8:26 NIV). With both Jesus and the Holy Spirit talking to the Father on your behalf, your victory is guaranteed. (2) Between the command to "Go" and your safe arrival on the other side, there's often a crisis. Jesus commanded them to cross to the other shore, but before the trip was completed, their world experienced upheaval. What's buffeting your life today—loss, guilt, loneliness, financial reversal, illness, addiction, rejection? When our faith is low and our fear high, we cry, "If only I had (or hadn't) ... If only I could ... " Learn to trust God. It's not over until He says so. And He hasn't!

April 20

"God is ... a very present help in trouble."
Psalm 46:1 (NKJV)

WALKING ON WATER (3)

Let's observe two final things: (1) Between the dread and the devastation, look for the Deliverer. Picture a boat lashed by huge waves and frightened disciples who thought they were going under. They forgot the promise: "God is . . . a very present help in trouble. Therefore we will not fear" (vv.1-2 NKJV). They didn't look for Jesus to rescue them. Yet as the night advanced and things looked hopeless, He "went to them, walking on the sea" (Matthew 14:25 NKJV). Did they rejoice? No, their fear intensified, and they said, "It is a ghost!" (v. 26 NKJV). Look out! Your fear can distort your perceptions and make you see the answer as just another problem. Often what appears as a threat is actually a blessing about to manifest itself. For example, you lose your job, and God opens up a better one, but your fear and inadequacy make you avoid the interview. Look to Jesus in your time of fear; when He takes away the lesser, it's always to give you the greater. (2) God's best always requires facing what you fear. Jesus called Peter to come to Him. Deciding it was safer in the storm with Jesus than in the boat without Him, Peter walked toward Him. But there's always a moment after you step out in faith when you hear, "What if I'm not up to this?" Peter heard it, and the waves began to engulf him. Panicked, he called, and Jesus immediately rescued him. Peter wasn't drowning; he was learning and growing! When you walk by faith, even your failures will lead to success. So step out with Jesus; He won't let you drown.

April 21

"You received the Spirit of adoption."
Romans 8:15 (NKJV)

IMAGINE BEING ADOPTED BY GOD! (1)

The Bible says, "[We] received the Spirit of adoption by whom we cry out, 'Abba, Father.' The Spirit Himself bears witness with our spirit that we are children of God, and if children, then heirs—heirs of God and joint-heirs with Christ" (vv.15-17 NKJV). Adoptive parents understand what it's like to have an emptiness in their hearts, to search, to set out on a mission, to take responsibility for a child with a troubled past and an uncertain future. And that's what God did for you. Knowing full well the trouble you'd be, and what it would cost, He sought you, found you, paid the price for you, took you home, gave you His name and the right to call Him "Abba," which means "Daddy," a term of endearment. Adoption isn't something you earn; it's a gift you receive. You'd never hear adoptive parents say, "We'd like to adopt little Mary, but first we want to know—does she have a house, money for tuition, a ride to school in the morning, and clothes to wear every day?" The adoption agency would say, "Hold on, you're not adopting her because of what she has, but because of what she needs. She needs love, hope, a home, and a future." You don't earn the Spirit of adoption – you receive it by faith. That's important, because if you can't gain it through your stellar efforts, you can't lose it through your poor performance. How reassuring! And it gets better; you're an "heir" to all your Father owns. That means you'll never have a need He cannot or will not meet. How good is that?

April 22

"Receive the kingdom of God as a little child."
Mark 10:15 (KJV)

IMAGINE BEING ADOPTED BY GOD! (2)

Jesus said, "Whosoever shall not receive the kingdom of God as a little child, he shall not enter therein." You need to become a little child again, to allow yourself the kind of relationship with the Lord that you may have missed, to allow Him to heal and adjust the damaged places of your past. God provides arms that allow adults to climb up like little children and be nurtured through the pain of earlier days. The new birth gives you a chance to start over. God will not abuse you when you come to Him. Through praise, you approach Him like a toddler on unskilled legs. In worship, you kiss His face and are held securely in His embrace. He has no ulterior motive, for His embrace is safe. That's why it's important that you learn how to worship and adore Him. Even if you were exposed to grown-up situations when you were a child, God can reverse what you've been through. Here's what He told His people: "I passed by you and saw you struggling…I said to you…'Live!' I made you thrive like a plant in the field; and you grew, matured, and became…beautiful…I…covered your nakedness…I…entered into a covenant with you and you became Mine…I washed you in water…I thoroughly washed off your blood, and I anointed you with oil. I clothed you in embroidered cloth and gave you sandals…I clothed you with fine linen and covered you with silk" (Ezekiel 16:6-10 NIV). And God can do that for you too.

April 23

"Lord, teach us to pray."
Luke 11:1 (NKJV)

LORD, TEACH ME TO PRAY (1)

In his book, With Christ in the School of Prayer, Andrew Murray writes: "None can teach like Jesus … therefore we call on Him, 'Lord, teach us to pray.' A pupil needs a teacher who knows his work, who has the gift of teaching, who in patience and love will descend to the pupil's needs. Blest be God! Jesus is all this and much more … Jesus loves to teach us how to pray." If you: (a) are not sure God is really listening when you talk to Him; (b) don't understand why some prayers seem to go unanswered; (c) wonder if you are praying "right" or generally feel frustrated in prayer; (d) are eager to know what to do to feel more connected with God and gain confidence that your prayers really do make a difference, say, "Lord, teach me to pray." Although there are principles of prayer that apply to everyone, God will lead each of us individually. He wants to take you just the way you are and help you discover your own rhythm of prayer, to develop a style of prayer that maximizes your relationship with Him. He wants prayer to be an easy, natural, life-giving way of communicating as you share your heart with Him and allow Him to share His heart with you. Prayer is so simple; it's nothing more than talking to God and taking time to listen to what He has to say to you. God has a personalized prayer plan for you, a way for you to communicate most effectively with Him. So begin by saying, "Lord, teach me to pray."

April 24

"Jesus . . . spent the night praying."
Luke 6:12 (NIV)

LORD, TEACH ME TO PRAY (2)

One of the dangers of being involved in God's work is that you can go for weeks or even months without praying. In a survey of a thousand pastors, half acknowledged that they often went for long periods without taking time to pray. They didn't have a personal prayer life beyond their function in church. Amazingly, they had preached entire sermons on the topic, yet they themselves didn't practice it. Can you relate? Jesus arose before dawn and spent hours in prayer. He even prayed all night. And it showed. His incredible success flowed out of the rich relationship He had with His Father. He made deposits every morning so that He could make withdrawals all day long. One Bible teacher writes: "I have gone from laboring and striving to pray for five minutes every few days to enjoying—and actually personally needing and wanting—beginning my day with prayer, then to praying throughout the day as things come to my heart, and finally ending my day communicating with the Lord as I fall asleep. I have moved from a sporadic, irregular prayer life to regular times of prayer that are disciplined without being legalistic. Where I once thought I was fulfilling an obligation to God by praying, I now realize that I absolutely cannot survive a day and be satisfied . . . if I do not pray. I realize that prayer is a great privilege, not a duty. I no longer approach God in fear, wondering if He will really hear me and send an answer to my prayers. I now approach Him boldly, as His Word teaches me to do, and with great expectation."

April 25

"Evening, morning and noon ... he hears my voice."
Psalm 55:17 (NIV)

LORD, TEACH ME TO PRAY (3)

God is far too creative to insist that every person interact with Him in exactly the same way. He designed each of us differently. There are prayer principles that apply to all of us, but God leads each of us as individuals. We are all at different places in our walk with Him. We are all at different levels of spiritual maturity. We all have different types of experiences in prayer. Yes, we need to learn the fundamentals of prayer. But then we need to move beyond intellectual knowledge about how to pray and take those principles to the Lord and say: "Teach me to apply this to my life, in my situation, to my heart. Show me how this idea is supposed to work for me. God, I'm depending on You to teach me to pray, to make me effective in prayer, to make my relationship with You through prayer the richest, most rewarding aspect of my life." When you say, "Lord, teach me to pray," you're asking Him to teach you to pray in a distinctly personal way, and to enable your prayers to be easy, natural expressions of who you are. You need to go before God just the way you are and give Him the pleasure of enjoying the company of the "original" that He made you to be. You need to approach Him with your own strengths, weaknesses, uniqueness, and everything else that so wonderfully distinguishes you from everyone else. God enjoys meeting you where you are, developing a personal relationship with you, and helping you grow to become everything He wants you to be.

April 26

"He fashions their hearts individually."
Psalm 33:15 (NKJV)

LORD, TEACH ME TO PRAY (4)

Your prayer style should be consistent with the way God designed you. Yes, you can learn from people who are more experienced in prayer than you are, but you need to be careful not to make them your standard or become a "clone." It's wrong to force yourself to do what others do if you are not comfortable with it in your spirit. Don't try to keep up with someone else or copy their prayer style. And don't feel compelled to work every prayer principle you have ever learned, every time you pray. Most of us are afraid not to be like everyone else. We are more comfortable following specified rules than daring to follow the leading of God's Spirit. When we follow man-made rules, we please people. But when we step out in faith and follow God's Spirit, we please Him. You don't need to feel pressured to pray a certain way, or for a certain length of time, or to focus on specific things because other people are doing so. "Untie the boat from the dock," so to speak, and let the tide of God's Spirit take you wherever He wills. When you are in control, you know what will happen next. But when you let God's Spirit take the lead, you are in for a lot of surprises in life. Wonderful surprises! You need to be determined to be yourself and refuse to spend your life feeling guilty because you're not like somebody else. The Bible says, "He fashions their hearts individually." So when it comes to prayer, the word for you today is, "Be yourself."

April 27

"Let us strip off every weight that slows us down."
Hebrews 12:1 (NLT)

STAY FOCUSED!

The Bible says, "Let us strip off every weight that slows us down . . . And let us run with endurance the race God has set before us." God has given you the two things needed to run and win your race in life: time and energy. And you can't afford to waste them. Why do we have such a hard time saying no? Two of the most common reasons are: (1) Fear of rejection. Ultimately, you must ask yourself this question: "Whose approval am I seeking, God's or people's?" (2) Fear of missing out on good opportunities. We assume that whenever opportunity knocks, we must answer the door and say yes to whatever's standing there. That's a mistake. Opportunity doesn't equal obligation. There will always be more opportunities than there is time to pursue them. So you must choose your opportunities prayerfully and wisely. Jim Collins, author of the book Good to Great, writes: "Most of us lead busy but undisciplined lives. We have ever expanding 'to do' lists, trying to build momentum by doing, doing, doing. But it rarely works. Those who built the good to great companies made as much use of 'stop doing' lists, as 'to do' lists. They displayed a remarkable discipline to unplug from all sorts of extraneous junk and channel their resources into only one or a few areas." In his groundbreaking book, Focus: The Future of Your Company Depends on It, Al Ries adds, "Great leaders, in spite of a multitude of distractions, know how to keep things focused. They know how to inspire and motivate their followers to keep pushing 'the main chance.' They don't let side issues overwhelm them." So stay focused!

April 28

"Your righteous laws are eternal."
Psalm 119:160 (NIV)

GOD'S WORD DOESN'T CHANGE

A publishing house advertised: Ten books to read before you die - and the Bible didn't make the list! Amazing. If there's one book you should read, it's the Bible! When a well-known Christian author replaced her favorite cookbook with a "New and Updated" version, she said: "It wasn't the same. It had been adapted for convenience. And people are trying to do the same with God's Word; adapt it to make it more convenient, time-saving, and easier to follow. The truth is, God's Word never changes. The results of sin are the same: 'The wages of sin is death, but the gift of God is eternal life in Christ' (Romans 6:23 NKJV). God's plan of salvation hasn't changed: 'By grace you have been saved through faith ... not of works, lest anyone should boast' (Ephesians 2:8-9 NKJV). His method for finding guidance is in the same place: 'The law of the Lord is perfect, converting the soul; the testimony of the Lord is sure, making wise the simple; The statutes of the Lord are right, rejoicing the heart; the commandment of the Lord is pure, enlightening the eyes' (Psalm 19:7-8 NKJV). His solution for anger is still the same: 'Rest in the Lord ... Cease from anger, and forsake wrath ... it only causes harm' (Psalm 37:7-8 NKJV). His method for finding peace hasn't changed: 'Be anxious for nothing, but in everything by prayer and supplication, with thanksgiving, let your requests be made known ... and the peace of God ... will guard your hearts and minds' (Philippians 4:6-7 NKJV). The Psalmist said, 'All your words are true; all your righteous laws are eternal.'" Bottom line: "new and improved" simply isn't in the book!

April 29

"Am I trying to please people?"
Galatians 1:10 (NIV)

TAKE THE STRESS OUT OF SERVING GOD (1)

Whether we are ordained ministers or lay people, we aren't exempt from stress. A deadly combination of traits seen frequently in those serving God produces inferiority and perfectionism—traits that make us obsessive-compulsive performers who think we're inadequate and that our service is never satisfactory. As a result, we become: (a) Over-responsible: We think we must do everything ourselves. (b) Irresponsible: We think nothing we do is acceptable, so we shouldn't tackle anything. (c) Uncertain: Vacillating between A and B, we feel like losers either way we go. Understand this: it's the stress we generate, not the demands of the service, that wears on us. And nothing stresses us like people-pleasing! Paul says, "Am I trying to please people? If I were still trying to please people, I would not be a servant of Christ," because he'd previously lived for people's acceptance. Now he found himself unable to be an effective servant of Christ and still worry about people's opinions. People-pleasing must not be your motivation for serving because: (1) It won't work. Every vote you capture loses you others. (2) It makes you attempt the impossible. The more you fail to please people, the harder you try. So you get caught in a cycle of pressure, failure, and discouragement. (3) You become the source of your strength. Jesus avoided this exhausting lifestyle. "The Son can do nothing by himself. He does only what he sees the Father doing" (John 5:19 NLT). Only when God is your source do your stress levels go down!

April 30

*"I . . . contend with all the energy
Christ so powerfully works in me."*
Colossians 1:29 (NIV)

TAKE THE STRESS OUT OF SERVING GOD (2)

You say, "Since serving successfully is a joint effort requiring cooperation with others who will often disagree with me, what's God's alternative to people-pleasing?" Paul answers, "Whatever you do or say, do it as a representative of the Lord Jesus" (Colossians 3:17 NLT). You represent the Lord Jesus! You are His servant, and He alone is qualified to judge your service. And it gets better; you are "God's handiwork, created in Christ Jesus to do good works, which God prepared in advance for us to do" (Ephesians 2:10 NIV). Regardless of people's opinions, God created you for a specific field of service. So celebrate your calling and embrace your destiny. When you do that, it takes the stress out of serving God. You are called by God, and all of heaven's resources are available to you. "God is working in you, giving you the desire and the power to do what pleases him" (Philippians 2:13 NLT). God is your source of wisdom and capability, so trust Him to carry the concerns of your ministry or career. "I . . . contend with all the energy Christ so powerfully works in me." Yes, there's some labor and struggle required, but you are never the sole proprietor. The energy is His, and it's working continually in you. You are the glove, and He's the hand that fills it, controls, and activates it. So relax, and just stay connected to Him. He will "equip you with all you need for doing his will . . . [and] produce in you . . . every good thing that is pleasing to him" (Hebrews 13:21 NLT).

May 1

"No temptation has overtaken you except what is common to mankind."
1 Corinthians 10:13 (NIV)

IT'S JUST PART OF LIFE'S JOURNEY (1)

Paul writes, "No temptation has overtaken you except what is common to mankind." Notice the word "overtaken." Suddenly you're "overtaken" by a set of circumstances you didn't create, don't want, and don't know how to get out of. Understand this: You don't pick the test; the test picks you! You don't get to choose who breaks your heart, or who gets on your nerves, or who lets you down. When you first held your child, you didn't think that one day you'd be down at a detention center trying to get them out of lock-up. You couldn't have known that a routine checkup would have you in the hospital fighting a life-threatening illness. Maybe your problem is so personal and embarrassing that you're afraid to even discuss it with anybody. So you walk the floor at night praying, "Lord, get me out of this or I'm finished!" Even Paul wrote, "We despaired . . . of life" (2 Corinthians 1:8). When you've been "overtaken" by a situation, you learn three things: (1) Don't judge others. The Bible says, "Every man is . . . drawn away of his own lust and enticed" (James 1:14). When you don't know what somebody's been through or the circumstances which have conditioned them, be quiet. If you have to talk about it, talk to God! (2) Don't tell your troubles to the wrong people. Look for people who will share your burden, not gossip about your problem. (3) Bring it to Jesus. "Let us then approach God's throne of grace with confidence, so that we may receive mercy and find grace to help us in our time of need" (Hebrews 4:16 NIV).

May 2

"But such as is common to man."
1 Corinthians 10:13 (KJV)

IT'S JUST PART OF LIFE'S JOURNEY (2)

The Bible says your struggle is not unique. It's "common to man." Your secret is not really a secret. It's just a secret shared by others who are equally afraid to talk. The only time we tend to be honest is when we're in trouble. As long as we think we can manage our dysfunction, we don't talk about it. You are not the only one who got married and then wanted a divorce, or lost control and lashed out, or quit a job and now doesn't have a job to go to. This is important to know because it takes away your feeling of isolation and enables you to overcome self-pity. It also helps you to say, "If others made it, then by God's grace, I can too." Perhaps you wonder if God is judging you, or the Devil is attacking you, or if you did something to bring it on yourself. No, it's just part of life's journey! You'll notice in Scripture that God doesn't whitewash His heroes. He doesn't exempt the people He uses from struggle and sorrow. "These things happened to them as examples and were written down as warnings for us" (1 Corinthians 10:11 NIV). Every age and every stage of life brings a different test and a different level of testing. You can't pray away the tests of life or quote Scripture and make them disappear. God never promised you a trouble-free trip to heaven. Jesus said, "I have told you these things, so that in me you may have peace. In this world you will have trouble. But take heart! I have overcome the world" (John 16:33 NIV).

May 3

"But God is faithful."
1 Corinthians 10:13 (KJV)

IT'S JUST PART OF LIFE'S JOURNEY (3)

Here's a promise you can stand on when your world has been shaken: "But God is faithful." Jesus said, "Heaven and earth shall pass away: but my words shall not pass away" (Luke 21:33). In a world of uncertainty, you can sing, "On Christ the solid rock I stand, all other ground is sinking sand." Your job, your health, your relationships, and your investments are all "sinking sand." But God's faithfulness is as solid as a rock. He will be faithful to you in the delivery room, in the operating room, in the nursing home, in the unemployment line, in the criminal proceedings, and in the divorce court. The Psalmist wrote: "I would have lost heart, unless I had believed that I would see the goodness of the Lord in the land of the living. Wait on the Lord; be of good courage, and He shall strengthen your heart" (Psalm 27:13-14 NKJV). Focusing on God's faithfulness will keep you from falling apart, giving up, having a nervous breakdown, or losing your mind. Be honest; hasn't God been better to you than you've been to Him? Hasn't He been faithful when you've been unfaithful and consistent when you've been inconsistent? "The gifts and calling of God are without repentance" (Romans 11:29). When God gives you a gift, He doesn't take it back. When He makes you a promise, He won't break it. Even when Abraham died, God remembered His promise and blessed his children down through the generations. Why is this important to know? Because when you begin to see God's faithfulness to you, it will make you want to be faithful to Him.

May 4

"He will not let you be tempted beyond what you can bear."
1 Corinthians 10:13 (NIV)

IT'S JUST PART OF LIFE'S JOURNEY (4)

The Bible says, "He will not let you be tempted beyond what you can bear." You have been tempered for the test! Like tempered steel or glass, certain additives have been placed within you to increase your ability to stand up to the pressure life will throw at you. The fact that you've been exposed to this level of testing is a sign that God has given you the grace to handle it. He's not going to let you escape this trial because He's equipped you to deal with it. So stop feeling sorry for yourself, or giving up, or saying you can't take it anymore. Not everybody in a gym can handle the same level of weight because each is at a different stage of development. But the trainer knows. He will push you to your limit, but he will never add one weight more than you can carry. God is a good trainer, and He's working according to a plan. He not only knows the right technique, He knows how much weight needs to be added in order to get you to the next stage of development. He will let you strain, shake, and sweat, but He won't let you break. While you are focused on temporary stuff like getting a better house or car or job, He has something entirely different in mind: "We . . . are being transformed into his image with ever-increasing glory, which comes from the Lord" (2 Corinthians 3:18 NIV). Once you understand this and line up your will with God's will, you'll begin to appreciate what He's doing and cooperate with Him.

May 5

"God ... will ... make a way to escape."
1 Corinthians 10:13 (KJV)

IT'S JUST PART OF LIFE'S JOURNEY (5)

Look at the last part of this verse: "[God] will ... make a way to escape, that ye may be able to bear it." Before the Army sends you into battle, it first sends you to boot camp. You're up at dawn running miles with a heavy backpack, climbing over barricades, crawling through mud with the sounds of gunfire all around you, taking orders from authority figures you don't like, who make you do stuff you don't want to do. But when you pass the test, you get to wear the uniform and fight for your country. Now with that picture in mind, reread these words: "But will with the temptation also make a way to escape, that ye may be able to bear it." The Living Bible says, "So that you can bear up patiently against it." God is looking for people who are able to bear up under training, then go out and win the battle with the enemy. For every problem, God has a solution. But it may not be the solution you have in mind! Satan's strategy is to defeat you by wearing you down, so winning is not a matter of escape but of endurance. Tenacious faith and commitment is one of the great themes of Scripture. It's also the secret of victory. When their prison doors miraculously opened, Paul and Silas realized that God's plan for them was not to escape but to stay there and win the jailer and his family to Christ. Sometimes God's "way of escape" is to keep you where you are and use you to bring glory to His name.

May 6

"The ... years of abundance ... came to an end."
Genesis 41:53 (NIV)

HOW TO ACHIEVE FINANCIAL SECURITY

The Bible says: "Joseph stored up huge quantities of grain ... The seven years of abundance in Egypt came to an end, and the seven years of famine began, just as Joseph had said. There was famine in all the other lands, but in the whole land of Egypt there was food" (vv. 49-54 NIV). In his book *Surviving Financial Meltdown*, Ron Blue teaches us some valuable principles for achieving financial security: (1) Think long-term. The longer term your perspective, the better financial decisions you'll make. Set goals in writing for the future. Invest for the long term and worry less about short-term ups and downs in your investment portfolio. (2) Spend less than you earn. To accomplish this, you need to know what you're earning and what you're spending. Make a spending plan (or, if we dare use that loathed term, a budget). Monitor how you're doing. Develop the self-control to avoid overspending. If you consistently spend less than you earn over a long period of time, you will do well financially. (3) Maintain emergency savings. A reserve set aside will help you ride out the curve balls life throws at you. You must spend less than you earn to build savings. Savings will then help you avoid debt. These principles work together. (4) Minimize the use of debt. Debt increases risk. It may allow you to do more and have more now, but it will reduce your ability to have more in the future. These four financial principles are so simple that they may easily be overlooked, yet they've stood the test of time.

May 7

"We are labourers together."
1 Corinthians 3:9 (KJV)

GROWING INTO LEADERSHIP (1)

A cartoon shows an executive sitting forlornly behind a big desk. Standing meekly on the other side of the desk is a man dressed in work clothes who says, "If it's any comfort to you, it's lonely at the bottom too." The truth is, you'll meet lonely people at the top, on the bottom, and in the middle. Loneliness is not a positional problem, it's a relational one. The Bible says, "A man who has friends must himself be friendly" (Proverbs 18:24 NKJV). The saying, "It's lonely at the top," was never made by a great leader. Stop for a moment and think about that. If you're all alone, nobody is following you. And if nobody is following you, you're not really leading. What kind of leader would leave everyone behind? An ineffective one. An insecure one. A dysfunctional one. Effective leadership is about lifting people, not elevating yourself. And to lift people, you must get close to them. As a leader, you must always remember these three things: (1) To have credibility, you must make it to the top. Many folks are willing to give you advice on things they have never experienced, but credibility comes from paying the price to achieve personal success. (2) To have respect, you must acknowledge that you didn't get to the top by yourself. Sir Edmund Hillary climbed Mount Everest because he had the right team. You need one too. (3) To have fulfillment, you must take others to the top with you. "We are labourers together." True success is shared success, and it only happens when you're willing to invest in the lives of others.

May 8

"I, Tertius, the one writing this letter for Paul, send my greetings."
Romans 16:22 (NLT)

GROWING INTO LEADERSHIP (2)

Paul surrounded himself with people who were willing to lay down their lives for him (See Romans 16:3-4). Some of them are virtually unknown. Ever hear of Tertius? He recorded Paul's thoughts so we could read them. We all know about Timothy, but do you know about Gaius? "He is my host and also serves as host to the whole church" (Romans 16:23 NLT). Many served in the shadows so Paul could work in the limelight. Sadly, when some leaders arrive at the top, they spend their time trying to push others off it. They play "king of the hill" because of immaturity, insecurity, and competitiveness. That may work for a time, but it doesn't last long. When your goal is to knock others down, your time and energy are spent watching out for people you think would do the same to you. It's a miserable way to live, and it's no fun for those who have to work with you. Jules Ormont said, "A great leader never sets himself above his followers except in carrying responsibilities." If you're in a leadership position, don't rely on your title to convince people to follow you. Build relationships. Win people over. When you don't love people, you're only a few steps away from manipulating them. When that happens, you'll have a high turnover. A few years ago the three great tenors—José Carreras, Plácido Domingo, and Luciano Pavarotti—were performing together. When a reporter tried to find out if there was any rivalry among the superstars, Domingo said, "No, you can't be rivals when you're together making music."

May 9

"Search me, O God, and know my heart; test me."
Psalm 139:23 (NLT)

GROWING INTO LEADERSHIP (3)

In his Pogo cartoon strip, Walt Kelly said, "We have met the enemy, and he is us." The hardest person in the world to lead will always be yourself. Human nature seems to endow us with the ability to size up everybody except ourselves. After having a victorious Goliath experience, followed by a devastating Bathsheba experience, the Psalmist wrote, "Search me, O God, and know my heart; test me and know my anxious thoughts. Point out anything in me that offends you, and lead me along the path of everlasting life" (vv. 23-24 NLT). That's a prayer you need to pray every day because we all have two problems. What are they? (1) We don't see ourselves as we see others. If we don't look at ourselves honestly and realistically, we will never understand where our personal difficulties lie. And if we can't see them, we won't be able to lead ourselves effectively. It's said that Frederick the Great of Prussia met an old man who was walking ramrod straight in the opposite direction. "Who are you?" Frederick asked. "I am a king," replied the old man. Frederick laughed. "Over what kingdom do you reign?" Proudly the old man replied, "Over myself." (2) We are harder on others than we are on ourselves. We judge others according to their actions, while we tend to judge ourselves according to our intentions. When we do the wrong thing, we let ourselves off the hook because we believe our motives were good. And the problem is, we are usually willing to do that over and over before requiring ourselves to change!

May 10

*"The heart of the discerning acquires knowledge,
for the ears of the wise seek it out."*
Proverbs 18:15 (NIV)

GROWING INTO LEADERSHIP (4)

The story's told of two Irishmen out hunting when one of them falls to the ground. He doesn't seem to be breathing, and his eyes are rolled back in his head. The other guy whips out his cell phone and calls 911. Frantically, he tells the operator, "Paddy is dead! What can I do?" The operator says, "Just take it easy. First, let's make sure he's dead." There is silence, then a shot is heard. The guy's voice comes back on the line and says, "Okay, he's dead, now what?" When you are under pressure, you can fail to hear what's being communicated, and the results can be fatal. So: (1) In order to lead people, you must first understand them. You must have insight into the human heart. Sensitivity toward the hopes and dreams of people is essential for connecting with people and motivating them. (2) Listening can keep problems from escalating. Good leaders are attentive to small issues. They pay attention to their intuition. Not only do they listen to what's being said they also hear what's not being said. They are secure enough to ask for honest feedback and not become defensive when they receive it. (3) Listening establishes trust. Dr. David Burns, Adjunct Clinical Professor of Psychiatry at the Stanford University School of Medicine, said, "The biggest mistake you can make in trying to talk convincingly is to put your highest priority in expressing your own ideas and feelings. What people really want is to be listened to, respected, and understood. The moment they are, they become more motivated to understand your point of view."

May 11

"Listen . . . and I will give you some advice."
Exodus 18:19 (NIV)

GROWING INTO LEADERSHIP (5)

As a leader, it's your job to see that things get done. But as the workload grows, you will have to find people with talents equal to the task; otherwise, you will stop growing. So what keeps us from seeking out the right people and delegating the right tasks to them? (1) Past hurts: Somebody let us down, so we're reluctant to trust anybody. (2) Pride: We don't want to share the credit with others. (3) Perfectionism: We are not willing to be put at risk while people with potential learn on the job, so our vision bottlenecks and everything bogs down. Moses had this problem with Israel. Here's how he solved it: "Moses' father-in-law replied, 'What you are doing is not good. You and these people who come to you will only wear yourselves out. The work is too heavy for you; you cannot handle it alone. Listen now to me and I will give you some advice . . . You must be the people's representative before God and bring their disputes to him . . . But select capable men from all the people . . . and appoint them as officials over thousands, hundreds, fifties and tens. Have them serve as judges for the people at all times, but have them bring every difficult case to you; the simple cases they can decide themselves. That will make your load lighter, because they will share it with you. If you do this . . . you will be able to stand the strain, and all these people will go home satisfied.' Moses listened to his father-in-law and did everything he said" (vv. 17-24 NIV). If you want to be a good leader, follow his example!

May 12

"I make known the end from the beginning."
Isaiah 46:10 (NIV)

GOD IS WORKING OUT HIS PLAN FOR YOU

You are not a mistake your parents made in the heat of passion. What your parents did may have been illegitimate, but you are not. You may wonder: "God, is it possible that You have a reason for my conception? Am I called to do something great in life? Is there something so unique to my personality, so connected to my life experiences, so relative to my sphere of influence, so dependent upon my color and culture, so necessary to my needs and shortcomings that nobody can do it exactly the way You want it done but me?" Yes. God says, "'I make known the end from the beginning . . . My purpose will stand.'" You are going to succeed because God has already determined your destiny. Before God establishes the procedure, He decides the purpose. When a builder is confused, he refers back to the blueprint and checks with the architect. God is the architect and builder of your life. He never gets confused about what He's planned or how it's to be built. When He builds something, it's built for maximum efficiency and optimal performance. We think, "Lord, why are You holding me back while others get to go forward? Why is it taking so long for my breakthrough to come?" God responds, "What does the blueprint say?" God is building a solid foundation under you so that you'll be able to handle the pressures that accompany His blessing and go through the storms of life without being moved or shaken. Anything that's made well is made slowly. Anything that's worth having is worth fighting for.

May 13

"Choose for yourselves this day whom you will serve."
Joshua 24:15 (NIV)

THE MOST IMPORTANT SKILL YOU CAN TEACH YOUR CHILD (1)

Good decision-making is the key to a happy life. But good decision-making is not a skill some of us are naturally blessed with, and poor decision-making is a struggle many experience in life. Courage, education, or the aging process don't automatically produce better decision-makers. Spending time with good decision-makers is wise, but it doesn't rub off on you. And the earlier you teach this skill to your children, the better (See Proverbs 22:6). So teach your children the following principles: (1) The consequences you get are the result of the choices you make. Let your children know it's not their circumstances but the decisions they make about them that govern their lives. You may think your kids know this, but they don't. Their "wiring problem" makes "cause and effect" difficult to connect until their brain reaches later adolescence. Asking, "What were you thinking about?" will just invite the famous shoulder shrug and blank stare. They're not stupid—they just need guidance. (2) You will always have options. Kids commonly feel powerless and hopeless when reacting to negative circumstances. They tend to be "either/or" thinkers, concluding that things are either all good or all bad. Teach them "both/and" thinking, because things can be bad, yet you can choose to make good decisions about them. "Either/or" thinking frequently produces kids who become pessimistic, disempowered, easily manipulated, depressed adults. Knowing they always have good options prevents circumstances from dictating their lives.

May 14

"A man reaps what he sows."
Galatians 6:7 (NIV)

THE MOST IMPORTANT SKILL
YOU CAN TEACH YOUR CHILD (2)

Somebody said, "Yard by yard life is hard, inch by inch life's a cinch!" For their life to go right, your children must learn to think right. So teach them to ask: (1) "What are my options in this situation?" But do it with the right attitude. If your face is like a thundercloud when you talk to them, they'll run for cover. Brainstorm with them, writing down every option that's offered. Tell them that no answers are wrong, and no idea will be judged silly; all suggestions are accepted and valued. You're priming their creative pump and encouraging them to think for themselves. (2) "What benefits come from each option?" The goal is not to coerce them but for them to discover and embrace the truth for themselves. And that comes through patience, not pressure. Have them list which benefits seem most important to them. (3) "What negative consequences come from each option?" Kids can be brutally honest. That's OK; it's just part of learning God's cause-and-effect law of sowing and reaping. Indeed, many adult regrets could have been avoided by following this law. Don't preach or rant about how terrible the consequences are. Teach them to question themselves, "Am I willing to accept the consequences? How would they change my life?" (4) "What personal values are involved in this decision?" Values-based decisions call us to the high road rather than the path of least resistance. Suggest some godly values as primers, such as truthfulness, trustworthiness, loyalty, responsibility, compassion, friendship, self-denial, courage, honor, faith, etc. Break it down small for younger kids, but don't miss your opportunity.

May 15

"Your thoughts ... are the source of true life."
Proverbs 4:23 (CEV)

THE MOST IMPORTANT SKILL YOU CAN TEACH YOUR CHILD (3)

Teach your child to ask themselves these two questions: (1) "How will I feel afterward?" What outlasts our decisions are the subsequent feelings of self-respect versus shame and positive self-worth versus negative self-worth. Our actions ultimately become history, but our thoughts about them continue to shape our future. "Carefully guard your thoughts because they are the source of true life." Kids with self-respect are much less likely to indulge in promiscuous sex, drugs, drinking, antisocial and illegal behaviors. Self-respect and self-worth are internal standards we are loath to violate. Giving in to selfish choices is like abandoning the moral core of our being—the sacred soul God gave us. (2) "How will the people I value feel about me after this decision?" The trust and respect of others is always needed to succeed. Reputation trumps money, even in the secular marketplace. "Choose a good reputation over great riches; being held in high esteem is better than silver or gold" (Proverbs 22:1 NLT). Poor decision-making can earn us a reputation that'll haunt our prospects indefinitely. "A person who plans (chooses) evil will get a reputation as a troublemaker" (Proverbs 24:8 NLT). When you get a negative reputation, it's hard to recover from it (See Proverbs 25:10 NLT). The short-term benefits of making poor decisions lead to long-term losses and regrets. The person God blesses must "exercise self-control, live wisely, and have a good reputation" (1 Timothy 3:2 NLT).

May 16

"[There is] a time to be silent and a time to speak."
Ecclesiastes 3:7 (NAS)

THE MOST IMPORTANT SKILL YOU CAN TEACH YOUR CHILD (4)

Teach your child to ask: (1) "Is this the best time to make this decision?" Decisions made in haste are often regretted. "There is a time to be silent and a time to speak." Poor decisions are situationally driven, caused by momentary stress, peer pressure, mood swings, and temporary emotions like loneliness, etc. When the situation changes, our feelings change, and our decisions often look doubtful. Can the decision be made later, reducing or eliminating the risk? Pressuring children often increases their desperation and leads to premature decisions. But assuring them that time is on their side lowers their reactivity and the likelihood of future regret. Helping them see that God "has made everything appropriate in its time" (Ecclesiastes 3:11 NASB) offers them space to think wisely about their options, allowing for God's guidance. (2) "If I were advising a friend (John or Susie), would I suggest they take this same option?" Shifting perspective often broadens the perceptions of our options. When emotionally influenced, our children often narrow their perspective, excluding many important possibilities. Often adults press logical, rational thinking on them, meeting resistance. But by bringing "John" or "Susie" into the equation, we open their perspective up. And one more thought: it's beneficial to "debrief" with your child, helping them to evaluate the effectiveness of their decision-making process. Talk through how they handled the situation. Ask, "How do you feel about that result?" If they're pleased, compliment them; if not, say, "I'm sorry about that. Any ideas what you'll change next time?" Instead of judging their failure, reward their success.

May 17

"Epaphroditus... ministered to my need."
Philippians 2:25 (NKJV)

ENCOURAGE SOMEONE TODAY

When people are hurting, they need your support until they can get back on their feet again. Medical researchers have developed a bone-bonding compound that illustrates this. It looks like toothpaste. Once injected into the body, it hardens in ten minutes. In twelve hours, it reaches the compression strength of natural bone. A study in the journal, *Science*, found the compound virtually identical to natural bone crystals. It so closely resembles real bone that the body doesn't reject it. Weeks after being injected into the body, the cement is replaced by real bone. According to the Associated Press, clinical trials "show the material has allowed patients to discard casts early—or altogether—and to resume walking more quickly and with less pain." Epaphroditus is introduced by Paul as "my brother, fellow worker, and fellow soldier... and the one who ministered to my need... Receive him therefore in the Lord with all gladness, and hold such men in esteem; because for the work of Christ he came close to death, not regarding his life, to supply what was lacking in your service toward me" (vv. 25-30 NKJV). You ask, "What was Paul lacking?" Encouragement! And who brought it? "Epaphroditus, a brother, a fellow worker, and a soldier." Epaphroditus worked side by side with Paul, and he fought for him. What an asset he was! We look for such people in times of crisis because they lift us. So today, ask God to make you an encourager whose words and actions bring comfort and support to others. There is no greater calling!

May 18

"All you need to say is simply 'Yes' or 'No'."
Matthew 5:37 (NIV)

SET BOUNDARIES (1)

When does "a good thing" become "too much?" Can I help you without hurting me? Can we share our lives without me giving up mine? When do you truly need my help? When do I need to let go and let you and God handle it? Finding the balance between "enough" and "too much" in relationships is a constant challenge and isn't easy. Especially when your role tends to be, "all things, at all times, to all people," and theirs is, "I'm helpless, you owe me, take care of me"; when you have no "no" and they have no "yes." Needing to be needed by needy people who always want someone to take care of them puts the needy person in the driver's seat—and puts you over the edge. They are never happy, whatever you do. So you do more to make them feel happier, and yourself feel less guilty, and you end up in a double bind. They resent you for not giving enough, and you resent them for not appreciating what you give. Yet neither of you knows how to break the cycle. So the relationship becomes what counselors call a "more-of-the-same" tangle where both parties resent and devalue the other, feeling stuck in a life-dominating trap you both fear to jettison. Marriages, families, friendships, workplaces, churches, and social groups get trapped in this "victim-rescuer" pattern where needy people and fixers become lock-stepped in a mutual dance they both "love to hate," but won't stop doing! Recognize yourself? If so, you're moving toward a healthier, less toxic relationship.

May 19

"Its parts should have equal concern for each other."
1 Corinthians 12:25 (NIV)

SET BOUNDARIES (2)

When you buy a house, you need clearly marked boundary lines to let you know what's yours and what's not. Good boundaries make good neighbors. The Bible says, "Seldom set foot in your neighbor's house—too much of you, and they will hate you" (Proverbs 25:17 NIV). So, how close is too close? Let's look at three kinds of boundaries we establish between ourselves and others. Rigid boundaries. These are designed to keep others at arms' length and protect your private, self-absorbed world. Without saying a word, your attitude says: "Keep out, trespassers will be prosecuted!" Why do we create such boundaries? Fear! We fear being known, controlled, hurt, or feeling inadequate and inferior. And our rigidity prevents intimacy. Our unwillingness to be vulnerable or to compromise leaves us defensive, isolated, and lonely. Closeness and intimacy are things we long for yet fear and avoid. We think, "You can't hurt me if I keep you at a safe distance." But it doesn't work. God designed us to share life's victories and defeats, not to live in isolation. We are to "have equal concern for each other. If one part [person] suffers, every part suffers with it; if one part is honored, every part rejoices with it" (1 Corinthians 12:25-26 NIV). Rigid boundaries rob you of life-enriching relationships. "So, what's the answer?" you ask. Reach out! You were created to give to others and to receive what they have to give back to you. In giving, you are fulfilled, and in receiving, you are made complete. Anything less is just existing.

May 20

"Like a city with broken-down walls."
Proverbs 25:28 (NLT)

SET BOUNDARIES (3)

Permeable boundaries. Well-adjusted people find the right balance between protecting their personal space, and allowing others to infiltrate, manipulate, and dominate them. They know how to say yes to what's healthy and no to what's not. Permeable boundary people, on the other hand, allow others to permeate their lives at will, siphon off their time and energy, dictate their options, and deprive them of other important relationships. Unable to say no, they permit others to make them feel guilty, obligated, uncaring, or even "unchristian" if they withhold what's demanded. They inconvenience themselves, their families, and their friendships to facilitate the endless demands of the seemingly helpless, disempowered, irresponsible user, believing they are being kind and helpful. The "helper's" toll is immense, often leading to emotional, physical, social, and spiritual overload, while the "helpee" feels increasingly dependent, irresponsible, and entitled, not appreciating, and sometimes even resenting the helper's efforts. Permeable boundary people are unaware that their "open" sign is always illuminated, attracting a deluge of other people's needs they feel personally responsible for. They carry the weight of much that's wrong in the world, feeling exhausted, anxious, inadequate, and guilty, taking it personally that they can't do more and fix things. And it leaves them feeling "used." "A person without self-control is like a city with broken-down walls." Understand this: You can't take charge of your own life while you're overwhelmed feeling responsible for other people's lives. Set some boundaries and live the life God gave you to live!

May 21

"I can make it through anything."
Philippians 4:12 (MSG)

SET BOUNDARIES (4)

Flexible boundaries. Rigid boundaries cause you to shut other people out and live unprepared and ill-equipped for the give-and-take that healthy relationships require. Permeable boundaries leave you defenseless against "users" who feel entitled to manipulate you and who expect to be taken care of at your expense. But flexible boundary people are competent for living their own life, yet with a balanced and healthy interest in others. They can be generous in sharing their time, compassion, and resources without becoming overly responsible or betraying their God-given duty to be the unique person He made them just to please others. They say, "I can be in relationship with you, without giving up being me!" They don't let you violate their boundaries, and they know how to keep from violating yours. Unlike rigid people, they bend and adjust as circumstances require, without becoming overwhelmed, defensive, resentful, blaming, or reactive. In tough situations, they roll with the punches, stay focused, and draw on a well of inner strength which God provides. Paul was such a person: "I've learned … to be … content whatever my circumstances … I can make it through (adjust to) anything in the One who makes me who I am" (vv. 12-13 MSG). People and circumstances don't control them; they flex, and let God take charge. They are helpful, but they don't feel guilty because they can't "fix" everybody. Their boundaries enable them to adjust to circumstances. They practice the principle, "Bear ye one another's burdens" (Galatians 6:2), without over-functioning or being responsible for others.

May 22

"It is [God] who gives you the ability to produce wealth."
Deuteronomy 8:18 (NIV)

ARE YOU STRESSED OUT ABOUT MONEY? (1)

The story of Elijah being fed by the ravens teaches us that God can take care of us in a bad economy (See 1 Kings 17:1-7). The story of Joseph teaches us that when we follow God's plan, we will have all that we need to get us through hard times (See Genesis 41:37-57). One of the dangers of living in a materialistic society is that you feel "entitled" to things, even when you can't afford them. To overcome financial anxiety, you must practice fiscal discipline. God doesn't bless recklessness. You can't go into debt, then pray that God will get you out of it. Sometimes He does. But if you don't learn from your mistakes, you'll just keep repeating them. A popular radio show in Atlanta is hosted by a guy called Clark Howard. He begins every program by saying, "Spend less, save more, and don't get ripped off." He talks about banks that charge extortionate rates for credit cards and encourages people to live within their means. "But I'm used to a certain lifestyle," you say. Get unused to it! If you want peace of mind, learn the art of contentment. Does contentment mean you can't have ambition? No, it means delaying gratification and enjoying where you are, on your way to where you're going. It means learning to live by these words: "I know how to live on almost nothing or with everything. I have learned the secret of living in every situation, whether it is with a full stomach or empty, with plenty or little. For I can do everything through Christ, who gives me strength" (Philippians 4:12-13 NLT).

May 23

"I am the Lord . . . who teaches you to profit."
Isaiah 48:17 (NASB 1995)

ARE YOU STRESSED OUT ABOUT MONEY? (2)

The best way to overcome financial anxiety is by trusting God to meet all your needs. You say, "That's nice, but what does God know about my business?" More than you think! He's the CEO of the whole world. When it comes to successful systems, nobody knows more than He. He created the universe in such precise order that if one star moves two degrees out of orbit without His permission, the whole thing dissolves into cosmic chaos. Yet when He needs to move a star, He can do it like He did for the wise men that first Christmas. Wall Street could learn a thing or two from Him! Here's part of His résumé: "I am the Lord your God, who teaches you to profit, Who leads you in the way you should go." If you want to become more profitable, go into partnership with God. Does that mean you can just stay home from work, go fishing, and God will pay your mortgage? No, God doesn't reward laziness and inefficiency! The story's told of a pastor who stopped by to admire the garden of one of his parishioners. "Isn't God's handiwork wonderful?" he said. The parishioner thought about it for a moment and then replied, "Yeah, but you should have seen it when God had it all by Himself." Understand this: (1) You've got to get up and go to work. (2) You've got to consult God before you make decisions. (3) You've got to honor God with your tithes and offerings (See Malachi 3:8-12). (4) When you've done your best, you've got to trust God with the rest.

May 24

"He has commanded us to love one another."
2 John verse 6 (NLT)

SHOW YOUR LOVE NOW

Each morning pray: "Lord, whether or not I get anything else done, help me to spend this day loving You and loving others, because that's what Your Word says life is all about." If you do that, you'll treat those around you more graciously. And people will notice it. You'll start winning in areas where you've lost. The more time you give to someone, the more you reveal their importance to you. It's not enough to tell them they're important. You must prove it by investing in them. The best way to spell love is T-I-M-E. Love is not what you think or feel about others; no, it's how much you give of yourself to them. Men, in particular, struggle with this. They say, "I don't understand my wife and kids. I provide everything they need. What more could they want?" They want you! They want your attention! Love concentrates so intently on another that it forgets itself. This kind of attention says, "I value you enough to give you my most precious asset—my time." Why is now the best time to express your love? Because you don't know how long you'll have the opportunity to do so. Circumstances change. People die and children grow up. The truth is, you've no guarantee of tomorrow. If you want to express your love you'd better do it now. So, who do you need to start spending more time with? What do you need to cut out of your schedule to make that possible? The best use of life is love, the best expression of love is time, and the best time to love is now.

May 25

"For we walk by faith, not by sight."
2 Corinthians 5:7 (NASB)

LEARNING TO WALK BY FAITH (1)

It's time to "get with it," when God tells you the same thing three separate times: "The just shall live by faith" (See Habakkuk 2:4; Romans 1:17; Galatians 3:11). This is not a suggestion for theological debate; it's His will for your life. Clearly, God has made faith the only way to live! No alternative is offered. "Without faith it is impossible to please God, because anyone who comes to him must believe that he exists and that he rewards those who earnestly seek him" (Hebrews 11:6 NIV). Let's take a moment and consider some questions arising from this life-transforming truth: (1) Who are "the just"? Paul writes, "Know that a person is not justified by the works of the law, but by faith in Jesus Christ. So we, too, have put our faith in Christ Jesus that we may be justified by faith" (Galatians 2:16 NIV). Justification (just-as-if-I'd-never-sinned) can't be earned. It's a free gift that comes by faith. If you have placed your trust in Christ then you are fully accepted in God's eyes. How good is that? (2) What is "walking"? Paul says, "We walk by faith and not by sight." Walking requires that you get up and start moving. You can't just sit around aimlessly, waiting for the rapture. Walking involves these things: Motivation—you're moved by a purpose. Direction—you've chosen a destination, a goal to reach. Motion—you're committed to mobilizing your energy and resources in the pursuit of your God-given destination and purpose. To walk by faith, you must be engaged in consistent, forward movement intended to bring you into God's destiny for your life.

May 26

"I do believe; help me overcome my unbelief!"
Mark 9:24 (NIV)

LEARNING TO WALK BY FAITH (2)

Here is another question to consider: What is "walking by sight"? (See 2 Corinthians 5:7). It's living your life based on how things look to the natural eye. It's deciding and acting in accord with your perceptions and circumstances, rather than God's Word. It's being dictated to by your feelings and thoughts. Your thoughts and feelings are—yours! Examine them. Don't let them hijack you. Use your spirit-controlled temperament to bring them under control. Too often, we are sandwiched between faith and doubt, in a "catch-22" between what our transformed spirit says and what our carnal mind says. One day a distraught father brought his son to Jesus for healing. Jesus told him, "Everything is possible for one who believes" (Mark 9:23 NIV). At that point, the boy's father said, "I do believe; help me overcome my unbelief!" At times we experience both faith and doubt. This man was honest about his doubts, yet Jesus still worked a miracle for him. If he had needed correcting, Jesus would have corrected him. If his faith was not genuine, the Lord would have known it. But Jesus accepted his declaration of faith, despite his doubts. There are three lessons here for us: (1) Don't be afraid to acknowledge your doubts. (2) Don't let your doubts overrule your faith. God's Word in the matter is God's will for you; stand on it. (3) Hand your doubts over to the Lord and say, "I do believe; help me overcome my unbelief!" How long does it take to learn to walk by faith? A lifetime!

May 27

*"Faith comes from hearing the
message... through the word."*
Romans 10:17 (NIV)

LEARNING TO WALK BY FAITH (3)

What does it mean to "walk by faith"? (2 Corinthians 5:7 NASB). It's radically different from walking by sight, reason, emotion, or intellect. It calls you to live above these things. It enables you to enter the realm of supernatural possibilities because Jesus said, "Everything is possible for one who believes" (Mark 9:23 NIV). Here are some scriptural principles about faith that will help you: (1) It's not rooted in human effort. Self-confidence and intellectual acumen don't qualify. Optimism, good luck, and social connections don't qualify. Learning religious formulas won't do it either. (2) It's rooted in God's unlimited power and unchanging Word. "Faith comes from hearing the message, and the message is heard through the word." The Word of God, received and residing within you, continuously produces faith within you. No teeth-gritting super-effort is required; you simply decide to believe what God says and respond to it. (3) Walking by faith calls for action. "Show me your faith without deeds, and I will show you my faith by my deeds" (James 2:18 NIV). Until you act, your faith is useless. "In the same way, faith by itself, if it is not accompanied by action, is dead" (v. 17 NIV). The moment you act, your faith springs to life, inviting God to move on your behalf. Today, He's waiting for you to act so that He can respond to you. Even if you don't feel like it, ask yourself, "What would my first step of faith be if I really felt like taking action?" Do it! You'll be walking by faith and reaping the rewards! (See Hebrews 11:6).

May 28

"Forgiving each other, just as ... God forgave you."
Ephesians 4:32 (NIV)

THE POWER OF FORGIVENESS (1)

The power of forgiveness is an awesome thing. No relationship can survive without it, much less thrive. Whatever the issue, forgiveness sets both sides free, takes a weapon out of Satan's hands, and opens the door for God to go to work in the situation. This is never more so than in your family. The truth is, it's easier to forgive an enemy you seldom see than a loved one you have to live with every day. But you must do it. George Herbert said, "He who cannot forgive others, breaks the bridge over which he must pass himself." Paul writes: "Clothe yourselves with compassion, kindness, humility, gentleness and patience. Bear with each other and forgive one another if any of you has a grievance against someone. Forgive as the Lord forgave you. And over all these virtues put on love" (Colossians 3:12-14 NIV). Teach your children how to forgive. If you expose them to your anger, make sure that they're around when you show grace. Teach them how to deal with the issue, without attacking the person. Let them know that a difference of opinion can lead to a decision that makes things better for everyone, and that as a family member you can be "wrong" and still be treated right. This may mean teaching them things you were never taught. If so, learn from the mistakes of your parents and pass it on to your children. "Do not let the sun go down while you are still angry, and do not give the devil a foothold" (Ephesians 4:26-27 NIV). In other words, forgive when you are hurt, and don't take your resentments to bed.

May 29

"Forgive one another if any of you has a grievance against someone."
Colossians 3:13 (NIV)

THE POWER OF FORGIVENESS (2)

In Restoring Your Spiritual Passion, Gordon MacDonald writes: "One memory that burns deep within is that of a plane flight on which I was headed toward a meeting that would determine a major decision in my ministry. I knew I was in desperate need of a spiritual passion that would provide wisdom and submission to God's purposes. But the passion was missing because I was steeped in resentment toward a colleague. For days I had tried everything to rid myself of vindictive thoughts toward that person. But try as I might, I would even wake in the night thinking of ways to subtly get back at him. I wanted to embarrass him for what he had done, to damage his credibility before his peers. My resentment was beginning to dominate me, and on that plane trip, I came to a realization of how bad things really were... As the plane entered the landing pattern, I found myself crying silently to God for the power both to forgive and to experience liberation from my poisoned spirit. Suddenly it was as if an invisible knife cut a hole in my chest, and I literally felt a thick substance oozing from within. Moments later, I felt as if I'd been flushed out. I'd lost negative spiritual weight, the kind I needed to lose. I was free. I fairly bounced off that plane and soon entered a meeting that did, in fact, change the entire direction of my life." Forgiveness: (1) frees you from the grip of a negative force; (2) positions you where God can bless you; (3) teaches little people how to be big people.

May 30

"The boat was now in the middle of the sea, tossed by the waves."
Matthew 14:24 (NKJV)

KEEP YOUR EYES ON JESUS (1)

Jesus had accompanied His disciples in a previous storm and calmed it. But now He was up on a mountain praying, and they were alone, "tossed by the waves." Why? Because sometimes, the teacher has to step back in order to see how much the pupil has learned. Is that what's happening in your life right now? The Sea of Galilee was only about thirteen miles long and seven and a half miles wide. But when the wind sweeps down from the Golan Heights, it can churn those waters into a blender for two or three days, and it could sink a fishing boat like the one the disciples were in. Note the words, "tossed by the waves." Is that where you are today? In the middle of a divorce, tossed by guilt. In the middle of a home foreclosure, tossed by creditors. In the middle of an illness, tossed by pain, and an even more painful prognosis. "Now in the fourth watch of the night Jesus went to them, walking on the sea. And when the disciples saw Him . . . they were troubled, saying, 'It is a ghost!' And they cried out for fear. But immediately Jesus spoke to them, saying, 'Be of good cheer! It is I; do not be afraid'" (vv. 25-27 NKJV). Here are words worth writing down and recalling often: "Take courage. I am here!" (v. 27 NLT). You will never go where Jesus cannot reach you. Look over your shoulder; that's Him following you. Look into the storm; that's Him coming toward you. Today, open your eyes and recognize Him.

May 31

"Jesus... went about doing good and healing all who were oppressed by the devil."
Acts 10:38 (NKJV)

KEEP YOUR EYES ON JESUS (2)

The Bible says: "Peter answered Him and said, 'Lord, if it is You, command me to come to You on the water.' So He said, 'Come.' And when Peter had come down out of the boat, he walked on the water to go to Jesus. But when he saw that the wind was boisterous, he was afraid; and beginning to sink he cried out, saying, 'Lord, save me!' And immediately Jesus stretched out His hand and caught him, and said to him, 'O you of little faith, why did you doubt?' And when they got into the boat, the wind ceased. Then those who were in the boat came and worshiped Him, saying, 'Truly You are the Son of God'" (Matthew 14:28-33 NKJV). The major message for you in this story is—where to stare in a storm. Whether or not storms come, we cannot choose. But where we stare during a storm, that we can choose. When you are staring into the face of cancer, heart disease, or some other life-threatening illness, some of the first questions that come to mind are: "Who is the doctor? What is his experience? Is he able? Is he available?" Yes, He is! Jesus' résumé reads: "God anointed Jesus of Nazareth with the Holy Spirit and with power, who went about doing good and healing all who were oppressed by the devil, for God was with Him." Note the word "all." He can meet all your needs. So keep your eyes on Jesus and draw strength from Him. The One who "went about doing good and healing all" is on your side today.

June 1

"You will also declare a thing, and it will be established for you."
Job 22:28 (NKJV)

CHANGE YOUR SELF-TALK

It's not what others say to you or about you that determines your future; it's what you say to yourself after others get through talking! The Bible says, "Death and life are in the power of the tongue, and those who love it will eat its fruit" (Proverbs 18:21 NKJV). You say, "I'd love to have a better relationship, but I'm afraid if I make the first move and they don't respond, I'll feel rejected." Or, "I'd like to pursue my education, but I'm afraid if I register for classes and can't do the work, I'll feel stupid." Such words become self-fulfilling prophecies. Until you replace your negative self-talk with faith-talk you'll always live in fear. Your mind is like the womb of your spirit; it nurtures each seed you sow until the time of delivery. If you don't want what a seed will ultimately produce, you must stop sowing it and feeding it. Your first step in breaking fear's hold over you is in recognizing the self-talk that got you into trouble in the first place. This is not easy to do. It takes vigilance, self-awareness, discipline, and scriptural reprogramming. But by changing your thoughts, you'll begin to change your life. Job says, "You will . . . declare a thing, and it will be established for you." And the amazing part is, at times you may not feel like you believe the particular Scripture you're standing on. That's okay; your inner-self accepts what it's consistently fed and begins to act accordingly. So starting today, serve an eviction notice to every negative thought that's holding you back and begin feeding your mind with God's Word.

June 2

"From one degree of glory to another."
2 Corinthians 3:18 (AMPC)

SPIRITUAL MATURITY COMES BY DEGREES

How would you describe someone who is spiritually mature? Leonard Wedel says: "A mature person does not take himself too seriously . . . keeps himself alert in mind . . . does not always view with alarm every adverse situation that arises . . . is too big to be little . . . never feels too great to do little things, and is never too proud to do humble things . . . never accepts either success or failure in themselves as permanent . . . is one who is able to control his or her impulses . . . is not afraid to make mistakes . . . has faith in themselves which becomes stronger as it is fortified by their faith in God." So, measured by that standard, how well are you doing? Are you able to evaluate your progress without getting discouraged or feeling condemned? Can you look at how far you still have to go, yet be able to appreciate and celebrate how far you have already come? The Bible says we are changed "from one degree of glory to another." Notice, spiritual maturity takes place by degrees. In small steps, not giant leaps. You must learn to live by God's Word, not by how you feel, for His Word states that as long as you believe, God is working in you: "The Word of God . . . is effectually at work in you who believe [exercising its superhuman power in those who adhere to and trust in and rely on it]" (1 Thessalonians 2:13 AMPC). There is a direct connection between your daily intake of God's Word and your maturity level. And the good news is, God hasn't left us to do it on our own. "We . . . are being transformed . . . from glory to glory . . . by the Spirit" (2 Corinthians 3:18 NKJV).

June 3

"They gather gossip, and ... spread it."
Psalm 41:6 (NLT)

CONFIDENTIALITY

A man approached Socrates one day to share some gossip. The wise philosopher asked, "First, are you certain it's true? Second, is it something good? Third, is it something useful?" When the man said, "Not really," Socrates replied, "Well, if it's not true, good or useful, why talk about it?" Gossip can feel like a form of intimacy, but it's actually a false bond motivated by the desire to diminish another person and make yourself look good. David said, "They visit ... as if they were my friends, but ... they gather gossip, and ... spread it." Solomon said, "Gossip separates ... best ... friends" (Proverbs 16:28 NLT), and it can cause you to lose "your good reputation" (Proverbs 25:10 NLT). Kevin Miller says: "A challenge in ministry is confidentiality—how open can you be? The following questions can help you decide. Are you telling someone who can do something about the problem by helping, or offering discipline or correction? Are you talking to someone wise enough to help you process your feelings and courageous enough to make you do the right thing by confronting the other person, or confessing where you're at fault? Is this news approved for sharing? Are you breaking a confidence, and if so, is it strictly because the person is endangering someone's life, including their own? Are you willing to divulge your source so it can be checked? When you say this, does it break your heart? Have you examined your own life and confessed where you've sinned in similar areas? Are you praying for the person? Would you be comfortable if someone was saying this about you?"

June 4

"Along unfamiliar paths I will guide them."
Isaiah 42:16 (NIV)

ADAPTING TO CHANGE

Change forces us out of the comfort of the familiar and into the discomfort of the unfamiliar. And while it can turn your world upside down, it makes you face your greatest fears and deal with the things that steal your joy, peace, and confidence. Change can be your friend or foe, depending on how you use it. Running away turns it into an enemy; embracing and learning from it makes it one of your greatest allies. C. Neil Strait said: "Change is always hardest for the man who's in a rut for he has scaled down his living to that which he can handle comfortably and welcomes no change or challenge that would lift him up." When you are facing the unknown, instead of automatically going into resistance mode, "Fix your eyes on what lies before you . . . stay on the safe path" (Proverbs 4:25-26 NLT). Ask yourself: What is God trying to teach me? How can I become stronger and wiser? What opportunities does it hold? John Mason says: "Correction and change always result in fruit . . . One change makes way for the next, giving you the opportunity to grow. Every time you think you're ready to graduate from the school of experience, somebody thinks up a new course . . . If you can figure out when to stand firm and when to bend, you've got it made." You don't have to fear what lies ahead. "Along unfamiliar paths I will guide them; I will turn the darkness into light before them and make the rough places smooth . . . I will not forsake them." God never closes a door without opening another one—but you must be willing to walk through it.

June 5

"Can two walk together, unless they are agreed?"
Amos 3:3 (NKJV)

E-V-A-L-U-A-T-E

A successful marriage is based on two things: "finding" the right person, and "becoming" the right person. And the second thing is harder than the first. Just because two people share the same bed and the same name, doesn't guarantee harmony. Here are some practical suggestions based on the word E-V-A-L-U-A-T-E: *Enjoy.* Do you enjoy the same things? Maybe it's no big deal now, but later when your husband is glued to the ballgame on TV and you want a little conversation, it will be. *Values.* The Bible asks, "Can two walk together, unless they are agreed?" Are you able to agree on major issues such as intimacy, child rearing, finances, in-laws, goals, and your relationship with God? You may disagree over many things, but these are make-or-break issues. *Accessibility.* Are you both emotionally accessible, or is he the strong silent type who doesn't communicate—or understand your need to? Love. Do you really love each other? Not the Hollywood version but the kind that listens to your spouse's opinions and concerns, overlooks their faults and failings, values them, and expresses itself through kindness? *Understanding.* As surely as God doesn't make two snowflakes alike, He doesn't make two people alike. So, can you understand and handle each other's differences? *Appreciation.* Your mate can't read your mind, so get into the habit of expressing your appreciation for one another. *Temperament.* If you're naturally upbeat but they're moody and introverted, you may have an oil-and-water mix. How will you handle this? *Environment.* If you're from different backgrounds, are you comfortable in the same social and spiritual settings? If you want a happy marriage, E-V-A-L-U-A-T-E these things.

June 6

"Given to hospitality."
Romans 12:13 (KJV)

SHOW HOSPITALITY

Making others feel loved and valued is a hallmark of discipleship (See John 13:34-35). Welcoming newcomers was important in the early church, and it's just as important today. Social customs may change, but God's Word doesn't. Jesus said, "Anyone who receives you receives me" (Matthew 10:40 NLT). As a follower of Christ, it's your job to make new people feel like part of "the household of faith" (Galatians 6:10). Established friendships within churches can easily become religious cliques where we smile and nod at newcomers but spend all of our time with a select group of people we already know. Most of us are satisfied with our existing circle of friends, so we need to be looking for ways to include others. People come to church hoping for love and acceptance, and if they don't find it within a month or two, they move on. So keep your spiritual antennae tuned to people who seem uncomfortable and out of place. Most folks have had at least one negative experience in church, so they need extra T.L.C. (Tender Loving Care). The Bible says, "Carry each other's burdens" (Galatians 6:2 NIV). Genuine warmth and caring attract people. First impressions count. Church should be a place where our love for people who are hurting is evident the minute they walk in the door. And remember, God doesn't just use these relationships to meet the needs of those coming out of bad situations—He uses them to mature us too.

June 7

"I bear him witness that he has a great zeal."
Colossians 4:13 (NKJV)

DON'T RUN OUT OF STEAM!

John Wesley, founder of the Methodist Church, travelled two hundred and fifty thousand miles on horseback, averaging twenty miles a day for forty years. He preached forty thousand sermons, produced four hundred books, and knew ten languages. At eighty-three, he was annoyed that he couldn't write more than fifteen hours a day without his eyes hurting. And at eighty-six, he was ashamed he couldn't preach more than twice a day. He complained in his diary of an increasing tendency to lie in bed until 5.30 a.m. One word described Wesley's life: zeal. Paul writes: "Epaphras . . . greets you, always laboring fervently for you in prayers, that you may stand perfect and complete in all the will of God. For I bear him witness that he had a great zeal for you" (vv. 12-13 NKJV). We speak of "getting up a head of steam." It's the language of the locomotive. Steam is literally water turned to energy. Kate Eaton wrote in the Chicago Tribune: "You may see it above your whistling tea kettle or on your bathroom mirror, but that's not it. Steam is the clear vapor between the hot water and the visible mist. As it forms at 212 degrees Fahrenheit, it expands to take up much more space than its liquid state. This explosive expansion, harnessed in a giant locomotive, is what powered 250-ton engines and enabled them to pull twenty or more railcars through the Blue Ridge Mountains, across the great plains and over the deserts to the west. It's a powerful force." If you work for God, you must spend time with God, otherwise you'll run out of steam!

June 8

"He ... guided them in the wilderness."
Psalm 78:52 (NKJV)

ARE YOU IN THE WILDERNESS?

The wilderness is a place where growth comes hard, water is scarce, and you plod on when there's no end in sight. You can have a wilderness experience anywhere: at a graveside, in an unemployment line, or in a divorce court. In the wilderness: (1) There seems to be no way out. In Scripture the number forty represents struggle. Noah experienced storms for forty days. Moses spent forty years alone in the desert. Jesus was tempted by the devil for forty days. (2) You begin to think the worst. The wilderness weakens your resolve. It makes you look for an easy way out. A troubled marriage can make you look the wrong way at somebody else's husband or wife. It's the breeding ground for dishonesty, depression, even pornography—things you normally wouldn't find appealing. "Jesus ... was led by the Spirit in the wilderness, where he was tempted by the devil" (Luke 4:1-2 NLT). Notice, going face to face with the devil was God's idea. Jesus, the last Adam, came to succeed where the first Adam failed. "Because one person disobeyed ... many became sinners. But because one other person obeyed ... many will be made righteous" (Romans 5:19 NLT). Jesus overcame the devil by using God's Word. Three times He said to Satan, "It is written" (Luke 4:4, 8, 12). And God's Word is still your wilderness-survival guide. After using it, Jesus left the wilderness clothed in the power of God's Spirit, ready to launch His ministry. And God can do the same for you. "He ... guided them in the wilderness ... He led them on safely, so that they did not fear" (Psalm 78:52-53 NKJV).

June 9

"Do not be afraid ... I am with you."
Acts 18:9-10 (NIV)

HAVE YOU BEEN REJECTED?

When Paul tried to share his new faith with his old friends, "They opposed him" (v. 6 NKJV). It hurts to be rejected by those you love. It seems like Paul was so hurt by their rejection that God had to encourage him, saying, "Do not be afraid ... I am with you, and no one is going to ... harm you." Later when Paul reached out to some of the apostles, they too were leery of him. They saw him as too Jewish to be Christian and too Christian to be Jewish. Throughout his ministry Paul suffered disappointment and rejection at the hands of those he loved. But when people fail you, it drives you into the arms of God. Being rejected by others can actually bring a greater intimacy with Him. When they stoned Paul and left him for dead, "he got back up" and went on to greater things (See Acts 14:19-20). Being rejected makes you lean on God like never before because you've nowhere else to turn! In fact, at times like that, unless you hear from God there's no other word of hope coming! When others reject you, God has a way of opening doors to new levels of blessing you'd otherwise miss. Your greatest spiritual growth will generally result from your greatest trials. The Psalmist wrote: "Thou preparest a table before me in the presence of mine enemies (vindication): thou anointest my head with oil (daily empowerment); my cup runneth over (greater blessing)" (Psalm 23:5). The truth is, without some pain and opposition you wouldn't get to sit at God's table and enjoy His best.

June 10

"The world and all that is in it is mine."
Psalm 50:12 (NRSV)

IMAGINATION AND FREEDOM OF CHOICE

The Bible says, "God formed man of the dust of the ground, and breathed into his nostrils the breath of life; and man became a living being" (Genesis 2:7 NKJV). Until then, we were just inanimate hunks of clay in human form. At that point God breathed into us two important things: (1) Imagination. It distinguishes us from all other living creatures. It's what makes us capable of going to the moon, inventing the Internet, having a dream, and worshipping our Creator. But even when God gives you a concept, you must work to make it a reality. God said, "The world and all that is in it is mine." That means that when you get ready to build and you have only a few bricks, you can pray for more bricks and God will give them to you. It also means that instead of complaining about what you don't have, you look at what you do have, and what you can make of it with God's help. (2) Freedom of choice. God has empowered you with the ability to make the right choices and act on them. But even though God has given you this ability, don't try to go it alone. Jesus said, "What is born of . . . [the physical is physical]; and what is born of the Spirit is spirit" (John 3:6 AMPC). Always depend on the Holy Spirit. He's called "the Helper" for a reason (John 14:26 NKJV). Jesus promised His disciples, "You shall receive power [ability, efficiency, and might] when the Holy Spirit has come upon you" (Acts 1:8 AMPC). Imagination and freedom of choice—use them to glorify God.

June 11

"God created mankind in his own image."
Genesis 1:27 (NIV)

TAP INTO YOUR CREATIVITY

The Bible says: "God created mankind in his own image... male and female he created them. God blessed them and said... 'Be fruitful and increase in number; fill the earth and subdue it. Rule over... every living creature that moves on the ground.' Then God said, 'I give you every seed-bearing plant on the face of the whole earth and every tree that has fruit with seed in it. They will be yours'" (vv. 27-29 NIV). God has given you everything required to succeed at whatever He's called you to do. But you must tap into your God-given creativity! The Bible says, "Where there is no vision, the people perish" (Proverbs 29:18). Every great accomplishment begins as a vision, and every God-given vision comes with the innate power to fulfill it. Others may be more educated and experienced, but they don't have a monopoly on creativity. The chances are there's a "God-idea" inside you right now that's just waiting to be released. By not tapping into it, you're settling for less than God wants you to have. Whatever you feel called to do—write, paint, preach, play a piano, build a business, be a nurse, teach—step out and do it. If you wait until you can do it perfectly or without criticism, you'll never do it! Walking on water begins with one step of faith. It also brings you closer to Jesus. You see, Jesus wasn't in the boat, He was out on the water saying to His disciples, "Come" (Matthew 14:29 NKJV). Only one of them did: Peter. And though he did it imperfectly, it changed his life. So don't be afraid, tap into your creativity and watch what happens.

June 12

"Let my words and ... thoughts be pleasing to you, Lord."
Psalm 19:14 (CEV)

WHO ARE YOU TRYING TO PLEASE?

Are you afraid to speak up in case you encounter disapproval? The Bible says, "Fearing people is a dangerous trap" (Proverbs 29:25 NLT). And fear is common among people-pleasers. One author writes: "A pleaser daughter is one who, at any age, still tries to please her parents. From report cards to parenting style ... her decisions are colored by the opinions of the people who raised her. But remember what Paul said, 'When I was a child ... I reasoned like a child. When I became a man, I put the ways of childhood behind me' (1 Corinthians 13:11 NIV). A pleaser friend is one who can't say no. Resentment may build up, but she always shows up and takes care of things. What she considers love and loyalty are often exploited by others who seek reliance, codependency, and caretaking. A pleaser employee consistently works long hours without compensation or appreciation, covers for others who don't pull their weight, and bites her tongue when her boss or colleagues take credit for her work. A pleaser wife is one who, in her desire to be perfect, ... becomes an altered version of the woman her husband fell in love with. A pleaser mom fears the loss of her children's love. She's afraid to set boundaries, even though they create an atmosphere of comfort and respect. She equates discipline with division, and by depriving her children of rules she ends up missing out on the later-life friendship that's the dessert of good parents." The only thing you should be concerned about is making sure that your "words and ... thoughts" please God. In the end, His approval is the only thing that counts.

June 13

"In everything give thanks."
1 Thessalonians 5:18 (NKJV)

GRATITUDE: IT'S CONTAGIOUS!

Author Barbara Johnson was frazzled; she was running late and had to stand while riding the bus to work. Her attitude was going downhill fast when a cheery voice from the front of the bus announced, "Beautiful day, isn't it?" She couldn't see the man, but she listened to his commentary as he described the lovely scenery... this church... that park... a cemetery... a firehouse. His grateful attitude lightened the mood of everybody around him. Then as Johnson got off the bus, she caught a glimpse of the speaker: an average-looking man wearing dark glasses and carrying a white stick! Paul said, "In everything give thanks: for this is the will of God." We don't thank God for trials, we thank Him in them. Gratitude is like a boomerang. It blesses the recipient, makes a 180-degree turn, and blesses the person who gives thanks. One Bible teacher says: "Whatever crisis there is in your life, before it ever came God made sure you'd be able to endure it... others have gone through exactly what you're going through... and made it through victoriously... with every temptation God promised to 'make a way to escape, that ye may be able to bear it' (1 Corinthians 10:13). Trials and 'escape ways' are inseparable. But the devil doesn't want you to know that, so every time you go through a test he tells you there's no way out. I learned long ago when the Devil keeps pressuring me, it's always an indication that 'the way out' is about to be revealed... We need to do what God says. Rejoice!" Remember, "The joy of the Lord is your strength" (Nehemiah 8:10). When you have His joy, it gives you strength for the journey.

June 14

"You will not grieve like people who have no hope."
1 Thessalonians 4:13 (NLT)

WHEN A BELIEVER DIES (1)

Our culture makes death a subject to avoid or to speak of with gloom. When the subject comes up, even Christians try to dodge the bullet by escaping into vague, irrelevant-sounding metaphors. But God's Word makes death clear and unthreatening for those who trust in Christ. "Dear brothers and sisters, we want you to know what will happen to the believers who have died so you will not grieve like people who have no hope." God's Word is direct, concrete, and encouraging on this subject. "Precious in the sight of the Lord is the death of His [godly ones]" (Psalm 116:15 NKJV). From our heavenly Father's perspective, death just opens the door for Him to enjoy perfect, eternal, delightful fellowship with each of His redeemed children. "I heard a voice out of Heaven, 'Write this: Blessed are those who die in the Master . . . how blessed to die that way!' 'Yes,' says the Spirit, 'and blessed rest from their hard, hard work. None of what they've done is wasted; God blesses them for it all in the end'" (Revelation 14:13 MSG). The Bible assures every believer that their death is not a tragedy but a triumphal entry into heaven. The Amplified Bible puts it: "Blessed (happy, to be envied)." God instructed John, "Write this." Why? Because God understands that when we lose a loved one, we tend to forget His perspective and adopt an emotion-driven perspective. Rejoice believer, "Whether we live or die, we belong to the Lord" (Romans 14:8 NIV). And the Lord takes good care of what belongs to Him!

June 15

"God will bring back with [Jesus] the believers who have died."
1 Thessalonians 4:14 (NLT)

WHEN A BELIEVER DIES (2)

Dealing with death separates us into two categories: the hopeless and the hopeful. The hopeless believe they have nothing to look forward to. Their losses feel permanent—the end of life and all that's good. But the hopeful have everything to look forward to. Their losses are temporary—the beginning of an endless life filled with God's finest gifts. God wants you "to know what will happen to the believers who have died so you will not grieve like people who have no hope" (v. 13 NLT). Our hope results from knowing these truths: (1) "We believe that Jesus died and was raised to life again" (v. 14 NLT). All hope begins here: believing in Jesus' death for our sin and His resurrection to represent us before God. (2) "Since we believe" this, "we also believe that . . . Jesus returns." Faith in Christ's physical return to earth gives us confidence that "God will bring back with him the believers who have died." God will raise us from our resting places and bring us back again with Jesus (See Romans 8:11). At that moment, "He will take our weak mortal bodies and change them into glorious bodies like his own" (Philippians 3:21 NLT). Never again will you be vulnerable to cancer, diabetes, heart disease, arthritis, strokes, Lou Gehrig's disease, paralysis, disabilities, weariness, weakness, grief, fear, depression, temptation, addictions, failure, remorse, suicidal thoughts, bipolar disorder, OCD, PTSD, or any kind of ailment. You'll be transformed into the very likeness of Christ. Isn't that wonderful!

June 16

"We tell you this directly from the Lord."
1 Thessalonians 4:15 (NLT)

WHEN A BELIEVER DIES (3)

What Paul wrote about death, he got directly from the Lord: "We tell you this directly from the Lord: We who are still living when the Lord returns will not meet him ahead of those who have died." The Lord reserves this high privilege exclusively for those who die in Him; they will be the first to experience the resurrection. Try to imagine that moment. Arising from their rest like we do after a good night's sleep, now dressed in Christ-like bodies, they awake to the sight of their Lord returning in glory with His angels. They meet Him—the first believers to witness His return, the initial wing of His airborne vanguard to escort Him back to earth. This is no pipe dream or mere fantasy; Paul got it "directly from the Lord." Our source is unimpeachable! He writes: (1) "Together with them, we who are still alive . . . will be caught up in the clouds to meet the Lord in the air" (v. 17 NLT). Living believers will rise to join with resurrected brothers, sisters, parents, grandparents, children, grandchildren, spouses, friends, family of God never-met-before, in a spectacular mid-air reunion with Christ. We'll be together, inseparable, eternal, one international, multicultural, love-based, Christ-centered family! (2) "Then we will be with the Lord forever" (v. 17 NLT). No speculating or imagining what He's really like. "For we will see him as he really is" (1 John 3:2 NLT). We will see, touch, and talk with Jesus as we do each other. And He will respond to us in real time! (3) "Encourage each other with these words" (1 Thessalonians 4:18 NLT).

June 17

"To go and be with Christ, which would be far better."
Philippians 1:23 (NLT)

WHEN A BELIEVER DIES (4)

No matter how much you enjoy where you are living right now, there's always a longing in your heart for the place you call "home." And how much more so for those who have been born again into God's redeemed family? The world has its beautiful shorelines and skylines, but deep down we yearn, like Paul, for our heavenly Father, heavenly family, and home. "For to me, living means living for Christ, and dying is even better... I'm torn between two desires: I long to go and be with Christ, which would be far better for me" (Philippians 1:21-23 NLT). Leaving this life to be with Christ, in Paul's judgment, "is far better." Far better than what? Anything else! Nothing here can compare with what awaits you there! "No one's ever seen or heard anything like this, never so much as imagined anything quite like it—what God has arranged for those who love him" (1 Corinthians 2:9 MSG). You ask, "How will this transition happen to us?" At death, "The dust [our body] returns to the ground it came from, and [our] spirit returns to God who gave it" (Ecclesiastes 12:7 NIV). Our bodies will "fall asleep in Christ" (See 1 Corinthians 15:18). Our God-indwelled spirits return to His presence, delighting in "the fullness of joy" and reveling in the "pleasures forevermore" that are found in abundance at His right hand (See Psalm 16:11). While we wait, anticipating our best days, heaven's hosts rehearse for the drama of the ages, the awesome return of Christ and our accompanying Him in our glorified bodies! We say, "Come, Lord Jesus" (Revelation 22:20 NIV).

June 18

"We believe that Jesus died and rose again."
1 Thessalonians 4:14 (NKJV)

CHRIST'S RESURRECTION, AND YOURS

The word "resurrection" means "the standing up of a corpse." Most religions teach the concept of immortality, but only the Christian faith teaches bodily resurrection. "If we believe that Jesus died and rose again, even so them, also which sleep in Jesus, will God bring with him." The patriarch Job, whose children all died tragically in a single day, asked, "If a man dies, shall he live again?" (Job 14:14 NKJV). We ask this question when death claims someone we love. So God gave Job, and us, the answer that dries our tears, heals our broken hearts, and focuses us on something greater than this temporal life with its troubles: "For I know that my Redeemer lives, and He shall stand at last on the earth; and after my skin is destroyed, this I know, that in my flesh I shall see God, whom I shall see for myself, and my eyes shall behold, and not another. How my heart yearns within me!" (Job 19:25-27 NKJV). The next time you see a butterfly soaring, stop and remind yourself, "That's my future!" No matter how you dress this body up, at best, it will always be a caterpillar. But when it emerges from the cocoon of death and rises to meet the Lord in the air, it will take on His beauty and His likeness. "The dead in Christ will rise first. Then we who are alive and remain shall be caught up together with them in the clouds to meet the Lord in the air. And thus we shall always be with the Lord. Therefore comfort one another with these words" (1 Thessalonians 4:16-18 NKJV).

June 19

"Be careful to do what is right."
Romans 12:17 (NIV)

BE HONEST

Jeremiah writes, "Like a partridge that hatches eggs it did not lay are those who gain riches by unjust means... in the end he will prove to be fools" (Jeremiah 17:11 NIV). Don't think that you can do whatever you like in small things and be okay as long as you've no major lapses. Whether you steal a dollar or a million dollars, you're still a thief. Webster's Dictionary defines integrity as—honesty. Every time you break a moral principle it becomes harder, not easier, to act with integrity. Everything you've done in the past, including the things you've neglected to do, comes to a head when you're under pressure. That's why developing integrity requires constant vigilance. John Morley observed, "No man can rise beyond the limitations of his own character." And that's particularly true when you're a leader. So: (1) Keep your promises. When you make a promise, you create hope. When you keep a promise, you create trust. (2) Acknowledge your mistakes. When your decisions don't turn out the way you intended, you owe people an explanation. (3) Apologize and try to make amends. When your actions hurt others, you need to admit that what you did was wrong and say you're sorry. This is usually very painful in the moment. But not only is it the right thing to do, it can actually shorten the agony and help you to put the incident behind you. That's why you should heed the advice of Thomas Jefferson on this subject: "If you have to eat crow, eat it while it's young and tender."

June 20

"We have fellowship with each other, and the blood of Jesus ... cleanses us from all sin."
1 John 1:7 (NLT)

THE FOUNDATION OF TRUE FRIENDSHIP

The Bible says, "Better a nearby friend than a distant family" (Proverbs 27:10 MSG). Sometimes it's easier to develop close friendships with those outside your immediate family circle. But there's another kind of "blood relative" mentioned in the Bible: brothers and sisters joined together through the blood of Jesus (See 1 John 1:7). It's the kind of relationship that doesn't allow you to go off and do your own thing (See Colossians 3:15 MSG). It requires us to "do the hard work of getting along with each other, treating each other with ... honor" (James 3:18 MSG). It calls for a long-term commitment not readily understood by the "me generation," where, when the going gets tough it's acceptable to bail out of a relationship and move on. One pastor points out that the world doesn't understand the Christian concept of brotherhood and sisterhood: "It says find friends among like-minded, like-income people who vote like you and have the same golf handicap. These friendships work until the bottom falls out of your life, you face a pressing problem, or a tragic loss, or a serious illness, and suddenly you realize that no one cares much about you. Why? Because you've made no investment in anybody's life, and now when you need to make a withdrawal there's no money in the friendship bank." Sacrificial love is the foundation of true friendship. Paul writes, "I have no one else like Timothy, who genuinely cares about your welfare. All the others care only for themselves ... But you know how Timothy has proved himself" (Philippians 2:20-22 NLT).

June 21

"We are God's masterpiece."
Ephesians 2:10 (NLT)

I MATTER, BECAUSE GOD LOVES ME

The fear of being nothing but a big zero can become a self-fulfilling prophecy. It works like this. When it's time to go for a job interview, your fear kicks in and you think, "I'll never impress them; I'll look stupid. They'll ask me questions I can't answer." A mouse in a lion's den has better odds of success. So you fail miserably and descend yet another level into the basement of self-defeat. Or consider the girl who's asked out on a date by a good-looking guy. So good looking, that she wonders what he sees in her. She's sure that once he gets to know her, he will drop her. Insecurity drives her to use the only tool she trusts, her body. She sleeps with him on the first date for fear there won't be a second, and she ends up feeling like the disposable woman she didn't want to become. The fear of insignificance creates the very result it dreads and arrives at the very destination it tries to avoid. Stop! You're disagreeing with God! You're questioning His judgment and second-guessing His taste. His Word says He can't stop thinking about you. If you could count His thoughts of you, "They would be more in number than the [grains of] sand" (Psalm 139:18 NKJV). Why does God love you so much? For the same reason an artist loves his paintings. "We are God's masterpiece. He has created us anew in Christ Jesus, so we can do the good things he planned for us long ago." So when you get up each morning, look in the mirror and tell yourself, "I matter, because God loves me!"

June 22

"Love covers over a multitude of sins."
1 Peter 4:8 (NIV)

A WORD TO SINGLE PARENTS

Are you struggling to raise children on your own? If so, teach them these three principles. As you do, they'll be reinforced in you. You'd be surprised how many instructors learn while they teach. (1) Teach them how to love imperfect people. Let them know that loving is a risk, but it's worth taking. Hearing you say that will help them to grow up and not become cynical because of what they've been through. Explain that when you love people, you must love what's good and accept what's still under construction. And it'll save them heartache if you teach them that sometimes we'll disappoint each other, and that God's remedy for this is, "Love covers over a multitude of sins." (2) Tell them that the future can be better than the past. We are fueled by the past, but fuel only works when it's combusted into another form. So allow the pain of the past to fuel your future with compassion, wisdom, and hope. Many of the people we admire have experienced failure. This year's winner was last year's runner-up. Learn from your mistakes and seize the new day. Once you do that, "All things are possible" (Matthew 19:26 NKJV). (3) Show them how to adapt to change. When you get stuck in the past, it's always at the expense of the future. After the initial shock is over and your anger has dissipated, start making plans. Draw closer to God and decide to live again. Don't get stuck in a stage that was just meant to be part of a process. This too shall pass; let it!

June 23

"Trying to become perfect by your own human effort?"
Galatians 3:3 (NLT)

BREAK FREE FROM PERFECTIONISM (1)

Columnist Ann Landers wrote, "Rose-colored glasses are never made in bifocals. Nobody wants to read the small print in dreams." The small print in every dream is—reality. You may fulfill your dream, but you won't do it perfectly. Looking back, you'll say, "If I knew then what I know now." But if you could live all over again, you'd probably say the same thing. The truth is, the journey will take longer than you hoped. The obstacles will be more numerous than you thought. The disappointments will be greater than you expected. The lows will be lower than you imagined. The price will be higher than you anticipated. Stop expecting more than what's reasonable. Stop seeing minor mistakes as major catastrophes. To break free from perfectionism, Dr. Chris Thurman says: "Humble yourself: repent of being so filled with pride that you think you're equal with God. Be reality focused: accept life as it is, not how you think it should be. Establish attainable goals: make them realistic and achievable in the here-and-now. Set reasonable time limits: instead of spending time struggling to do one thing perfectly, prioritize, and allot a reasonable amount of time to each activity. In less-important areas, accept good-enough; not every job has to be (or can be) done exceptionally well. Lose the all-or-nothing thinking: not every situation is black and white . . . most contain shades of gray. Learn from your mistakes, then move on. Confess your shortcomings. Acknowledging your weaknesses releases you from the pull of perfectionism. Find your worth in God, not in 'your own human effort,' in what you do and how well you do it."

June 24

*"We have different gifts, according
to the grace given . . . us."*
Romans 12:6 (NIV)

BREAK FREE FROM PERFECTIONISM (2)

One Christian writer says: "When my friend had her first child, she applied all her career talents to making a smooth transition into motherhood. She kept a rigid schedule, napped her son on time, planned time for grocery shopping, and always managed to have a nice dinner prepared by the time her husband got home. She kept up this façade till she could handle the stress no longer. Finally, she cracked. She left the house a mess, forgot to shower, never went to the grocery store, and when her husband came home, she handed him the dirty baby . . . and declared the house a dinner-free zone! What did her husband do? He fell to his knees in an exaggerated 'Hallelujah!' then spun his long-lost wife into a magnificent hug. 'You're back!' he declared . . . Her gifts, apart from being a great wife, mom, and businesswoman, are her sense of humor, her sass, her fun, and her authenticity . . . all the things her husband missed when her personality went on a postpartum hiatus." If you're "trying to become perfect by your own human effort" (Galatians 3:3 NLT), it's not going to happen! "We have different gifts, according to the grace given us." When you strive to be somebody other than the person God intended, you end up feeling angry, inadequate, and frustrated. God purposely gifted us all in different areas. Once you realize that, you can start to minister from your particular area of giftedness. Remember, every one of us is a work-in-progress, so cut yourself some slack. Instead of trying to become perfect, begin to thank God for making you one-of-a-kind.

June 25

"I sat where they sat."
Ezekiel 3:15 (NKJV)

DO YOU KNOW ANY NEEDY PEOPLE?

In an attempt to insulate ourselves against the evils in the world, we can isolate ourselves from those God's called us to reach out to. At the beginning of Ezekiel's ministry he wrote, "The hand of the Lord was strong upon me. Then I came to the captives... and I sat where they sat and remained there astonished among them seven days" (vv. 14-15 NKJV). True ministry begins with sitting in the other person's seat. Former President Jimmy Carter was a Sunday school teacher in his church. Recalling it in an interview, he said: "Most church members—including me—rarely reach outside to people who are different from us or less fortunate. Quite often my Sunday school class will say, 'Why don't we take up a collection and give a nice Thanksgiving meal to a poor family?' The next question is: 'Who knows a poor family?' Nobody does! We have to call the Welfare Office to get the name and address." So, do you know any needy people? Compassion is putting yourself in the other person's place. It's asking God to help you understand what's really going on with them. It's hearing what they're not saying as well as what they are. It's understanding that sometimes their anger is only masking their fear, that they're crying out for help in the only way they know how. Before Peter denied the Lord, Jesus said to him, "When thou art converted, strengthen thy brethren" (Luke 22:32). When God's grace touches your life, you will always reach back for others! And here's why: people don't care how much you know until they know how much you care.

June 26

"A hard worker has plenty of food."
Proverbs 28:19 (NLT)

KEEP YOUR JOB AND EARN A PROMOTION! (1)

Even in a bad job market, "good help is hard to find." So when employers find it they do all they can to keep it. Even in a long economic downturn there are still practical rules that increase the likelihood you'll keep your job, and maybe earn a promotion. These rules line up with what's taught in God's Word: (1) Understand that hard work is a blessing. God created paradise, then He created us. Then He put us to work, saying, "By the sweat of your brow you will eat your food" (Genesis 3:19 NIV). God rewards "sweat" (See Proverbs 28:19). Giving your job, even a menial one, your best, pleases Him. And ultimately, He, not your boss, controls your future. (2) Accept reality. Wishing away your present circumstances while feeling entitled to better, will just make you feel worse and get you nowhere. Your "God . . . [turns] the curse into a blessing" (Deuteronomy 23:5 NIV). He gives "beauty for ashes" (Isaiah 61:3 NKJV). In hard times God raises up people with fresh ideas that actually make the future better than the past—not only for themselves, but for others. And you can become one of those people. (3) Make God your source. "I am the Lord thy God which teacheth thee to profit, which leadeth thee by the way that thou shouldest go" (Isaiah 48:17). Make God your life coach. Give your boss the hard work he or she deserves, but trust only in the One Who promised to "use his wonderful riches . . . to give you everything you need" (Philippians 4:19 NCV).

June 27

"Get wisdom ... get understanding."
Proverbs 4:7 (NKJV)

KEEP YOUR JOB AND EARN A PROMOTION! (2)

In his book, Emotional Intelligence, psychologist Dr. Daniel Goleman says that IQ amounts to only 20 percent of success. To keep your job and earn a promotion you need more than intelligence. Goleman suggests several things to help you succeed on the job: (1) Confidence. Confident workers trust their God-given abilities. And where do you get this confidence? From God! "It is better to trust in the Lord than to put confidence in man" (Psalm 118:8). Confidence in God gives you the assurance that you "can do all things through Christ who strengthens [you]" (Philippians 4:13). (2) Curiosity. "Get wisdom: and with all thy getting get understanding." Curiosity is eagerness to know, learn and understand more. Curious workers are interested in what's not obvious. Others presume that a solution doesn't exist or is too difficult, so they quit at the point at which they should be starting. But when others are saying, "It's way beyond me," the curious employee says, "There's an answer. There's a better way. We just need more understanding." Every boss wants curious workers. (3) Decisiveness. "God has not given us a spirit of fear, but of power and of love and of a sound mind" (2 Timothy 1:7 NKJV). Fear is a "spirit." It's an attitude that makes you pull back, freeze in place, or give up. That spirit doesn't come from God, so resist it. Don't be afraid to take a prayed-over risk or accept responsibility for an outcome.

June 28

"Clothe yourselves with compassion, kindness, humility, gentleness and patience."
Colossians 3:12 (NIV)

KEEP YOUR JOB AND EARN A PROMOTION! (3)

Succeeding at your job requires these things: (1) Empathy. Always show consideration for other people's situation, needs, feelings, and perceptions. Try to understand what it's like to walk in their shoes. By doing this you increase their motivation, improve the working environment, and raise the productivity level. "Clothe yourselves with compassion, kindness, humility, gentleness and patience." You are supposed to "wear" these qualities to work every day. (2) Flexibility. It's the capacity to adapt, adjust, and advance. In an environment driven by economic difficulty and downsizing, rigid, reactive employees are often the first to be laid off or fired. Learn to "roll with the punches." Paul did that. "I have learned to be content whatever the circumstances... in any and every situation... I can do all this through him who gives me strength" (Philippians 4:11-13 NIV). When the winds of change blow, flexible people bend rather than break. They live to stand again, and even get promoted. (3) Humor. Start seeing yourself and the world around you with a sense of enjoyment. Refuse to take yourself too seriously. Look for the humor hidden in life's serious moments and you'll find it. People who are dispensers of misery just drag everybody down. God's Word says: "A cheerful disposition is good for your health" (Proverbs 17:22 MSG). "A cheerful heart is good medicine" (v. 22 NIV). A good sense of humor improves things and makes the workplace better for everybody.

June 29

"Work from the heart for your real Master . . . God."
Colossians 3:22 (MSG)

KEEP YOUR JOB AND EARN A PROMOTION! (4)

Keeping your job and earning a promotion calls for the following: (1) Initiative. Think outside the box. Better still, throw the old box away and ask God for a new one! Intelligence is more than just IQ. The average employee with initiative will always excel over the degreed one without it. If you don't believe it, read history. Education alone won't make you productive, but the Spirit and the Word of God will. Paul writes, "Let the Spirit renew your thoughts and attitudes" (Ephesians 4:23 NLT). Peter writes, "I have written . . . to stimulate you to wholesome thinking" (2 Peter 3:1 NIV). Let God stimulate your mind with ideas that make you an in-demand employee. (2) Perseverance. What is it? It's the energy and desire to achieve; it's motivation, determination, commitment, faithfulness, patience, resilience in the face of difficulty, and a willingness to work hard. Those who avoid the more demanding route and choose the easy way are costly to employ, decrease morale, reduce quality, and lessen the company's productivity. Paul challenges his readers to persevere in their assignment. "Here is my advice . . . you should finish what you started. Let the eagerness you showed in the beginning be matched now" (2 Corinthians 8:10-11 NLT). (3) Respect. Always consider the rights and needs of others. Treat them sensitively, kindly, courteously, and within the limits of law, conscience, and Scripture. "Do what you're told by your earthly masters . . . Do your best. Work from the heart for your real Master, for God." When you become such a worker God guarantees your financial security and professional success.

June 30

"In the day of my disaster ... the Lord was my support."
2 Samuel 22:19 (NIV)

GOD'S DISASTER-PREPAREDNESS KIT

A phone call in the wee hours, a malignant tumor, a police cruiser at your door, a child addicted to drugs—if you live long enough, you'll be confronted with "the day of ... disaster." And it's the strength of your relationship with God that will dictate your response. C. S. Lewis said that we can either acquire the wisdom assigned to a trial or keep repeating it until we "get it." One author points out that God's "disaster-preparedness kit is found in Psalm 31:24 NIV: Be strong. Why? Because God is fighting for you. You must know God, know your convictions, and know how to tap into God's unlimited power. You are not who you, or anyone else thinks ... God says you are strong. Believe Him! Take heart. Don't let your pain shut you down. Take the broken pieces and offer them to God ... choose to live with love. A closed heart isn't worth fighting for. You've worked too hard to get this far, so work with Him to see your healing all the way through. Hope in the Lord. Put no stock in emotion, circumstances, or chit-chat ... Place your hopes and dreams at the altar ... God makes all things new and possible. Any other counterfeit will fail ... No matter how long I've spent in God's workshop my progress is proven only in the moment of peril. We prepare in advance, so our responses are involuntary ... There isn't a situation, a temptation, or a question where Ephesians 6:10 doesn't apply: 'Be strong in the Lord and in his mighty power' (NIV). On multiple-choice tests it's the answer ... God isn't telling you to be tough on your own ... rely on His strength and let Him do for you what He knows is best."

July 1

"Don't begin until you count the cost."
Luke 14:28 (NLT)

EARNING THE RIGHT TO LEAD (1)

Earning the right to lead calls for the following things: (1) Prayerfully evaluating before you act. The very thing that makes leading others so appealing to your ego, makes you vulnerable to their pressures and praise. "When Jesus perceived that they were about to... make Him king, He departed again to the mountain by Himself alone" (John 6:15 NKJV). Let's be honest; who amongst us doesn't want to be "king" sometimes? But Jesus wasn't led by the applause of the crowd, He was led by the will of His Father. And you must be too. (2) Not just filling the slot – but filling it with the right person. Sometimes we give people jobs because we can't find anybody else to do them. But what happens when the job outgrows them? There's more at stake here than sparing somebody's feelings. Your fear of confrontation will permit people to languish in the wrong slot, slowing down the vision and discouraging the gifted folks around you who keep wondering, "How long are you going to put up with this?" (3) Seeking the best counsel you can find. "Be with wise men and become wise" (Proverbs 13:20 TLB). Don't pay twice for the same information. Seek advice from someone you respect; someone who's already done what you want to do, particularly when your decision affects others and will be called upon to stand the test of time. What looks good to you today, or in somebody else's polished sales pitch, may not look so good tomorrow when you're presented with better options. Jesus bottom-lines it: "Don't begin until you count the cost."

July 2

*"If God has given you leadership ability,
take the responsibility seriously."*
Romans 12:8 (NLT)

EARNING THE RIGHT TO LEAD (2)

Earning the right to lead calls for asking yourself: (1) Can I live with the results of this decision? Before you launch out into something be sure you have what it takes to handle it. If you can barely cope now, how will you handle more? Before God builds the ministry, He builds the man or woman because added success brings added responsibility. (2) Is the return worth the investment? When you overcommit and overextend yourself, the first thing that suffers is your time with God. The next thing that suffers is your family. And without the covering of both, you'll be vulnerable. There are a lot of good causes in this world, but God will only prosper you when you focus on what He has called you to do. (3) Are my expectations realistic? Hudson Taylor said, "Attempt great things for God and expect great things from God." When human wisdom and ability won't take you a step further, faith will, because faith holds the hand of God. And with God, "All things are possible" (Matthew 19:26 NKJV). Just make sure you're operating in faith and not presumption! (4) How can I survive today in order to thrive tomorrow? Obstacles and opposition are inevitable; they're part of the journey. But you must not allow them to make you doubt God and what He's called you to do. Be like Abraham—don't "stagger," stand on God's Word. "He staggered not at the promise of God through unbelief; but was strong in faith, giving glory to God; and being fully persuaded that, what he had promised, he was able also to perform" (Romans 4:20-21).

July 3

"Lord, 'Increase our faith.'"
Luke 17:5 (NKJV)

FAITH IS

Faith answers the question, "How?" in one word: "God!" The Bible says, "Faith is the substance of things hoped for, the evidence of things not seen" (Hebrews 11:1 NKJV). Notice: (1) Faith is a "substance." Some people see faith as something ethereal and "other worldly." But it's not; we use faith every day. For example, you pick up the phone, call a department store, place an order, and they ask for your credit card number. Then they send you a receipt. The receipt is what you hold on to while you're waiting for the item to arrive; it gives you the assurance that the product is on the way. And the same is true in the spiritual realm. God promises to answer your prayer, you believe Him, but your faith is the "substance" or the receipt you hold on to while you're waiting. (2) Faith is also "evidence." Why would you believe that someone you can't see on the other end of a phone line would send you something just because you order it? Because it happens every day for others, and it's probably happened to you before. Therefore, you're not being presumptuous or silly when you go to your mailbox expecting it to be there. You are not the first person to trust God and you won't be the last. "Lord, You have been our dwelling place in all generations" (Psalm 90:1 NAS). People have been trusting God for thousands of years and He has never let them down. His faithfulness is all the "evidence" you need. So it's not foolish to put your trust in a God like that, is it?

July 4

"Godly sorrow brings repentance . . . and leaves no regret."
2 Corinthians 7:10 (NIV)

DON'T LIVE IN REGRET

There's the kind of regret that leads to despair because you don't think God's grace is sufficient to cover your sins. Then there's "sadness . . . used by God [which] brings a change of heart . . . and . . . no regret" (GNT). This kind draws you closer and makes you more dependent on Him. You become "more alive, more concerned, more sensitive, more reverent . . . more passionate, more responsible . . . [and] come out . . . with purity of heart" (2 Corinthians 7:11 MSG). Jon Walker writes: "As the economy closed in, I began to regret not buying a less expensive home. If only we'd bought a cheaper house. If only we'd rented. If only we'd stayed in our first house. I can 'if only' myself into depression and stagnation where I'm stuck between regret and forward motion. When my focus is not on the One who provides . . . I let regret become bigger than God . . . and following that logic, I believe past choices, an event, a tragedy, a compromise, a mistake—is more powerful than the God who spoke the world into existence . . . We live in 'if only/what if' moments more than we realize. They wrap us in a sense of hopeless paralysis; we fear the bad choices we made [and] the choices we face. God pours His grace into the present . . . our walk is one where we make a decision and stick with it, trusting that even if we make mistakes, God's big enough to turn them around. When regret becomes ungodly sorrow versus godly sorrow, you find yourself submerged in self-pity instead of looking to Him to work things out for the good of 'those . . . he has called according to his purpose'" (See Romans 8:28).

July 5

"Don't excite love ... until ... you're ready."
Song of Solomon 2:7 (MSG)

DON'T RUSH INTO THIS RELATIONSHIP (1)

When we feel hurt and rejected there's something inside us that wants to prove we're still worthy and desirable; as a result, we can jump into the next relationship too quickly. But just like an infant doesn't go from crawling to driving overnight, there's a process involved, and if you try to circumvent it you'll end up back at square one, wondering what happened. One author says: "A new relationship won't successfully heal you, avoid aggravating inflicted wounds, or instantly clean up a mess ... Regardless of the temporary bliss, sooner or later you'll end up faced again with your old stuff ... If this is your situation, do things the right way. Take your time ... These things can't be feigned ... rushed or ... pursued. They'll be given to you when you're ready, and not a moment sooner ... you want the real deal this time ... and [God] wants to be your filter, so in order to reach the treasure of your heart, a person must first pass through Him." Solomon writes, "Don't excite love, don't stir it up, until the time is ripe—and you're ready." Don't be in such a hurry to take the edge off your pain that you run ahead of God. It takes time for Him to make you into the person He wants you to become. While He's working on you, He's preparing the heart of the right partner to show up at the right time. In the meantime, there's a way to fill the emptiness inside; work on developing a closer relationship with God and He will "fill you with ... joy and peace" (Romans 15:13).

July 6

*"No one who drinks the water I give
will ever be thirsty again."*
John 4:14 (CEV)

DON'T RUSH INTO THIS RELATIONSHIP (2)

We all want to be loved and appreciated for who we are. And when it doesn't happen on our timetable, it's tempting to rush into another relationship hoping it'll make everything better. One author writes: "There's no Prince Charming to sweep you off your feet and make you happy with yourself. Even when the first part of the story seems to go well, Sleeping Beauty wakes up to discover her prince is just a common frog . . . You can't expect a person to give you what only your heavenly Father can provide. Mere mortals, even with good intentions, can never come close. When you pin all your hopes and dreams on someone else you're bound to be disappointed . . . When you sell your soul in an attempt to attain the unattainable . . . the cost is high and the potential for peril is steep. Don't let obsessive desire lead you down a path of despair . . . obsession is powerful. It fuels fantasies and drives you to reckless behavior . . . You won't find love till you love and respect yourself enough to stop looking for someone or something outside yourself to give you worth." One day Jesus met a woman who'd been married five times and was pursuing yet another relationship. Recognizing that her need was not for another man, but a relationship with God, He said, "No one who drinks the water I give will ever be thirsty again" (vv. 13-14 CEV). Jesus saw beyond her sin to her real need and restored her sense of self-worth. Bottom line: only the water Jesus gives will quench your soul's thirst.

July 7

"Your sins are forgiven."
Matthew 9:2 (NAS)

CONFIDENCE BEFORE GOD

Jesus said to a quadriplegic lying on a cot, "Take courage, son; your sins are forgiven." Perhaps you're asking, "What sins could a quadriplegic commit?" There are three ways to sin: (1) Commission: the things we do. (2) Omission: the good we fail to do. (3) Disposition: our wrong attitudes. Why didn't Jesus just say, "Arise, take up your bed and walk?" Because when you know that your sins are forgiven you have the confidence to ask God for what you need, and the courage to rise up in faith and do what He tells you. Knowing his sins were forgiven enabled this man to do what everybody thought was impossible. There's an important lesson here. After Adam sinned, he hid from God. When God said to him, "Where are you?" he replied, "I heard Your voice in the garden, and I was afraid" (Genesis 3:9-10 NKJV). How can you know when something is wrong for you? When it causes you to hide from God! When it makes you avoid prayer, Bible reading, and fellowship with God's people. The Bible condemns sins such as stealing and lusting, but what about other things that are not so clearly spelled out in Scripture? To know whether something is right or wrong for you, you need only ask one question: "How will this affect my confidence before God?" You'll never go wrong asking that question. "If our heart does not condemn us, we have confidence toward God. And whatever we ask we receive from Him, because we keep His commandments and do those things that are pleasing in His sight" (1 John 3:21-22 NKJV).

July 8

"I ... lifted my eyes to heaven, and ... I was restored."
Daniel 4:34-36 (NKJV)

LET GOD RESTORE YOU

When King Nebuchadnezzar repented, his "understanding...reason...honor and splendor returned...and...[he] was restored." But when we have an image to maintain we're reluctant to ask for help in case people think less of us. One author writes: "To fall is bad enough, but to fall and not cry out for help is worse ... Some people are so full of pride and self-sufficiency they think, 'If I can't get up myself, I won't let anyone help me.' Stop being so proud; that's what caused you to fall in the first place! The Bible says: 'Those who walk in pride [God] is able to put down' (Daniel 4:37 NKJV). Pride is dangerous; it forces you to lie needlessly in a helpless state for days—and sometimes years. If you'd asked for help immediately, you could have gotten up and gone on with your life." Proverbs 14:12 says, "There is a way that seems right to a man, but its end is ... death" (NKJV). Have you ever tried to rescue an injured animal? It doesn't know your only desire is to help; it just knows it's in pain, and as a result it strikes out at the person who least deserves it. This is especially true when you've been wounded by someone close to you and didn't see it coming. You can hurt so much that you stop trusting everybody, including God. You stop praying and reading the Bible, you avoid those who want to help, and you refuse to let anybody pray for you. The Bible says, "Do not harden your hearts" (Hebrews 3:15 NKJV). Today, acknowledge that you've fallen and let God restore you.

July 9

"So that nothing will hinder your prayers."
1 Peter 3:7 (NIV)

HINDRANCES TO PRAYER (1)

Here are two hindrances to answered prayer: (1) Unconfessed sin. "Your sins have hidden his face from you, so that he will not hear" (Isaiah 59:2 NIV). As a believer, God expects you to walk in obedience. "What does the Lord require of you? To act justly and to love mercy and to walk humbly with your God" (Micah 6:8 NIV). Notice, these are "requirements." If you don't meet them, you're wasting your time praying, unless it's a prayer of repentance. You must seek God's forgiveness, then He will hear your prayers. (2) Unresolved conflict. "Husbands . . . be considerate as you live with your wives, and treat them with respect . . . so that nothing will hinder your prayers." There's no point praying if you are always fighting with one another. "Anyone who claims to be in the light but hates a brother or sister is still in the darkness" (1 John 2:9 NIV). God will answer when you come out into the light, deal with the thing that drove you apart, and attempt to mend the relationship. Now, sometimes it isn't possible to make amends. "If it is possible, as far as it depends on you, live at peace with everyone" (Romans 12:18 NIV). Sometimes the other person would rather keep the issue alive than accept your apology. When that happens look into your heart. Do you really want restoration, or would you rather "blame place" and let things fester? If your attempts have been wholehearted and honest, God won't let a broken relationship stand in the way of your prayers. But if your attempts have been half-hearted and self-serving, try again—this time for real.

July 10

"You do not have because you do not ask."
James 4:2 (NIV)

HINDRANCES TO PRAYER (2)

Here are two more hindrances to answered prayer: (1) Failure to pray. It's estimated that out of the 667 prayers for specific things mentioned in the Bible, there are 454 specific answers. That means the Bible is a book of prayers—and answers. Our problem is, we spend a lot of time talking about prayer and fail to get down to the business of praying. Charles Trumbull said, "Prayer releases the energies of God." The goal of prayer is not to overcome God's reluctance, but to believe Him and take hold of His willingness. His Word says: "You do not have because you do not ask." C. E. Cowman wrote: "No praying man or woman accomplishes so much with so little expenditure of time, as when he or she is praying." Until you learn to pray in faith and wait on God for the answer, you'll get nowhere. (2) Failure to care. When the Israelites complained that God wasn't answering their prayers He told them, "Stop oppressing those who work for you and treat them fairly . . . share your food with the hungry . . . Clothe those who are cold, and don't hide from [those] who need your help. If you do these things . . . the Lord will answer" (Isaiah 58:6-9 TLB). Sin and unbelief are not the only things that hinder your prayers; self-centered living will! A little girl prayed for several weeks asking God for a certain thing. Finally in frustration she said, "By the way, Lord, I've mentioned this to You several times before." If that's your situation, stop thinking about your own needs and focus on the needs of others.

July 11

"I am innocent... It is your responsibility!"
Matthew 27:24 (NIV)

THE BLAME GAME (1)

More and more, we are becoming a blame-oriented culture. Today our misfortunes are deemed to be somebody else's fault. "I'm this way because of them. They did it to me." And it didn't begin with us. It goes all the way back to Adam in the Garden of Eden when he told God, "The woman... You gave... me, she gave me of the tree, and I ate" (Genesis 3:12 NKJV). It's in our DNA! We say the breakdown in our marriage was our partner's fault, or we drink too much because somebody drives us to it, or we're sick because of the fast-food industry; let's sue them! Shifting responsibility may alleviate momentary guilt, but it's a deadly game with no winners. In sentencing Christ to die, Pilate said, "I am innocent of this man's blood... It is your responsibility!" He thought by dumping the blame onto the Jews he would avoid upsetting either his wife or his critics and prove himself innocent. But the buck stopped at his desk! Understand this: God holds you responsible for your decisions and actions (See Romans 2:6). And your failure to make the right decision, or take the right action, also earns you His guilty verdict. Paul writes, "You cannot mock the justice of God. You will always harvest what you plant" (Galatians 6:7 NLT). Others may be guilty of offending you, and that's their harvest to reap. But your harvest depends on your reactions. Accepting responsibility before God is how you alleviate your guilt, discouragement and stress.

July 12

"The woman you put here ... gave me some ... and I ate it."
Genesis 3:12 (NIV)

THE BLAME GAME (2)

Blaming came naturally to Adam and Eve, the father and mother of the human race. After all, who could fault them? God did! Their blaming was a result of how sin had changed them. Their relationship to themselves, each other, their environment, and even God, was radically changed by their irresponsibility. And since God can do nothing with people who won't take responsibility for their decisions, He dismissed them from Paradise. What a price to pay! Here are two good reasons for giving up the blame game: (1) It makes you a victim. When you make someone else responsible for your circumstances, you put the power to change things in their hands. That means nothing will change unless they decide to change it. You make them master of your fate. Only by accepting personal responsibility can you retain the power to change your circumstances. (2) It makes you miserable. You say, "But they hurt me." Yes, and by harboring resentment you are hurting yourself over and over. The Bible says, "Keep a sharp eye out for weeds of bitter discontent. A thistle or two gone to seed can ruin a whole garden in no time" (Hebrews 12:14-15 MSG). Before you know it, your entire outlook gets distorted. "Watch out for the Esau syndrome: trading away God's lifelong gift in order to satisfy a short-term appetite ... Esau later regretted that ... and wanted God's blessing—but by then it was too late, tears or no tears" (vv. 16-17 MSG). Forgive, take back your life, and get out of the blame game!

July 13

"You can't get forgiveness... without... forgiving others."
Matthew 6:15 (MSG)

THE BLAME GAME (3)

Blaming creates enemies. The person you are blaming will ignore you, compile numerous proofs of their innocence, and resent you. And their friends will defend them and become your enemies. Even your own friends will get fed up with your complaining and distance you. Your "root of bitterness" will spread, causing "many [to be] defiled," and making things worse (Hebrews 12:15 NKJV). Blaming rubs off. Blamers beget blamers. Your family gets pulled in, so they suffer too. "Don't hang out with angry people; don't keep company with hotheads. Bad temper is contagious—don't get infected" (Proverbs 22:24-25 MSG). Stop it, you're passing on your misery and dysfunction to those who love you! Blaming is addictive. The justification we feel in blaming hooks us for the long run. It manipulates our anger, making us feel okay about shifting responsibility. It gets progressively easier to complain rather than to resolve the problem. Like any addiction, it has to be fed more and more to achieve its reward. Sooner than you think, you'll become a skilled, confirmed "blame-aholic." Blaming sabotages forgiveness. You can't forgive someone while you're judging and resenting them. And while you're squandering your time and energy blaming them, you forfeit your right to receive God's forgiveness. "But if you do not forgive others their sins, your Father will not forgive your sins" (Matthew 6:15 NIV). It's time to give up the blame game, own responsibility for your life, and take back your God-given power to respond to things according to His Word!

July 14

"Here am I, and the children the Lord has given me."
Isaiah 8:18 (NIV)

YOU OWE IT TO THEM

You may not be able to give your children everything you'd like to, or everything they want, but here are four things you owe them: (1) Connect with them. The story's told of a couple who decided to buy a new playpen for a friend, on the arrival of her sixth child. A year later the friend wrote back saying, "Thank you for the pen. It's wonderful—I sit in it every afternoon and read, and the children can't get near me." Seriously, what do you really know about your child? Their struggles, their heroes, their music, their friends, their fears, their dreams? If your answer is "not much," start making changes right away! (2) Listen to them. If some of us paid as much attention to our garden as we did to our children, we'd be living in a weed patch. You'll never understand your child until you take time to listen to what they're saying—and what they're not saying. (3) Believe in them. As a child, the great Caruso was told by a music teacher that he had no talent at all. Parent, make sure your voice is the loudest. Build their confidence; give them the faith and the self-worth required to overcome the obstacles they'll face in life. (4) Let them see God in you. Three kids were discussing their fathers. One said, "My father knows the mayor." Another said, "My father knows the governor." Confidently the third said, "That's nothing; my father knows God!" Dad, Mom, do you know God? If you don't, commit your life to Him today.

July 15

"Stop being bitter and angry and mad at others."
Ephesians 4:31 (CEV)

YOU CAN OVERCOME BITTERNESS

A man who had been bitten by a rattlesnake was rushed to the hospital. When he asked the doctor, "Is it life-threatening?" the doctor said, "The bite isn't, but the poison is." The "bites" you suffer at the hands of others are painful and upsetting, but they're not lethal. What happens to you normally doesn't destroy you, but what happens in you afterwards can. Like venom, bitterness first poisons your mind, then your relationships. It causes you to replay the hurt until it controls you, stealing the future God planned for you. But it doesn't have to be that way. You can overcome bitterness. God says, "Stop being bitter and angry and mad at others." And what God commands, He will give you the grace to do. When Peter asked Jesus, "Should I forgive my brother seven times?" Jesus said, "No, you must forgive him seventy times seven" (See Matthew 18:21-22). In other words, "Forgive, and keep on forgiving until it no longer bothers you." What causes bitterness? Anger that's allowed to take residence in your thought-life. God's purpose for anger is to motivate you to tap into His power for solving problems; otherwise, they become permanent. Solving the problem resolves and relieves your anger. But anger can become long-term bitterness when you fixate on "who did it to me," making you hostile, critical, blaming, and punitive. You say, "Can I really stop my anger?" Yes, with God's help you can control your reactions and behaviors and starve your anger to death. "The fruit of the Spirit is . . . self-control" (Galatians 5:22-23 NIV).

July 16

"Run in such a way as to get the prize."
1 Corinthians 9:24 (NIV)

THE HEALTHY EDGE OF COMPETITION

We say things like, "It's a rat race out there, and the rats are winning," "Nice guys finish last," "Winning isn't everything; it's the only thing!" Such sentiments characterize our culture, driving workaholic lifestyles that destroy health, fracture family life, and eliminate the spiritual discipline required to have a growing relationship with God. So what should we do? Avoid all competition? Opt out of the race? Retire and watch the world go by? No, those are not options for a follower of Christ. (1) Beware of competitiveness that leads to jealousy. Cain's competitiveness toward his brother Abel led him to murder (See Genesis 4:1-8). He tried to put his brother down in order to lift himself up. King Saul tried to kill David when the crowd sang, "Saul has slain his thousands, and David his ten thousands" (1 Samuel 18:6-11 NKJV). Those words caused jealousy to grow like a cancer in him. (2) Understand that by seeking to excel in your calling, you exalt Christ. Paul writes: "You've . . . seen the athletes race. Everyone runs; one wins. Run to win. All good athletes train hard . . . for a gold medal that tarnishes and fades. You're after one that's gold eternally" (1 Corinthians 9:24-25 MSG). No second-rate effort, no settling for mediocre outcomes. "I'm running hard for the finish line. I'm giving it everything I've got. No lazy living for me! I'm staying alert and in top condition" (1 Corinthians 9:26 MSG). Getting ahead of others isn't what it's about; it's about maximizing all you do for God's glory! "Whatever you do, work at it with all your heart, as working for the Lord, not for human masters" (Colossians 3:23 NIV).

July 17

"The Lord is my helper; I will not be afraid."
Hebrews 13:6 (NIV)

EVICT YOUR WORRIES

Worry is a squatter; you must evict it. In certain situations, if a house lies empty long enough, whoever likes can move in and occupy it. Worry does that too. It roams around looking for an empty mind, then moves in. Has worry taken up residence in your mind today? Is it there when you wake in the morning and go to bed at night? As a follower of Christ, you have the authority to serve worry an eviction notice and it must leave. The only thing that enables it to stay is your ignorance of that truth. When your mind is occupied with God's Word, worry sees a "no vacancy" sign and moves on. Paul writes: "For though we walk in the flesh, we do not war according to the flesh. For the weapons of our warfare are not carnal but mighty in God for pulling down strongholds, casting down arguments and every high thing that exalts itself against the knowledge of God, bringing every thought into captivity to the obedience of Christ" (2 Corinthians 10:3-5 NKJV). The weapons God has given you to fight with are greater than the fears you face. But you must know your weapons, keep them in good repair, and be able to use them. "Therefore thus says the Lord God of hosts: 'Because you speak this word, behold, I will make My words in your mouth fire, and [your worries] wood, and it shall devour them'" (Jeremiah 5:14 NKJV). When you believe God's Word with all your heart and begin to speak it in the face of your worries, "It shall devour them."

July 18

"We will stand in your presence... cry out to you... and you will hear us and save us."
2 Chronicles 20:9 (NIV)

WHEN YOU FEEL DOWN (1)

A parishioner asked his pastor, "Do you ever feel down?" "Sure," he responded. "What do you do about it?" the parishioner said. "I get up again. Being down isn't my problem—staying down is. I'm either up, or I'm getting up. I've learned not to park in between." Although feeling down is universal, sociologists warn us to guard against its two most common causes: fear and fatigue. Let's look at them. Fear—when Edomite armies marched against Israel's king, fear gripped him and his nation. Feeling powerless, they feared losing their God-given land and possessions. If the stress of the last few years has left you feeling fearful, do what Israel's king did. He turned to God and prayed: "Whenever we are faced with any calamity... we can... stand in your presence... We can cry out to you... and you will hear us and rescue us" (v. 9 NLT). Don't let fear cause you to abandon your hope and your vision. Instead, stand in God's presence, cry out to Him, and watch Him rescue you. Throughout the Old Testament God reminded Israel of His track record of goodness. He wanted them to remember it and take courage. But sometimes fear would cloud their memory and they'd begin to doubt. Sound familiar? So He told them, "Do not be... discouraged... the battle is not yours, but [mine]" (v. 15 NIV). In other words, "You don't have to defeat the foe, that's My job. I'm in charge; trust Me to work it out." Remember Who's in control of your circumstances today. Stand in His presence; believe His promise!

July 19

"Let us not grow weary while doing good."
Galatians 6:9 (NKJV)

WHEN YOU FEEL DOWN (2)

Fatigue. Remember the old saying, "You can't burn the candle at both ends?" Today, we've gone from candle power to atomic power, and few of us pay heed to that old saying anymore. We want bigger homes, fancier cars and more exotic vacations. So we start earlier, work harder, and finish later. Then we stagger home and fall asleep in front of the television, worn out and feeling guilty about spending so little time with our family. We forget that God designed us to need one work-free day a week for rest and spiritual renewal (See Exodus 20:8-11). As a result, fatigue saps our creative energy, distorts our outlook, diminishes our joy, erodes our confidence and drains us spiritually. Elijah is a great example of this. Single-handedly he defeated the prophets of Baal (See 1 Kings 18). In answer to his prayer, God sent fire from heaven that consumed the altar and turned Israel back to God. It was a spectacular victory, yet on the heels of it, he got so down that he actually asked God to take his life. Now that's a major league downer! What did God do? Like any good doctor, He diagnosed the man's problem and prescribed three things: proper diet, adequate rest, and a good assistant: Elisha. Many of us who love what we work at, tend to get out of balance. We have no boundaries, so we risk burning out. We "grow weary while doing good." What's the answer? "He restores my soul" (Psalm 23:3 NKJV). The word "restores" has two parts: "rest" and "store." Relax physically and replenish spiritually. That's what to do when you feel down!

July 20

"Death and life are in the power of the tongue."
Proverbs 18:21 (NKJV)

THE ANSWER TO YOUR WORRIES

Your words either work for you or against you. The Bible says, "Death and life are in the power of the tongue, and those who love it will eat its fruit." The old saying, "You'll eat your words," is more than a meaningless cliché, it's the truth! Jeremiah the prophet writes, "Your words were found, and I ate them, and Your word was to me the joy and rejoicing of my heart" (Jeremiah 15:16 NKJV). The Psalmist writes, "They cried out to the Lord in their trouble, and He saved them out of their distresses (worries). He sent His word and healed them" (Psalm 107:19-20 NKJV). God's Word is the medicine that heals worry. What God has to say about the issue must be what you have to say about it too; otherwise, you're contradicting Him and disconnecting yourself from the source of all blessing. If you're wise, you will surround yourself with like-minded people who speak God's Word into your life and limit your time with those who have no interest in it. If you want to grow the right kind of fruit, you must have the right climate. And the words you speak (and listen to) determine the climate of your life, the direction in which it goes, and the results you get. There is no "secret" to success. The Bible says that when you learn to "meditate day and night" in God's Word, you "will prosper in all you do" (See Psalm 1:1-3). The answer to your worries is in God's Word!

July 21

"This, then, is how you should pray."
Matthew 6:9 (NIV)

PERSIST IN PRAYER

If prayer came naturally, God wouldn't have to remind us so often to do it. A consistent prayer life requires crucifying our selfish nature. But when prayer doesn't seem rewarding, we're apt to abandon it. So how can you pray and get results? (1) Before you ask, adore! Any prayer that begins with asking can become self-centered and shallow. "Enter his gates with thanksgiving and his courts with praise; give thanks to him and praise his name" (Psalm 100:4 NIV). When God's love, goodness and faithfulness are your starting point, you're lifted out of yourself, your spirit is prepared to "connect" with God, the content of your prayer becomes more scriptural, and you get results. In the Lord's Prayer Jesus directs our attention first to God's name, then His kingdom, then His will. After that, we ask for "our daily bread." Thanksgiving doesn't condition God to bless you—it conditions you to receive His blessing. (2) When you pray, persist! God's not an automated teller. You are supposed to stay engaged with Him until He decides to answer you. This involves an attitude of faith, persistence, and patience. Jesus gave us a parable about a woman who kept pleading with a hardhearted judge to grant her petition. When she finally wore him down, he gave her what she asked. Jesus had only one purpose for the parable: "To show them that they should always pray and not give up" (Luke 18:1 NIV). The point is not that persistence forces God's cooperation, it's that God wants you to pray and not quit. When you persist God will answer, "and quickly!" (v. 8 NIV).

July 22

"A man of two minds [is] . . . unstable and unreliable and uncertain about everything."
James 1:8 (AMPC)

STOP TRYING TO CONTROL EVERYTHING

Do you have a compulsive need to find a solution to every problem, and to control everything? Do you always have a back-up plan in case things don't go the way you think they should? Have you noticed that the more you try to "fix" things, the more anxiety you experience? The Bible says, "The mind of the flesh [. . . sense and reason . . .] is death . . . But the mind of the . . . Spirit is life" (Romans 8:6 AMPC). "Fixing" is the opposite of "trusting." Now God doesn't want you to be mindless or helpless, He just wants you to live by faith and not head knowledge alone. When you learn to trust God and operate in "the mind of the Spirit," you experience peace even when you're surrounded by tough circumstances. One of the pitfalls of human reasoning is that it causes you to become double minded and stuck: "A man of two minds [is] unstable and unreliable and uncertain about everything." What frame of mind do you live in? Instead of always trying to figure everything out, learn to be comfortable not knowing and trust the One who does. Decide that each time you feel anxious you'll stop and pray: "Lord, I'm not going to try to figure this out myself, I'm bringing it to You, trusting You for the answer." When you stop struggling with the when, where, why, and how, you start experiencing God's peace in a way you never have before. You also put yourself in a position where God can intervene on your behalf. So stop trying to control everything.

July 23

"The prudent [wise] considers well his steps."
Proverbs 14:15 (NKJV)

TAKE THE PLUNGE (1)

After you've prayed, planned, and prepared, there comes a point where you've got to take the plunge. Is it scary? Absolutely! There are two kinds of people. Those who leap before they look; they are driven by impulse. Then there are those who look, and look, and look but never leap; they are controlled by fear. Which are you? To get to the Promised Land, Israel had to cross the River Jordan at flood tide. It must have made the strongest heart skip a beat. God had promised that when the feet of the priests carrying the ark stepped into the water it would roll back. Can you imagine their thoughts? "Couldn't we wait until the tide goes down? Why do I have to go first? What if the waters don't roll back and I drown?" The step between prudence and paranoia is short and steep. Prudence wears a seatbelt; paranoia avoids cars altogether. Prudence washes with soap; paranoia avoids human contact altogether. Prudence saves for old age; paranoia clings to every penny. Prudence prepares and plans; paranoia panics. Prudence calculates the risk and takes the plunge; paranoia never enters the water. To reach your God-ordained destiny you must quit holding back, obey God and step into the water. The moment you do, doors will begin to open, and resources will be released where there now seems to be only shortage. God will provide the means, the method, and the manpower. So stand on His promise: "I have loved you; therefore I will give men for you, and people for your life. Fear not, for I am with you" (Isaiah 43:4-5 NKJV).

July 24

"Underneath are the everlasting arms."
Deuteronomy 33:27 (NKJV)

TAKE THE PLUNGE (2)

Picture this: a father and his two small children are at play. He's in the pool, and he invites them to run and jump into his arms. One does, the other doesn't. The one who doesn't, watches gleefully, applauds, and jumps up and down. But when her dad invites her to do the same, she shakes her head and backs away. Is that you? Living on the edge of the pool, never taking the plunge, happy to experience life vicariously through others? Preferring to take no risk, rather than any risk? For fear of the worst, you never enjoy the best. You say, "But I'm not sure what I'm jumping into!" Read this: "Underneath are the everlasting arms." Foolishness is closing your eyes and jumping before you know there's even water in the pool, or that your father has said, "Come, I'll catch you." Faith is knowing that the only way to conquer your fear of the water is to take the leap, because the One who is calling you has been there for you from the moment you became His child. Nothing is more important to Him than your safety, the development of your faith, and your total success in life. God told Joshua, "Arise, go over this Jordan . . . to the land which I am giving [you] . . . Only be strong and very courageous, that you may observe to do according to all the law which Moses My servant commanded you; do not turn from it to the right hand or to the left, that you may prosper wherever you go" (Joshua 1:2, 7 NKJV). Note the words, "Arise, go, be strong." In other words, take the plunge!

July 25

"But his sons did not walk in his ways."
1 Samuel 8:3 (NKJV)

WHAT'S A PARENT TO DO?

At times, every parent experiences despair over their child's decisions and actions. "I did my best to raise them right; did I fail as a parent?" Failure is a fact of life—and of parenting—and nobody does it perfectly! Parents assume a heavier load of guilt than they deserve. Consider some Bible examples of real-world parenting: Isaac had, at best, a 50 percent success rate with his sons, Jacob and Esau. Aaron struck out completely with Nadab and Abihu. Manoah's boy, Samson, didn't win the "son-of-the-year award!" And Samuel, a recognized moral and spiritual giant, watched his sons reject his example and teaching and pursue lives of bribery and shame. Since Adam, kids "doing their own thing" have broken their parents' hearts! So what's a parent to do? (1) Realize you're not responsible for their decisions. They make their own choices. Condemning yourself just discourages you, and it undermines your ability to be the parent they need. The Bible says, "Salvation is of the Lord" (Jonah 2:9). He saves and delivers—not you. (2) Pray for them and give them to God. Anxiety and frustration will only make you the kind of parent they don't enjoy being around, and who can't enjoy them. You're not built to carry such a load; your heavenly Father is, and He wants to carry it for you! (See 1 Peter 5:7). (3) Remember that God loves them more than you do! He gave His only child to save yours. He knows their heart, and how to reach it and turn it toward Him (See Jeremiah 17:9-10). Give your child to Him!

July 26

"The poles... are not to be removed."
Exodus 25:15 (NIV)

YOU CAN CARRY GOD'S PRESENCE WITH YOU (1)

The ark of the covenant represented the presence of God in the midst of His people. When the Philistines captured it, they were smitten with tumors. When they placed it in their temple, their god, Dagon, fell to the ground (See 1 Samuel 5). The moral of this story is—don't mess around with the things of God! Even if you are not prepared to serve God, at least be wise and reverence Him. When Israel conquered the Philistines, David decided to bring the ark, the symbol of God's presence, back home to Jerusalem. Now, when God designed that ark He put rings on the side of it, and poles through those rings, saying it must only be carried on the shoulders of special priests. But somebody thought up "a better way," so they put it on a new cart pulled by an ox. And that's when everything went wrong. When the ark started to slip off the cart, a well-meaning bystander decided to steady it. And he died for it! You say, "That's pretty extreme." There's a lesson here for those who want to package God's presence, market it, and "take it on the road." Who is qualified to carry God's presence? Only believer-priests who have been cleansed by the blood of the Lamb, are washed by the Word at the laver, who fellowship with God at His table, who worship Him at the altar of incense, and who walk in the light of truth represented by the seven-branched lampstand. Away with newfangled carts! "The Lord added to the church" (Acts 2:47 NKJV). If we are going to carry God's presence and build His church, we've got to do it His way.

July 27

"I am the Lord your God... who directs you."
Isaiah 48:17 (NIV)

YOU CAN CARRY GOD'S PRESENCE WITH YOU (2)

The ark of the covenant represented three things to the people of Israel. And these are three things you need in your life. Let's look carefully at each: (1) Victory. When Israel went into battle, they must have looked strange to their enemies, because the priests who carried the ark of the covenant went ahead of the army. Indeed, when their enemies saw it, they may have laughed and said, "What's that all about? What's the big deal with the box?" But after they had been humbled by defeat, they realized they weren't fighting man, but God. And when you are in right standing with God, He will go before you and fight your battles. And the great thing is, God has never lost a battle. (2) Guidance. When the Israelites needed direction, God spoke to them in the place where the ark rested in the tabernacle. And they discovered what you will discover: when you seek God's guidance and listen to Him, you won't get it wrong. His guidance system is infallible: "I am the Lord your God... who directs you in the way you should go." (3) Prosperity. Prosperity simply means, "Having enough to do the will of God." And that's how much God wants you to have, no more and no less. When the ark rested for a three-month span in the house of a man called Obed-Edom, all that he had was blessed and multiplied (See 2 Samuel 6:10-12). Could you use more victory, more guidance, and more prosperity? Spend time in God's presence, and then carry it with you wherever you go.

July 28

"So he is first in everything."
Colossians 1:18 (NLT)

YOU CAN CARRY GOD'S PRESENCE WITH YOU (3)

The ark of the covenant is mentioned in Scripture about 185 times, so it must be important. Every bit of activity in the outer court and inner court of the tabernacle was for one purpose, to lead you into the Holy of Holies where God's presence was. Old Testament symbols, such as the ark, are a picture of New Testament realities. In this regard, the ark, which was the most important piece of furniture in the tabernacle, is a picture of the Christ we love and serve. He is Lord. He is supreme. There's no one like Him. And He alone is worthy of all praise! Paul writes: "Christ is the visible image of the invisible God. He existed before anything was created and is supreme over all creation, for through him God created everything in the heavenly realms and on earth. He made the things we can see and the things we can't see—such as thrones, kingdoms, rulers, and authorities in the unseen world. Everything was created through him and for him. He existed before everything else, and he holds all creation together. Christ is also the head of the church, which is his body. He is the beginning, supreme over all who rise from the dead. So he is first in everything. For God in all his fullness was pleased to live in Christ, and through him God reconciled everything to himself" (vv. 15-20 NLT). If your faith is "me-centered," you'll get nowhere with God. But when your faith is "Christ-centered," then everything Christ has becomes available to you!

July 29

"But they all... began to make excuses."
Luke 14:18 (NKJV)

WHAT'S YOUR EXCUSE?

Let's look at some of the excuses we offer for not pursuing the dream God has given us: (1) "Dreams don't come true for ordinary people like me." The Wright brothers wanted to fly. Winston Churchill envisioned a free Europe. Dr. Martin Luther King, Jr. dreamed of racial equality. But you don't have to be a world figure to have a dream. No, the pursuit of a dream is what makes the difference between ordinary and extraordinary people. Ordinary people live extraordinary lives when they follow their dream. Why do we say that? Because a God-given dream will motivate you to make important changes in your life. You won't just change who you are in order to live out your dream; you pursue your dream, and the process changes who you are and what you can accomplish. In other words, your dream is both your goal and your change-agent. (2) "If the dream isn't big, it's not worth pursuing." Size doesn't determine significance. Your dream doesn't have to be big; it just has to be bigger than you. Mother Teresa said, "We can't all do great things, but we can all do small things with great love." (3) "Now is not the right time to pursue my dream." Permission to pursue your dream comes from two sources: God and yourself. Novelist George Eliot said, "It's never too late to become what you might have been." The timing will never be perfect for you to pursue your dream so you might as well start now. If you don't, next year you'll be one year older and not a step closer to it.

July 30

"Let the Spirit renew your ... attitudes."
Ephesians 4:23 (NLT)

GET RID OF THE "CLUTTER"

When you sell a house, it feels great to get rid of stuff you've accumulated. You wonder why you lived so long with it weighing you down. It's the same with mental and emotional clutter. Jon Gordon says, "We fill our minds with thoughts that hold us back, habits that limit us, distractions that derail us, negative people who drain us, fear that paralyzes us, and time-zappers that sabotage our productivity. We spend so much time and energy on things that don't matter—we fail to focus on what does matter. We fill up with so many things that generate negative energy, there's no room for positive energy in our lives." Paul writes, "Throw off your ... former way of life ... let the Spirit renew your thoughts and attitudes" (vv. 22-23 NLT). The clutter you need to lose includes: believing that you're alone, trying to please everybody, feeling insecure, putting yourself down, needing everybody to like you, jumping to negative conclusions before you know the facts, thinking you're always right, recalling all the times you messed up, wanting to know how it all turns out, needing to have all the answers, worrying that if you let go of the memorabilia you'll lose the memories, agonizing that you're not rich enough, good enough or smart enough, surrounding yourself with people who remember the bad times and not the good, making energy-sucking comparisons, viewing life like a movie instead of participating, believing that your best days are over, waiting at all times for the right moment, fearing you will look foolish, focusing on negative type-casting ... and anything else you don't want to pass on to your kids. How can you get rid of the clutter? "Let the Spirit renew your ... attitudes."

July 31

"A righteous person may fall ... but he gets up again."
Proverbs 24:16 (GW)

RESPONDING TO FAILURE

You can tell a lot about somebody by how they respond to life. Everybody gets knocked down, but how fast you get up again is what counts. Verla Gillmor says: "Failure teaches us things we can't learn any other way . . . Treat it as a visitor allowed to deliver unpleasant news, but don't let it take up residence. Remember, all failures aren't equal. For example, when a beautiful, talented young woman is first-runner-up in the Miss America Pageant, we say she failed. Yet some people would give their right arm to be named the second most attractive female in a national competition. It's a matter of perspective . . . [examine] your failures and weigh them according to their importance in the overall scheme of things . . . I once received a 'D' in college . . . it's ridiculous, but that sticks in my mind like a pebble in my shoe. Why do I fixate on that and not the fact that it happened the semester I carried nineteen credit hours, worked part-time, got engaged, and spent six weeks in the college health center with mononucleosis? When I put the experience in context, it loses its power to undermine my confidence. Failure teaches us what's important. I've a friend who was downsized out of a job . . . It caught her by surprise because she was good at her work. 'I tended to be full of pride,' she says. 'I got away with it because I was so successful. Losing my job . . . humbled me. With pride you have no permission to fail. It's a heavy yoke . . . and I don't wear it anymore. I feel lighter in my spirit without the burden of having to be perfect.'"

August 1

*"When you have done the will of God, you
will receive what he has promised."*
Hebrews 10:36 (NIV)

PROMISES, PROMISES! (1)

Many of us remember singing in church, "Every promise in the Book is mine!" Exciting words, but are they entirely true? If you've prayed for the fulfillment of a Bible promise that didn't materialize, you may have wondered, felt disillusioned, or even stopped trusting. What's true is that every promise in the Book intended for you, is yours! God is committed to keeping every promise He has made (See Matthew 24:35). So how can you know which Bible promises are yours? Here are some scriptural guidelines to help you: (1) Be sure you understand the promise. God is committed to His Word, not to your interpretation of it. When Jesus said, "Destroy this temple, and in three days I will raise it up" (John 2:19 NKJV), His audience completely misunderstood Him, thinking He meant the literal temple when He meant His body. (2) Walk in the Spirit, not the flesh. Walking in the Spirit, Peter received divine understanding of Christ's deity. When Jesus asked, "Who do you say I am?" Peter answered, "You are the Messiah, the Son of the living God." Jesus replied, "This was not revealed to you by flesh and blood, but by my Father" (See Matthew 16:13-18). Soon afterwards, walking in the flesh, the same man totally misunderstood Jesus and was severely rebuked by Jesus (See vv. 21-23). Why? Because "the natural man does not receive the things of the Spirit of God . . . nor can he know them, because they are spiritually discerned" (1 Corinthians 2:14 NKJV). Submit your thoughts to God; pray for His guidance, and in due time you'll get the insight you need.

August 2

"No . . . Scripture is . . . of one's own interpretation."
2 Peter 1:20 (NAS)

PROMISES, PROMISES! (2)

Here are two more principles for discerning which promises in Scripture are for you: (1) Try to understand the context. No Scripture stands in isolation but should be read in conjunction with every other Scripture on the same topic. If you isolate "I can do all things through Christ who strengthens me" (Philippians 4:13 NKJV), believing "all things" includes leaping from a twelfth-story window, don't blame God's Word for your unexpected demise! You should also have read the context which says, "I have learned both to be full and to be hungry, both to abound and to suffer need. I can do all [these] things through Christ who strengthens me" (vv. 12-13 NKJV). This Scripture doesn't mean you can do anything you want, but that God will enable you to get through anything you encounter while doing His will. (2) Test Scripture by Scripture, not by your own desires. "No prophecy of Scripture is a matter of one's own interpretation." Some Bible promises are universal in application, and some are personal. The personal ones apply to the intended hearer; the universal ones apply to all believers. Know which is which. If you think the Scripture, "Believe on the Lord Jesus Christ, and thou shalt be saved, and thy house" (Acts 16:31), guarantees your entire household's salvation, you might be disappointed and think that God failed. No, that was a personal promise made and fulfilled to the Philippian jailer. A universal word for you and your family is, "In fact, God . . . wants everyone to turn from sin and no one to be lost" (2 Peter 3:9 CEV). He wants your entire family to be saved!

August 3

"Help us for the glory of your name."
Psalm 79:9 (NLT)

FREEDOM FROM SEXUAL ADDICTION

For fifteen years Mike Cleveland, airline pilot and founder of "Setting Captives Free," seemed powerless as his addiction to online pornography devastated his life, his marriage, and his family. The spiral of lust enslaved him "until there wasn't a moment of his days free from its tortured domination." The cycle of prayers for deliverance, followed by repeated indulgence in porn, XXX DVDs, and sex chat rooms, plunged him deeper into the darkness of despair and self-loathing. He longed to escape the slimy, secluded underworld of secret soul-destroying sin, but every pathetic attempt left him unchanged, unhinged, and uncertain that freedom was possible for him. Mike turned to self-help books, counselors, and friends without success. His repeated disappointment, when every effort failed, led to increasing guilt and self-incrimination. When his wife insisted on a last-ditch visit with her pastor (all other remedies had been exhausted), the lights in their bleak prison cell suddenly came on. Mike learned that "deliverance belong(s) to the Lord" (Jonah 2:9 AMPC), and its rules are all dictated by Him. Mike's old motivations for getting clean—"saving my marriage for my kids' sake; I'm a Christian, a seminary graduate and preacher"—were full of "loopholes and escape clauses" and produced one botched disaster after another. His pastor taught him that the only viable motivation for getting clean and staying clean was a commitment to glorifying God in all of his decisions, because God delivers the powerless, "For the glory of [His] name." When Mike learned, "Whatever you do, do it all for the glory of God" (1 Corinthians 10:31 NIV), the doors to freedom from years of sexual addiction began to open. Yours can too!

August 4

"Command that these stones become bread."
Matthew 4:3 (NKJV)

THREE LEVELS OF ATTACK (1)

The Bible says, "Jesus was led up by the Spirit into the wilderness to be tempted by the devil" (v. 1 NKJV). This seems to be God's standard operating procedure. Why? Because He's a good general; before He puts you into battle, He puts you into boot camp. Imagine it: you're up at dawn, running for miles with a heavy backpack, crawling under barbed wire barriers with bullets whizzing over your head, taking orders from authority figures you don't know and probably don't like. But if you pass the test you get to wear the uniform. On the threshold of His ministry, God led His Son into a situation where He would face three levels of attack. You will face them also. Let's look at the first one: The attack over the bread. Did Jesus need bread? Yes, He'd been without food for forty days. But He knew that His greatest need was not for natural food but spiritual food. So He told Satan, "Man shall not live by bread alone, but by every word that proceeds from the mouth of God'" (v. 4 NKJV). Only when you're convinced God will take care of all your material needs, will you start putting spiritual things first in your life. Until that happens, you'll think you have to take care of yourself. As a result, you will walk in fear and not faith. That's not how God wants you to live. "Seek first the kingdom of God and His righteousness, and all these things shall be added to you" (Matthew 6:33 NKJV). When you worry, you don't trust God. When you trust God, you don't have to worry. The choice is yours.

August 5

"Then the devil... set Him on the pinnacle."
Matthew 4:5 (NKJV)

THREE LEVELS OF ATTACK (2)

The attack on the pinnacle. Let's look at the second temptation Jesus faced: "Then the devil took Him up into the holy city, [and] set Him on the pinnacle of the temple." Here you deal with the fear of failure. Satan will whisper, "You're on the pinnacle of success now, but you could easily fall off." He will bring up your past failures. He will remind you of leaders who crashed and burned. He will say, "If people realized how little you really know, or the issues you're struggling with, they wouldn't respect you." There are two kinds of fear: healthy fear and unhealthy fear. Healthy fear will keep you dependent on God; it will protect you from pride and self-sufficiency. "Therefore let him who thinks he stands take heed lest he fall" (1 Corinthians 10:12 NKJV). But there's an unhealthy fear that will keep you in the boat when Jesus is calling to you to step out and walk with Him on the water. You say, "But Peter almost drowned." Sure, but he was the only one of the disciples who experienced the joy of walking on the water! Having faith doesn't mean you won't experience a sinking feeling at times. You have a choice. You can give in to fear, or trust the God who has called you, sustained you, and never failed to give you the strength needed to cope with whatever you face. If your own intellect or talents are the basis of your confidence, you have good reason to fear. But if God is the basis of your confidence, you have nothing to fear.

August 6

"All these things I will give You."
Matthew 4:9 (NKJV)

THREE LEVELS OF ATTACK (3)

The attack over the cross. Let's look at the third temptation Jesus faced: "The devil took Him up on an exceedingly high mountain and showed Him all the kingdoms of the world and their glory. And he said to Him, 'All these things I will give You if You will fall down and worship me'" (vv. 8-9 NKJV). Satan's third attack was over a cross-less life. In essence, he told Jesus, "You don't have to carry the cross. Just bow to me and you can have it all." Jesus said, "Away with you, Satan!" (v. 10 NKJV). "Away" with any teaching that says God is your bellhop and He has to wait on you! Or that He's like a vending machine; all you have to do is put in a few coins and out will come whatever you want. Paul writes, "I have been crucified with Christ; it is no longer I who live, but Christ lives in me; and the life which I now live in the flesh I live by faith in the Son of God, who loved me and gave Himself for me" (Galatians 2:20 NKJV). Has God promised to bless you? Absolutely! But that doesn't mean you'll never get hurt, or face lack, or battle sickness, or be betrayed and disappointed by others. Jesus said, "Unless a grain of wheat falls into the ground and dies [to self], it remains alone; but if it dies [to self], it produces much" (John 12:24 NKJV). Have you ever heard the expression, "Dead man walking?" To do God's will you have to die to your own will and do it daily. But if you're willing to, God will take you to a new level of blessing.

August 7

"They that wait upon the Lord."
Isaiah 40:31 (KJV)

LEARN TO WAIT

The word "wait" gives us a picture of two things. The first is of a waiter at your table attending to your needs. The second is of a lower-level person making a request of a higher-level one. Your success depends on approaching them the right way, and on their willingness to grant your request. Since they hold the power, you must be patient and wait for them. Are you getting the idea? Our problem is twofold. First, we want God to wait on us, instead of the other way around. Second, we don't want to wait for anything! We drive to work listening to the radio and talking on the phone; some of us even put ourselves and others at risk by text-messaging. Vance Havner points out that in the Old West if someone missed a stagecoach they said, "That's okay, another one will come around in three or four weeks. Now we don't even want to wait for a revolving door." What God does in you while you are waiting is often more important than what you're asking God to do. Waiting on God brings rewards that nothing else will. Here are a few of them: (1) Vindication. "Do not fret because of those who are evil or be envious of those who do wrong . . . delight in the Lord, and he will give you the desires of your heart" (Psalm 37:1,4 NIV). (2) Strength. "Wait on the Lord . . . and He shall strengthen your heart" (Psalm 27:14 NKJV). (3) Deliverance. "I . . . waited for God . . . He lifted me out of the ditch" (Psalm 40:1-2 MSG). Relax, wait on God and He will come through for you.

August 8

"I . . . am the Lord, and besides Me there is no savior."
Isaiah 43:11 (NKJV)

THERE'S NOBODY LIKE HIM! (1)

The Israelites were commanded not to make any "graven image" of God. Why? Because God made us, we didn't make Him. A god you can make is a god you can control and make do whatever you wish. The ancient Greeks had a host of gods, all created by men. Some demanded human sacrifice; others permitted prostitution, and even promoted it in their temples. When we reverse the order and start to create God in our own image (according to our own imagination) we get the following things: (1) A god who's liberal or conservative, a hawk or a dove; this is a god that politicians conveniently pull out of a box at election time to garner votes even though they don't truly serve Him. (2) A flexible god who permits you to do whatever you want, and you can then say, "I just felt led to do it." (3) A god who promises to bless His children but never discipline them. (4) A god you can "keep in his place" until you need Him. (5) A god who is not supreme, but happy to be one of many deities offering many ways to heaven. Not so! God says, "I, even I, am the Lord, and besides Me there is no savior." Jesus said, "I am the way, the truth, and the life. No one comes to the Father except through Me" (John 14:6 NKJV). Jesus doesn't need a makeover to bring Him into alignment with the internet and the space age. He is Lord! Indeed, if He is not Lord over all, He is not Lord at all!

August 9

"The fear of the Lord is the beginning of wisdom."
Proverbs 9:10 (NKJV)

THERE'S NOBODY LIKE HIM! (2)

In a world out of control, we like a god we can control: a comforting presence who blesses, provides, and advises. Kind of like "God in a box." But when it comes to Christ, no box works. His contemporaries designed an assortment of boxes for Him, but He never fit in any of the boxes. They called Him a revolutionary, but He paid taxes. They labeled Him a country carpenter, but He confounded scholars. They came to see His miracles, but He refused to entertain them. He was a Jew who attracted Gentiles, a rabbi who gave up on synagogues, a holy man who hung out with streetwalkers. In a male-dominated society, He recruited females. In an anti-Roman culture, He opted not to denounce Rome. He talked like a king yet lived like a pilgrim. People tried to put Him in a "box," but they couldn't. And we can't either; indeed we must not! "Skilled living gets its start in the Fear-of-God, insight into life from knowing a Holy God" (v. 10 MSG). Most of our fears are unhealthy. They rob us of peace and joy. But the fear of the Lord does the opposite. One author writes: "There is nothing neurotic about fearing God. The neurotic thing is not to be afraid, or to be afraid of the wrong thing. That is why God chooses to be known to us, so that we may stop being afraid of the wrong thing. When God is fully revealed to us and we 'get it,' then we experience the conversion of our fear . . . 'fear of the Lord' is the deeply sane recognition that we are not God."

August 10

"This is My beloved Son, in whom I am well pleased. Hear Him!"
Matthew 17:5 (NKJV)

THERE'S NOBODY LIKE HIM! (3)

On the Mount of Transfiguration, Moses, the law giver, and Elijah, who represents the prophets, stood side by side with Jesus. But Jesus outshone them all. The Bible says, "His clothes shimmered, glistening white, whiter than any bleach could make them" (Mark 9:3 MSG). In that moment Jesus was God in His purest form. Awed by Him, Peter said, "Lord . . . if You wish, let us make here three tabernacles: one for You, one for Moses, and one for Elijah" (Matthew 17:4 NKJV). It was a sincere sentiment, but it was sincerely wrong. "While he was still speaking, behold, a bright cloud overshadowed them; and suddenly a voice came out of the cloud, saying, 'This is My beloved Son, in whom I am well pleased. Hear Him!'" The word beloved implies "unique." There is no one else like Jesus! Not Moses. Not Elijah. Not Peter. Not Zoroaster, Buddha, or Muhammad. No one in heaven or on earth. Three shrines would have made Moses and Elijah equal with Christ, and God would have none of it. Only one shrine should be built, because only one person on the mountain deserved to be worshipped. "When the disciples heard it, they fell on their faces and were greatly afraid" (v. 6 NKJV). The One who hung the stars in space and left Pharaoh dead at the bottom of the Red Sea stood among them. The sight of Him took their breath away, removed every trace of arrogance and caused them to finish up face-down on the ground. How long has it been since you felt such reverence for God?

August 11

"Let all that I am praise the Lord."
Psalm 103:2 (NLT)

THERE'S NOBODY LIKE HIM! (4)

The Bible equates God with light, and light with holiness. "God is light; in him there is no darkness at all" (1 John 1:5 NIV). Paul said that God dwells in "unapproachable light" (1 Timothy 6:16 NIV). Scripture refers to Christ "who is holy, blameless, pure, set apart from sinners" (Hebrews 7:26 NIV). So how should you approach such a God? As you would an auditor when your books don't balance? Or a dictator who holds the power of life and death? No, Jesus told us to pray, "Our Father which art in heaven, Hallowed be thy name" (Matthew 6:9). There's your answer! You must come to God as a father who loves you dearly and desires only what is best for you, while always regarding Him with profound reverence. As your awe of God expands, your fears in life will diminish. A big view of God translates into big courage; a small view of God generates no courage at all. A puny God can't help you when cancer strikes, your family is in trouble, or you've no way to pay your bills. A "do-me-a-favor" Jesus may look good stuck on your dashboard, but that image can do nothing for your fears. You need an awesome God who, while diminishing your ego, enlarges your faith and blows your mind. David wrote: "Let all that I am praise the Lord; may I never forget the good things he does for me. He forgives all my sins and heals all my diseases. He redeems me from death and crowns me with love and tender mercies. He fills my life with good things" (Psalm 103:2-5 NLT).

August 12

"The Lord is my light and my salvation; whom shall I fear?"
Psalm 27:1 (NKJV)

THERE'S NOBODY LIKE HIM! (5)

We all need an encounter with the transfigured Christ; the One Who is greater than Moses the law giver and Elijah the prophet, and all the other prophets who have ever lived. The One who wears the true crown of the universe, God's beloved Son. We need to fall on our face and see Him as the Holy One, the Highest One, the Only One. As you do, all your fears, save the fear of Christ Himself, will melt like an ice cube on a summer day. You will agree with David: "The Lord is my light and my salvation; whom shall I fear?" In the book *Prince Caspian,* there is a great illustration of this. Lucy sees Aslan the lion for the first time in many years. He has changed since their last encounter. His size surprises her, and she tells him as much. "Aslan," says Lucy, "you're bigger." He replies, "That is because you are older, little one." Lucy says, "Not because you are?" He replies, "I am not. But every year you grow, you find me bigger." And so it is in our walk with Christ. The longer we serve Him, the greater He becomes. It's not that He changes, but that we do. We see dimensions, aspects, and characteristics we never saw before, increasing and astonishing increments of His purity, power, and uniqueness. Only when we have fallen at His feet in humility and total dependence will He say to us what He said to His disciples on the Mount where He was transfigured: "Arise, and do not be afraid" (Matthew 17:7 NKJV).

August 13

"You are the salt of the earth."
Matthew 5:13 (NKJV)

TAKE GOD TO WORK WITH YOU

Jon Gordon says: "I speak to a lot of organizations on the importance of positive leadership and the benefits of building a positive culture that fuels performance. Yet the most common question I receive is, 'How do I stay positive when my boss isn't?' Here are a few suggestions: Even though you're not the leader ... focus on being the best and bringing out the best in the people you work with ... tune out negativity and negative comments. Remember, you can't control what other people say and do, but you can control how you react. Dr. David Hawkins says, 'Eighty percent of the population vibrates to a negative frequency. It's all around us. Stay above the fray.' There's an old adage, 'Never wrestle with a pig because you'll both get dirty—and the pig will enjoy himself!' Jesus said, 'You are the light of the world. A city set on a hill cannot be hidden.' Make up your mind to be the beacon that shines in your workplace. Bottom line: most people don't enjoy being negative. Many times, they're that way because of stress, busyness, and fear. Most of them just need a wake-up call to break out of their rut, and contrary to what you may think, you can be that instrument of change. Jesus also said, 'You are the salt of the earth,' and salt has two functions. It stops things from going bad, and it adds taste and flavor. Your job as a Christian is to preserve, reconcile, and give hope to those around you, including the people you work with every day." So, take God to work with you.

August 14

"If My people . . . will humble themselves, and pray . . . I will hear."
2 Chronicles 7:14 (NKJV)

PRAY FOR OUR NATION

In August 1984, President Ronald Reagan spoke at the national prayer breakfast in Dallas and stated: "We poison our society when we remove its theological underpinnings. We court corruption when we leave it bereft of belief. All are free to believe or not believe; all are free to practice faith or not. But those who believe must be free to speak of and act on their belief, to apply moral teaching to public questions. I submit to you that the tolerant society is open to and encouraging of all religions. And this does not weaken us; it strengthens us . . . without God, there is no virtue, because there's no prompting of the conscience. Without God, we're mired in the material, that flat world that tells us only what the senses perceive. Without God, there is a coarsening of the society. And without God, democracy will not and cannot long endure. If we ever forget that we're one nation under God, then we will be a nation gone under." When Abraham prayed on behalf of Sodom and Gomorrah, God told him that He would spare those cities if only fifty righteous people could be found. Sadly, ten righteous people couldn't be found, much less fifty, so the cities were destroyed. But there's hope in this story—a righteous minority can move God, bring revival, and save our nation! "If My people who are called by My name will humble themselves, and pray and seek My face, and turn from their wicked ways, then I will hear from heaven, and will forgive their sin and heal their land."

August 15

"He ... earns wages to put into a bag with holes."
Haggai 1:6 (NKJV)

FOUR KINDS OF GIVERS (1)

There are four kinds of givers noted in the Bible. For the next few days let's look at each. Bag people. In the days of Haggai the prophet, the Israelites were so busy making money that they had no time for God. Sound familiar? So He said to them: "'Is it time for you yourselves to dwell in your paneled houses, and this temple to lie in ruins? ... Consider your ways! You have sown much, and bring in little ... and he who earns wages, earns wages to put into a bag with holes ... You looked for much, but indeed it came to little; and when you brought it home, I blew it away. Why?' says the Lord of hosts. 'Because of My house that is in ruins, while every one of you runs to his own house'" (Haggai 1:4-9 NKJV). If you want God to be interested in your house, be interested in His house. If you want God to bless your house, begin to bless His house. If you want God to provide for your house, start providing for His house. You say, "How much should I give?" God sets the baseline at one-tenth of your income (See Malachi 3:10). Whatever you give beyond that will be determined by three things: (a) Your ability. "Every man shall give as he is able, according to the blessing of the Lord your God which He has given you" (Deuteronomy 16:17 NKJV). (b) Your desire to reap. God will "multiply the seed that you have sown" (2 Corinthians 9:10 NKJV). (c) Your love. "You shall love the Lord your God with all your heart, with all your soul, and with all your mind" (Matthew 22:37 NKJV).

August 16

"The bin . . . shall not be used up."
1 Kings 17:14 (NKJV)

FOUR KINDS OF GIVERS (2)

Bin people. In the middle of a devastating famine God sent the prophet Elijah to Zarephath, saying he'd meet a widow there who would feed him. Why did God not send Elijah to a wealthy family? Because they didn't need a miracle, she did! When Elijah asked this woman for something to eat she told him that she'd "only a handful of flour in a bin" (v. 12 NKJV). She had just enough for one more meal, then she and her son would die. Perhaps you're thinking, "Typical preacher! They'll take the last bite out of your mouth and the last penny out of your pocket." No, this was the best day of her life! She was about to step into miracle territory. But first she had to overcome the fear of giving. "Elijah said to her, 'Do not fear . . . make me a small cake from it first, and bring it to me . . . For thus says the Lord God of Israel: 'The bin of flour shall not be used up . . . until the day the Lord sends rain on the earth'" (vv. 13-14 NKJV). How does this story turn out? "So she went away and did according to the word of Elijah; and . . . The bin of flour was not used up" (vv. 15-16 NKJV). Day after day, without fail, she reached into the bin and found more flour. She discovered that when you obey God's Word, He will meet your every need. Are you a bin person? Are you afraid of letting go of what you have in case you don't have enough? Don't be. You will never out-give God! Whatever you give to Him, He has promised to give back "good measure, pressed down, and shaken together, and running over" (Luke 6:38).

August 17

"They took up twelve baskets full."
Mark 6:43 (NKJV)

FOUR KINDS OF GIVERS (3)

Basket people. A boy gave his lunch to Jesus and He used it to feed five thousand people. Afterward, "They took up twelve baskets full of the fragments." Basket people find a need greater than their own and say, "Lord, here's what I have; take it, bless it and use it." What a contrast this boy was to the disciples. Notice: (1) They tried to escape the problem. "Send them away, that they may go . . . and buy themselves bread" (v. 36 NKJV). Your faith only grows by facing your problems and looking to God for answers. Indeed, when you solve the problem, you position yourself to receive what God has in store for you next. (2) They didn't know what they had. Jesus said, "How many loaves do you have? Go and see" (v. 38 NKJV). Moses had a rod, but it parted the Red Sea. David had a slingshot, but it brought down a giant. You may not know it, but God has given you the answer. He's given you something capable of multiplying once you put it into His hands. The key is, "Go and see." (3) They despised the day of small things. "There is a lad here who has five barley loaves and two small fish, but what are they among so many?" (John 6:9 NKJV). Instead of looking at your lack, look at God's abundance and His willingness to work on your behalf. "Do not despise this small beginning, for the eyes of the Lord rejoice to see the work begin" (Zechariah 4:10 TLB). Factor God into the equation. The formula for success is you—plus God!

August 18

"Joseph opened all the storehouses [barns] and sold grain to the Egyptians."
Genesis 41:56 (NIV)

FOUR KINDS OF GIVERS (4)

Barn people. God used Joseph to feed the nations during a time of worldwide famine. When Pharaoh's advisers couldn't interpret his dream, Joseph did. He actually gave Pharaoh a plan that would not only feed Egypt during seven years of famine, but also feed the world and cause Pharaoh to come out of this crisis a richer man. When you serve God, He can give you information about the future. He can give you not only the wisdom to survive, but to thrive when you're in a recession. But you can't build such a relationship with God overnight! Joseph's journey to the throne of Egypt led him through years of delay, detours, and discouragement. He experienced betrayal at the hands of his family, temptation and slander at the hands of his employer's wife, false imprisonment, years of waiting and wondering when God would fulfill His promise to make him a leader. But he never doubted God. And you must not either! If God can take an ex-con like Joseph and make him the prime minister of Egypt, no obstacle and no enemy can keep Him from fulfilling His promise to you. So, if you're a bag person, "consider your ways" and start putting God first in your finances. If you're a bin person, "be not afraid," give, and God will give back to you. If you're a basket person, place what you've got into God's hands and watch Him multiply it. If you're a barn person with a heart that longs to meet the needs of a hurting world, nothing your enemies do will stop you.

August 19

"Mind your own business; do your own job."
1 Thessalonians 4:11 (MSG)

AVOID TRIANGLES

We're not very good at knowing the difference between helpfulness and interference! Suppose two people we care about are in conflict, and we think we can solve their problems. Ultimately, we discover we're in over our heads. Looking back, we say, "I'll never do that again"—until the next time! Here are some healthy relationship boundaries. Sometimes, when two people are at odds with each other they "triangle in" a third person to focus on, attempting to lower their stress. Whoever they "triangle in" gets caught in the middle, becomes enmeshed in their unresolved issues, and ultimately becomes their shock absorber. Unfortunately, when that person's rescue attempt backfires, they become part of the problem, keeping the issues and themselves stuck. So what should you do? (1) Unless God puts you in the middle, stay out! The Bible says, "Mind your own business; do your own job." If your name's not on it, don't pick it up! Try saying, "I care about you both too much to complicate things with unqualified advice. I'll pray that God gives you the wisdom to do what's right for each other." (2) Maintain a caring relationship with both people. Relationship specialist Edwin Friedman says, "The way to bring change to the relationship of two others is to maintain a well-defined relationship with each and avoid taking responsibility for their relationship." Don't take sides. Don't let them pull you in. If they try, remind them that you're praying and trusting God to help them resolve the problem, and that you're confident He will do it.

August 20

"Change the way you think."
Romans 12:2 (GW)

A NEW ATTITUDE

For things to change for the better, you must "change the way you think." Consider these examples: (a) View setbacks as detours, not dead ends. Winners don't just face adversity; they embrace it, knowing it leads to future success. (b) Tune out the critics and focus on doing your best. Anybody who accomplishes anything worthwhile has to overcome naysayers. (c) When you're afraid, praise God until your faith rebuilds. It may take a while, but praise and thanksgiving never fail, and will give you the strength to go on. (d) When you fail, look for the lesson and remember all the times you've succeeded. Weed out self-doubt and replace it with scriptural self-talk. (e) When you're heading into battle, visualize yourself winning in God's strength—with Him "all things are possible" (Matthew 19:26). (f) Instead of focusing on the past and worrying about the future, focus on the now—that's where your influence is greatest. Remember, God said, "As your days, so shall your strength be" (Deuteronomy 33:25 NKJV). (g) Instead of complaining, work on identifying solutions, and more will come to you. (h) When you're distracted, focus on your breathing, take a walk and clear your mind, think on what you can control, and surrender the rest to God. (i) When you're lonely, remember the people who've helped you this far and who love and support you. (j) When you're fatigued, take time to rest—but never ever give up! Finish strong in everything you do. (k) When you're under pressure and under scrutiny, smile and have fun. You only live once. Life is short—seize the moment!

August 21

"Let there be no strife between you and me."
Genesis 13:8 (NAS)

WHEN CONFLICT COMES HOME (1)

The conflict between Abram and Lot teaches us important principles about our families. Lot had lived peacefully in his Uncle Abram's home. Abram had taken him along on the journey of faith, when suddenly conflict arose. And because conflict reveals character, Lot showed his true colors. Since their growing herds were too big to share the same pastures, Abram suggested they split the land between them, offering Lot first choice. Lot "chose for himself" the best land, leaving the rest to his uncle (v. 11 NAS). Lot moved to rich, sinful Sodom; Abram built an altar to the Lord. Same genes—totally different values! (1) Consider the facts. Abram was God's appointed leader and Israel's primary patriarch. God had promised him a homeland, fatherhood of a great nation, blessing and protection. And above all these, God promised that in him, "All the families of the earth will be blessed!" (Genesis 12:3 NAS). In practical, day-to-day terms, Abram was the senior partner and major stockholder in the family business. He had shown love and generosity to his nephew, and in the crunch, valued their relationship over personal interests. Abram, therefore, deserved consideration and deference from his nephew. But Lot never gave it to him. (2) Consider the point. For the family's sake, Abram chose not to "pull rank," or "insist on his rights," or "show who's boss." He proved that God alone vindicates us! We shouldn't even attempt to vindicate ourselves. Abram chose grace over law, humility over pride, self-denial over "rights," mercy over justice, love over lust, and character over popular opinion. Think about it!

August 22

"Let there be no strife between you and me... for we are brothers."
Genesis 13:8 (NAS)

WHEN CONFLICT COMES HOME (2)

Family conflict brings out the worst and the best in all of us. But conflict itself isn't the problem—character is! Conflict just reveals what's important to us. Abram's priority was the family; Lot's was "getting rich." Abram's concern was harmony; Lot's was self-preservation. Abram was driven by his faith, Lot by his greed. Abram was a giver; Lot was a taker. But watch how the story turned out. (1) What should have happened? The junior partner should have submitted to the senior; the follower should have deferred to the leader; the less-spiritual should have acknowledged the more-spiritual. But Lot failed on all counts! (2) What could have happened? As the God-appointed leader Abram could have assumed top dog status and enforced his will, but he didn't. He could have been concerned about winning, but he wasn't. He could have called in his debts with Lot, but he refused to. (3) What did happen? First, Abram elevated relationship above personal advantage. Second, he relinquished his "rights" to keep peace in the family. Third, he "turned the other cheek" and deferred to Lot. The greater gave way to the lesser. The stronger made allowance for the weaker. The mature showed mercy toward the immature. Did it make Abram the weaker man and Lot the stronger? Did Abram lose and Lot win? No! God always has the last word. And it was this: "Look... northward and southward and eastward and westward... all the land which you see, I will give it to you and to your descendants forever" (vv. 14-15 NAS). Doing things God's way is the sure road to peace and prosperity.

August 23

"I have set before you life and death ... choose life."
Deuteronomy 30:19 (KJV)

TAKE CONTROL OF YOUR LIFE

Choice is the greatest power God gave you. Too many of us just accept our lives—we don't become leaders of ourselves. As a result, we can't get out of our own way. Holocaust survivor Elie Wiesel wrote in *Souls On Fire*, that when you die and go to meet your maker, you're not going to be asked why you didn't become a Messiah or find a cure for cancer. All you're going to be asked is, "Why didn't you become you? Why didn't you become all that you are?" Fulfilling God's will for your life requires taking responsibility for yourself and your life. How do you do that? By saying yes to God first—then to yourself. Every time you say yes, you open yourself up to your God-given potential and to the greatest of possibilities. If you're used to saying no, you may find this difficult. If that is true in your case, then at least be willing to say "maybe." One day a father whose child was chronically ill asked Jesus to heal him. "Jesus said to him, 'If you can believe, all things are possible to him who believes.' Immediately the father of the child cried out and said with tears, 'Lord, I believe; help my unbelief!'" (Mark 9:23-24 NKJV). If you're a self-doubter, pray that same prayer. God will answer it. Never forget that you are unique, possessing talents, experiences and opportunities that no one else has ever had—or ever will have. You're responsible to become all God made you to be, not only for your own benefit but for everyone else's.

August 24

"Faith comes by hearing, and hearing by the word of God."
Romans 10:17 (NKJV)

GROWING IN FAITH

If you want to know how strong your faith is, pay attention to what's coming out of your mouth. "The word which they heard did not profit them, not being mixed with faith in those who heard it" (Hebrews 4:2 NKJV). It's not enough to read God's Word; you must internalize it, then vocalize it. We say all kinds of things, but the truth is that we don't really believe them because they don't show up in the way we live. You should live in such a way that if God is not who He says He is, you'll fall flat on your face. This means: (1) looking for opportunities to trust God more; (2) trusting Him to come through for you regardless of the situation; (3) strengthening your faith for the tough times ahead. And here's how you do it: "Faith comes by hearing, and hearing by the word of God." If someone could stick a thermometer under your tongue and take your spiritual temperature, the thing that would cause it to rise or fall would be the time you have spent in God's Word. You say, "Right now my faith is very low." Then start spending more time reading God's Word. You say, "I wish I had the faith of so-and-so." There's no mystery about how to close the gap between your faith and that of others—just log more time in the Scriptures. Rearrange your priorities, take control of your time and put Bible reading at the top of your to-do list. If you're serious about growing in faith, it's a price you must be willing to pay.

August 25

"You are not your own."
1 Corinthians 6:19 (NKJV)

GOD'S CLAIMS ON YOUR LIFE (1)

Picture two people standing outside of a house. One says, "This is my house." The other replies, "How come?" The first one says, "For three reasons. I built it. I paid for it. I live in it." Let's look at the first reason why you belong to God: Creation. Some folks think we all came from an amoeba. The problem is, they can't tell us where the amoeba came from! The Bible says, "God created man in His own image . . . male and female He created them" (Genesis 1:27 NKJV). Some folks say that the earth came into existence as a result of the "big bang" theory. Yet if you told them, "The car you drive right now was the result of an explosion at an assembly plant in Detroit," they'd question your sanity. If there's a design, there must be a designer. If there's a creation, there must be a Creator. And since God made you, He holds ownership rights over you. The Bible says: "Do you not know that your body is the temple of the Holy Spirit who is in you, whom you have from God, and you are not your own? For you were bought at a price; therefore glorify God in your body and in your spirit, which are God's" (1 Corinthians 6:19-20 NKJV). Not only did God create you, He gave you certain gifts so that you could fulfill His purposes and bring glory to Him. So before they tag your toe and write your obituary, ask God what you were born to do. Only by finding and fulfilling His purpose, can you fill the God-shaped space within you that you were born with.

August 26

"Ye are bought with a price."
1 Corinthians 6:20 (KJV)

GOD'S CLAIMS ON YOUR LIFE (2)

God's second claim on your life is Calvary. The story's told of two friends went to law school. One became a judge, the other became a law breaker and ended up in court. Guess who was sitting in the judge's seat? His friend. So how could the judge be merciful, yet still be just? Taking off the black robes of justice, he walked over to the dock where the prisoner stood and said, "Not only am I this man's friend, today I'm his savior. I will stand chargeable with all his debts." At the cross God took all your sin and put it on Christ's account, and took all Christ's righteousness and put it on your account. And the moment you trust Christ as your Savior you're no longer under the sentence of death. The value of something is determined by the price a buyer is willing to pay for it. At Calvary God said, "This is how much I love you!" Your creator became your redeemer. "The maker of the universe, as Man for man was made a curse. The claims of law that He had made, unto the uttermost He paid." To fulfill His purposes in the earth, God always had a man. To deliver the Israelites from Egypt, He used Moses. To challenge the prophets of Baal, He used Elijah. But when it came to your salvation, God "saw that there was no man, and wondered that there was no intercessor; therefore His own arm brought salvation" (Isaiah 59:16 NKJV). The good news is: when God could not find a man, He Himself became a man; that we who are the sons of men, might become the sons of God. Awesome!

August 27

*"Therefore glorify God in your body, and
in your spirit, which are God's."*
1 Corinthians 6:20 (KJV)

GOD'S CLAIMS ON YOUR LIFE (3)

God's third claim on your life is consecration. It's not a word we hear very much these days. It means "to be set aside for the exclusive use of." You say, "But I have so many faults." God's not looking for perfection, He's looking for willingness. The Bible says, "Every high priest [was] taken from among men" (Hebrews 5:1 NKJV). The people God calls and uses are all human and flawed in some way. Why would God call someone like that? Because they "can have compassion on those who are ignorant and going astray, since [they also are] subject to weakness" (v. 2 NKJV). You say, "My parents want me to go to Bible school and be a minister." Well, there's good news and bad. The good news is that Bible school can deepen your devotion to Christ and give you insights into His Word. The bad news is that your parents can't call you, only God can! "No man takes this honor to himself, but he who is called by God" (v. 4 NKJV). You say, "How will I know I'm called to a ministry?" Fruitfulness! When controversy broke out in Israel over who should be in leadership, God told Moses to pick a man from each of the twelve tribes. That man's rod was placed in the ark of the covenant overnight, and the one whose rod "budded" was the one God had called. The Bible says, "A man's gift makes room for him" (Proverbs 18:16 NKJV). When God calls you, He will open the doors, make the connections, and provide the resources. All He asks of you is a life that's consecrated to doing His will.

August 28

"Let us keep in step with the Spirit."
Galatians 5:25 (NIV)

LEARN TO BE LED BY GOD'S SPIRIT

If the Christian life is about having a personal relationship with God, then God must still speak to us today. But a relationship can't be built on one-way speeches. First, it requires commitment. Then it requires communication between two people in which each speaks and listens to the other. "You … are in the realm of the Spirit, if indeed the Spirit of God lives in you" (Romans 8:9 NIV). That means having Spirit-controlled responses and making Spirit-led decisions. When you follow God, life no longer consists only of that which can be seen, felt, or figured out. It includes walking by faith, trusting Him, and learning to know His voice and the leadings of His Spirit. Some of us are reluctant to do that because we've seen people who claim to be doing it and their approach scares us. So when we sense the Spirit's leading we doubt it, analyze it, conclude it isn't logical, and don't pay attention to it. Some of us want to obey the Spirit, but we're not sure we know that He's really speaking to us. We wonder, "Is this God's voice or my own desires?" We've all experienced this; it's a normal part of the Christian life. This is why Paul writes, "Since we live by the Spirit, let us keep in step with the Spirit." Spiritual guidance is learned—one step at a time. Even the most mature believer will stumble and get it wrong at times. No problem. "The Lord makes firm the steps of the one who delights in him; though he may stumble, he will not fall, for the Lord upholds him with his hand" (Psalm 37:23-24 NIV).

August 29

"The fruit of that righteousness will be . . . confidence."
Isaiah 32:17 (NIV)

CONFIDENCE (1)

Never mistake competence for confidence; one is ability-based, the other comes from knowing who you are in Christ; that you're "complete in them" (1 John 2:5 NIV). One author says: "The first thing I learned about confidence was I didn't possess it . . . I had a thin glaze of arrogance covering a core of fear. All those years of being a success in the eyes of the world left me deathly afraid of failure. Worldly success requires taking risks beyond the comfort zones of previous accomplishments. Spiritual success requires letting go of outcomes and allowing God to move on your behalf. I was so afraid of failure . . . I never found success in it either . . . the false confidence I'd known was built on my own abilities . . . However if you suddenly find a lump in your breast, or your spouse says he never loved you, or you get fired from your job, or your child is seriously ill, every tactic you've ever employed and every skill you've ever mastered will get you nowhere . . . The Bible says, 'Have a sane estimate of your [abilities]' (Romans 12:4 PHPS) . . . once you realize you aren't perfect . . . you can exhale and start the task of being good enough . . . When your confidence stems from knowing the Almighty, unchanging One, you cannot be shaken by change or circumstances. You . . . exude competence, peace, contentment, and fortitude." Isn't it time you got out from under the pressure of acting like God and having all the answers? "We have different gifts, according to the grace given to each of us" (Romans 12:6 NIV). When you use your gift to glorify God, you're doing what He intended you to do.

August 30

"Who told you . . . you were naked?"
Genesis 3:11 (NKJV)

CONFIDENCE (2)

It's impossible to feel confident when you're telling yourself you're not good enough and that you'll never amount to anything. One pastor says: "After Adam and Eve ate the forbidden fruit, they hid. God came to them and said, 'Where are you?' They said, 'We're hiding because we're naked.' I love how God answered . . . 'Who told you . . . you were naked?' In other words, 'Who told you there was something wrong with you?' God immediately knew the Enemy had been talking to them. And God's saying to you today, 'Who told you . . . you don't have what it takes to succeed . . . that the best grades you can make are C's . . . that you're not attractive enough to succeed in your relationships . . . or talented enough to flourish in your career . . . or that your marriage isn't going to last? Those are lies from the Enemy. God said, 'No good thing will He withhold from those who walk uprightly' (Psalm 84:11 NKJV); 'Delight yourself . . . in the Lord, and He shall give you the desires of your heart' (Psalm 37:4 NKJV). The potential is inside you . . . and it doesn't change because you don't believe it, or because you've been through negative experiences. 'The gifts and the calling of God are irrevocable' (Romans 11:29 NKJV). He's never going to take back the potential He poured into you . . . or say, 'I'm tired of dealing with you . . . you've failed too often and made too many mistakes. Give Me back My gifts.' No . . . His calling on your life will be with you till the day you leave this earth, but it's up to you to . . . tap into it." When the Enemy starts chipping away at your confidence, take authority over him in Jesus' Name; resist him and he will flee (See James 4:7).

August 31

"Run to win!"
1 Corinthians 9:24 (NLT)

WINNING

In the Roman Empire, athletes stripped down to a simple loincloth so that nothing prevented them from running their best race. Referring to it, Paul writes: "Don't you realize that in a race everyone runs, but only one person gets the prize? So run to win! All athletes are disciplined in their training. They do it to win a prize that will fade away, but we do it for an eternal prize. So I run with purpose in every step" (vv. 24-26 NLT). How about you? Do you just want the fun of being in the race, or are you running to win? To succeed at being what God has redeemed and called you to be, you'll have to stop doing certain things, even enjoyable things, and begin doing other things that support your goals and help you to fulfill your God-ordained purpose. Sometimes this will mean saying no to well-intentioned people who try to involve you in things that steal your time and produce the wrong results. It will also mean dealing with "the sin that so easily entangles" (Hebrews 12:1 NIV). When God says something is wrong, it's wrong! You don't need to rationalize, make excuses or feel sorry for yourself. You just need to agree, ask His forgiveness and get it out of your life. Who gets the prize? Those who pay the price! Paul knew he couldn't win the race without first bringing his body, mind, and emotions under the control of God's Spirit. The same goes for you. And you can't expect somebody else to make you do what's right; you must listen to what God's saying to you and take action.

September 1

"Clothed and in his right mind."
Mark 5:15 (NKJV)

THEN JESUS CAME!

One of Christ's greatest miracles was the healing of a man who was controlled and tortured by evil spirits (See v. 2 NKJV). The Bible says: "His dwelling [was] among the tombs; and no one could bind him, not even with chains . . . neither could anyone tame him . . . always, night and day, he was . . . crying out and cutting himself with stones" (vv. 3-5 NKJV). Notice four things about this man's condition: (1) He kept hurting himself. Now he used stones to do it, but some of us use drugs, food, sex, alcohol, overwork, and negativity. What are you doing today that's hurting you? Until you can acknowledge it, you won't get free of it. (2) He was preoccupied with death. Why else would someone choose to live in a graveyard? Life's troubles can bring you to the place where you lose your very desire to live. (3) He had no peace, day or night. The downside of godless living is restlessness, irritability, and discontent. Nothing satisfies or is ever enough. (4) He lived in isolation. Satan's job is made easier when you don't have a spiritual support system. Fellowship wrecks his plans. Then Jesus came! He made a boat trip across storm-tossed Galilee to get to this man. Just one word from Jesus, and we read: "They . . . saw the one who had been demon-possessed . . . sitting . . . clothed and in his right mind." Out of gratitude the man wanted to join Jesus' disciples. But Jesus told him, "Go home to your friends, and tell them what great things the Lord has done for you" (v. 19 NKJV). When Christ sets you free, your first responsibility is to stay free and help set others free.

September 2

"When you come, bring ... my scrolls."
2 Timothy 4:13 (NIV)

KEEP GROWING (1)

In prison with no possibility of release and facing the certainty of death on the chopping block, Paul asked Timothy to bring his books. Why? Because he wanted to keep growing. The truth is: (1) When you finish growing, you're finished. When the poet Longfellow was old, an admirer asked him how he was able to keep writing so beautifully. Pointing to a nearby apple tree he replied, "That tree is very old, but I never saw prettier blossoms. The tree grows a little new wood every year, and out of that new wood those blossoms come. So I try to grow a little each year." (2) Growth doesn't come easy. It will stretch you. It will challenge you to rethink assumptions you've always believed to be right. Indeed, it can cost you friends and money. But when you're committed to growth you cannot settle for ignorance. (3) Growth is your responsibility. When you were a child, your parents were responsible for your growth, but now you are. The poet Robert Browning wrote, "Why stay we on earth except to grow?" Yet few dedicate themselves to the process. That's because growth requires change, and we're uncomfortable with the things change brings. Gail Sheehy said, "If we don't change we won't grow, and if we don't grow we're not really living. Growth demands the temporary surrender of security. It means giving up familiar but limiting patterns, safe but unrewarding work, values no longer believed in, or relationships that have lost their meaning. Taking a new step is what we fear most, yet our real fear should be the opposite." Can you think of anything worse than a life devoid of growth?

September 3

"Let the wise listen and add to their learning."
Proverbs 1:5 (NIV)

KEEP GROWING (2)

When it comes to growth, Christ is our example. The Bible says that He "grew in wisdom and stature, and in favor with God and man" (Luke 2:52 NIV). To enjoy favor with God and others you must keep growing spiritually, mentally, and emotionally. That requires you to do two things: (1) Never stop learning. Every experience in life, including the ones you don't enjoy, yields knowledge that can make your future better than your present. But you have to look for it. The downside to the internet and the iPhone is that you get endless "hits" of information you don't process or glean anything from. Instead of letting life just "happen" to you, you need to stop and ask yourself, "What's really happening here? I'm hearing it, but what does it mean?" You are body, soul, and spirit, so you need to ask, "Am I healthy physically, mentally, emotionally, and spiritually?" No one can answer that question but you. (2) Never stop developing your talents. When one of the world's greatest violinists was an old man, he was asked why he still practiced six to eight hours every day. He replied, "Because I think I'm getting better." What a great attitude! It's not enough just to live longer, you're supposed to live better! Paul told Timothy, "Stir up the gift ... which is in you" (2 Timothy 1:6 NKJV). Wesley Tracy said, "Some people have the notion that following your spiritual gift is spending the days and years of your life doing only those things which come naturally, easily, with no effort, discipline, or practice. No, your gift can either be mediocre or excellent; it's up to you."

September 4

"The more you grow like this, the more productive and useful you will be."
2 Peter 1:8 (NLT)

KEEP GROWING (3)

Let's look at two more things you need to grow: (1) Don't just grow in knowledge, grow in character. The truth is, God is more interested in your character than He is in your career. Why? Because success without character has the potential to hurt you and those around you. The Bible says: "Make every effort to respond to God's promises. Supplement your faith with a generous provision of moral excellence, and moral excellence with knowledge, and knowledge with self-control, and self-control with patient endurance, and patient endurance with godliness, and godliness with brotherly affection, and brotherly affection with love for everyone. The more you grow like this, the more productive and useful you will be" (vv. 5-8 NLT). Note the words "make every effort." You've got to work at it! (2) Always stay fresh. Did you hear the old story about the country pastor who was preaching when his notes flew out the church window and a cow grazing nearby ate them? Three days later the cow went dry. Hello! Stay thirsty. Stay hungry. Jesus said, "Blessed are those who hunger and thirst for righteousness, for they will be filled" (Matthew 5:6 NIV). Ultimately, it's not your talents but your desire that determines your destiny. One of Paul's highest compliments was given to the believers in the Thessalonian church: "We ought always to thank God for you, brothers and sisters, and rightly so, because your faith is growing more and more, and the love all of you have for one another is increasing" (2 Thessalonians 1:3 NIV). Let that be said of you.

September 5

"He will show you a way out."
1 Corinthians 10:13 (NLT)

THE WAY OUT

The Bible says, "When you are tempted, he will show you a way out so that you can endure." Maybe you are in a situation—a relationship or a financial condition—that's not what you wanted. You can lie down and die. But when you don't—when you show up, when you offer the best you have—something good is happening inside you that far outweighs whatever is happening outside you. Jesus was facing adversity when He told His followers that if they had faith, they could command a mountain and it would be cast into the sea. Now when your focus is on the mountain, you are driven by your fear. But when your focus is on God, you are made alive by faith. But if you didn't face the mountain, you'd never know that faith was in you or to what extent. Adversity has a way of changing your values and priorities for the better. When you're on the treadmill of money, security, or success, and adversity knocks you off, you start seeing the folly of chasing temporal things. And if you're wise you resolve not to return to your old way of life when things normalize. But the key to accomplishing this is taking action before normal life takes over again. You have a finite window of time to make changes; otherwise, you'll drift back into your old patterns. While the memory of your adversity is still fresh, pray and ask God what changes He wants to make in your attitudes, your relationships, your habits, and your lifestyle, and "He will show you a way out."

September 6

*"For to you it has been granted on
behalf of Christ ... to suffer."*
Philippians 1:29 (NKJV)

SUFFERING WITH GRACE

You need the kind of faith that not only believes God for good things, but also sustains you through bad things. The Bible says, "If you suffer for doing what is right, God will reward you for it. So don't worry or be afraid... Instead... worship Christ as Lord of your life" (1 Peter 3:14-15 NLT). God has foresight but we have only hindsight. So whether the path you've been called to walk is rough or smooth, your attitude should be one of "worship," acknowledging "Christ as Lord of your life." Joseph's kidnapping led to the saving of his family. The lions' den led Daniel to a cabinet position. Christ entered the world by a surprise pregnancy and redeemed it through an unjust murder. Do you believe what the Bible teaches—that no disaster is ultimately fatal? Chrysostom did. He was the archbishop of Constantinople from AD 398 to 404. He gained a following by his eloquent denunciations of corruption in the church. Twice banished by the authorities, he asked: "What can I fear? Will it be death? But to know that Christ is my life, and that I shall gain by death. Will it be exile? But the earth is the Lord's and its fullness is the Lord's. Will it be by loss of wealth? But we have brought nothing into the world, and we can carry nothing out. Thus all the terrors of the world are contemptible in my eyes; and I smile at all its good things. Poverty I do not fear; riches I do not sigh for. Death I do not shrink from." That's suffering with grace!

September 7

*"Despite all these things, overwhelming
victory is ours through Christ."*
Romans 8:37 (NLT)

POST-TRAUMATIC GROWTH (1)

Just as there is a condition known as "post-traumatic stress," researchers are now talking about "post-traumatic growth." One line of thinking is that adversity can lead to growth. Another is that the highest levels of growth cannot be achieved without adversity. But adversity doesn't automatically bring growth. Much of the outcome depends on how you respond to adversity. Ernest Hemingway wrote, "Sooner or later, the world breaks everyone, and those who are broken are strongest in the broken places." Sometimes that's true. But sometimes people write beautiful things and believe them to be true—or hope they're true—and yet they don't help. Hemingway himself had a brokenness that ended his life because the pain was too great. On the other hand, Joseph, who was betrayed by his family, falsely accused of rape and unjustly imprisoned, looked back and said, "God intended it all for good" (Genesis 50:20 NLT). The key to post-traumatic growth is in seeing God in all things, drawing close to Him, trusting Him when you can't understand the situation, and knowing He only has your best interests at heart. When it comes to serving God there are two sides to the coin: success and suffering. We like the first and try to avoid the second. But they're both part of God's plan. God called Paul into the ministry, saying, "I will show him how much he must suffer for my name's sake" (Acts 9:16 NLT). But hard times didn't make Paul doubt his faith, or the God he served: "No, despite all these things, overwhelming victory is ours through Christ, who loved us."

September 8

"God intended it all for good."
Genesis 50:20 (NLT)

POST-TRAUMATIC GROWTH (2)

Rising to a challenge reveals hidden abilities within you that otherwise would have remained dormant. Just as you find out what's inside a tube of toothpaste when it gets squeezed, adversity reveals what you're made of. Sometimes we say, "I could never go through what that person went through. I would die." Then you go through it, and guess what? Your heart keeps beating. Your world goes on. You don't know what you're capable of until you have to cope. Wise people have always understood the connection between suffering and growth. Meng Tzu, the Chinese sage, said, "When heaven is about to confer a great responsibility on any man it will place obstacles in the path of his deeds so as to stimulate his mind, harden his nature, and improve wherever he is incompetent." God could have let Abraham stay in the comfort of Ur, and Moses in the splendor of Pharaoh's courts. He could have kept Daniel out of the lions' den, Nehemiah out of captivity, Jonah out of the whale, John the Baptist away from Herod, Esther from being threatened, Jeremiah from being rejected, and Paul from being shipwrecked. But He didn't. In fact, God used each of these trials to bring them closer to Himself—to produce perseverance, character, and hope. It's said, "The school of hard knocks produces the greatest scholars." And guess who the teacher is? Adversity! You either face it with God, or without Him. And those without God are watching you. When they see your faith sustain you and God bring you through, they'll get interested in what you have to say. And not before!

September 9

"My grace is sufficient for you."
2 Corinthians 12:9 (NKJV)

POST-TRAUMATIC GROWTH (3)

One of the classic stories of adversity in the Bible is about Joseph. At the beginning of his life, he is the favorite son, envied by his brothers, with dreams of being someone everybody bows down to. Then he's kidnapped by his brothers and ends up serving as a slave in Potiphar's house. He loses his home, his culture, his security, and his status as favorite son. What does Joseph have left? He is in a strange bed, in a strange house, in a strange land, with no friends, no prospects, and no explanation. But he has one gift—one that makes all the difference. "The Lord was with Joseph" (Genesis 39:2 NIV). What happens when you lose everything but God, then find out that God is enough? You experience His presence in a way you never did before! Paul writes: "Does it mean he no longer loves us if we have trouble or calamity, or are persecuted, or hungry, or destitute, or in danger, or threatened with death... No, despite all these things, overwhelming victory is ours through Christ, who loved us" (Romans 8:35-37 NLT). God wasn't at work producing the circumstances Joseph wanted, He was at work in bad circumstances producing the Joseph that God wanted. Just as a diamond is formed out of common carbon placed under millions of pounds of pressure—so the character of Christ is formed in you by adverse circumstances. So the question is, will you hold up or fold up? When Paul thought he couldn't stand any more, God told him, "My grace is sufficient for you" (2 Corinthians 12:9 NKJV). And do you know what? His grace is sufficient for you too.

September 10

"Blessed (happy, to be envied ...) are the poor in spirit (the humble, who rate themselves insignificant)."
Matthew 5:3 (AMPC)

MARITAL HAPPINESS

When the rosy glow diminishes and reality sets in, what makes some marriages happy while others slide into misery? Luck? Good genes? Hanging tough? Hardly! Marital happiness that transcends changing circumstances is built on the qualities Jesus taught. Let's look at them: (1) Happy are the humble. "Blessed (happy ...) are the poor in spirit (the humble, who rate themselves insignificant)." Pride that's self-promoting and always demanding its rights brings misery, while humility, self-denial and considering your mate's needs brings happiness. (2) Happy are the meek: the gentle, patient, and kind. Handling your spouse's struggles with kindness, sensitivity, and long-suffering is an expression of love that brings healing into the painful chapters of life and marriage. (3) Happy are the merciful. Sooner or later, we'll inflict injury on one another. Hurt, disappointment and anger will rise up, followed by a desire to make them pay. But just as revenge begets revenge, mercy begets mercy. Mercy isn't "letting them get away with it." Treating your spouse mercifully is reciprocal. It creates an atmosphere, where, when you fail, you "shall obtain mercy." Mercy ends disputes when nothing else works! (4) Happy are the peacemakers. The need to be "right" and "win" only intensifies conflict. In marriage, when one "wins," both lose! Giving up personal victory to be a peacemaker is ultimate victory. You'd be eternally lost if Jesus hadn't willingly surrendered His rights for your wrongs. The ring is not the sole symbol of Christian marriage, but the cross superimposed on the ring. Christlike surrender of our uncrucified self, promotes marital happiness!

September 11

"We love because he first loved us."
1 John 4:19 (NIV)

FORGIVENESS (1)

One author writes: "Think of an area of unforgiveness and see if any of these reasons to hold a grudge resonate with you. (a) Anger keeps more potent emotions at bay; once it's gone you fear the emotional flood that may follow. (b) A grudge takes time and energy, and you're not sure who you'd be without it. (c) You've replayed your 'personal-betrayal-and-hurt movie' so often you know it by heart. (d) The idea of moving on is terrifying, whereas misery is familiar. (e) The offender has done nothing to deserve forgiveness. (f) Harboring resentment stops you from getting hurt again because nobody can get close." Jesus said, "Why . . . look at the speck of sawdust in your brother's eye and pay no attention to the plank in your own?" (Matthew 7:3 NIV). This author says, "I've banged my plank into walls and around corners so often I'm certain I have retina damage!" Now consider these reasons for releasing a grudge. (a) Relinquishing past hurts frees you to embrace the present and future. (b) When you're not spending time and energy feeding a grudge, you can nourish new, healthy ideas. (c) The offender can't keep hurting you when you shake off the shackles and move on. (d) Holding a grudge feels like a form of control, but actually you're the one being controlled. (e) Once you lower your defenses you can start to heal, love, and be loved. (f) Feeling angry feels good temporarily; but being healed feels so much better. (g) God mandates us to love because He first loved us. You've held onto it long enough; it's time to let it go and enjoy the freedom that comes from forgiveness.

September 12

"Forgiving each other, just as ... God forgave you."
Ephesians 4:32 (NIV)

FORGIVENESS (2)

The Bible says, "Be kind ... forgiving each other ... as ... God forgave you." Kristin Armstrong says: "After you forgive ... you get to walk out the process ... it's a collaborative effort of God's power and your hard work. Letting go isn't always as simple as opening your tightly-clenched fist, although deliverance sometimes is immediate. For example, some people quit smoking cold-turkey, while others chew nicotine gum for years! Old habits die hard and letting go of resentment means: (a) Recommitting to your decision as many times as old thoughts of unforgiveness pop into your head. (b) Making peace with the space formerly occupied by bitterness, regret, and thoughts of revenge until the Holy Spirit takes up full-time occupancy in the new digs! (c) Releasing old, toxic relationships and people whose only purpose is keeping your old wounds fresh. When people change around unchanging people, it makes them aware of their own need for change, and it scares them. (d) Just as your salvation is immediate yet you have to walk out your sanctification, the release of your forgiveness is immediate, but you have to walk out your healing. (e) Living a life free from the burden of resentment and the toxicity of unforgiveness is a choice followed by a series of choices. Each one becomes easier ... as we move farther from our old ways and into the light ... Paul said, 'It is for freedom that Christ has set us free' (Galatians 5:1 NIV) and every time we let something or someone go free, we receive freedom for ourselves in overflowing proportion. It's a time-tested, guaranteed spiritual principle backed by the promise of Scripture."

September 13

"Do you see someone skilled in their work?
They will serve before kings."
Proverbs 22:29 (NIV)

HAVE A WORK ETHIC GOD CAN BLESS

Journalist William Zinsser's first job was writing for *The New York Herald Tribune*. Traditionally "cub" reporters often start by writing obituaries, but Zinsser was frustrated with his assignment. "I could be doing Pulitzer Prize-winning investigative reporting," he thought to himself, "and I'm stuck writing obituaries." Finally, he worked up enough courage to ask his editor, "When am I going to get some decent story assignments?" His crusty old editor growled at him and said, "Listen, kid, nothing you write will ever get read as carefully as what you are writing right now. You misspell a name, you mess up a date, and a family will be hurt. But you do justice to somebody's grandmother or somebody's mom, you make a life sing, and they will be grateful forever. They will put your words in laminate." "Things changed. I pledged I would make the extra calls," Zinsser said. "I would ask the extra questions. I would go the extra mile." That is essentially from the Sermon on the Mount—write obituaries for others as you would want others to write an obituary for you—obituaries that deserve to be laminated—because someday, somebody will. Zinsser eventually moved on to other kinds of writing, including a book on writing itself that has sold more than a million copies. But none of it would have happened if he had not devoted himself to obituaries. Understand this: if you cannot experience the spirit in the work you are doing today, then you cannot experience the spirit today at all.

September 14

"He rewards those who earnestly seek him."
Hebrews 11:6 (NIV)

GETTING "UNSTUCK"! (1)

Ever notice how icy winters cause multiple car pile ups, leaving drivers in ditches waiting for tow trucks to rescue them? In life, we each have different reactions. Some surrender to feelings of being powerless, others get frustrated and deepen the rut they're in. But the wise think rationally of steps they can take to get unstuck. Getting stuck isn't always an option—staying stuck is! Good news: no matter how long you've been stuck, the right attitude can get you moving again. So here are some attitude changers: (1) Forgiveness. The guilt that follows failure can immobilize you long-term, but forgiveness liberates you—freeing up your energy and creativity. Forgiveness is two-dimensional: first, you must receive God's forgiveness for your failures. Things you've done: betrayal, angry words, dishonesty, broken promises, etc. Things you haven't done: love unexpressed, responsibility avoided, a child, parent or spouse neglected, the truth withheld. Heartfelt confession always brings God's forgiveness! (See 1 John 1:9). Second, you must forgive those who've failed you—parents, siblings, children, bosses, spouses, friends, enemies, etc. Severing the chains to your past restores your options for the future. (2) Faith. When you've been stuck a long time, forward momentum can seem impossible. You lack direction, energy, and confidence. What to do? Getting traction requires a willingness to act in spite of your feelings. God calls this "faith," and He always responds to it! "He rewards those who earnestly seek him." When you act like you believe, God will reward your faith—and the feeling of faith will follow your action!

September 15

"I'm off and running, and I'm not turning back."
Philippians 3:14 (MSG)

GETTING "UNSTUCK"! (2)

Though you've settled the issues of forgiveness and faith, getting unstuck involves two more challenges. You will need to learn the following: (1) Flexibility. When your faith runs into obstacles, your flexibility keeps you in the race. You need the ability to "roll with the punches," to bend without breaking. Don't marry your methods! Be willing to make a mid-course correction when it's needed. Flexibility, however, isn't ambivalence or wishy-washiness. Flexibility is: (a) An attitude of determination to adjust to life's challenges and stay on course; to trust God for wisdom; to fine-tune your responses to changing circumstances. (b) A commitment to take action. A positive mind-set alone won't get you unstuck. You'll have to "do something!" Remember, big doors swing on little hinges; taking small steps of faith will move you forward! (2) Firmness: resolve not to quit. You'll encounter problems that leave you no option but to stand still, like the Israelites between the Red Sea and the Egyptian army. In the tightest of spots, they received this five-fold counsel: (a) Don't give in to fear. Don't let it decide your response. (b) Stand still. Stop your irrational, emotion-driven behaviors. (c) Quit talking. Don't talk yourself into defeat. (d) Look for God's way forward. Expect Him to take action that will get you unstuck. (e) Be ready to move forward when He opens the way. These are simple but powerful steps you can take when you don't know what to do. And what about when you blow it? Acknowledge it. Relabel it as a "valuable lessons learned," and put it in your "what not to do next time" file!

September 16

*"The curtain of the temple was torn
in two from top to bottom."*
Matthew 27:51 (NIV)

YOU CAN APPROACH GOD WITH CONFIDENCE

One day a year, on the Day of Atonement (at-one-ment), the high priest could go beyond the thick curtain in the tabernacle and into the "Holy of Holies" where God's presence was. What qualified him to go there was the fact that the blood of a sacrificial lamb was covering the mercy seat, under which rested the ark of the covenant. You ask, "What was in the ark?" The Ten Commandments—which all of us have broken. God arranged it like that. The only way God could look at the evidence of His people's guilt was through the blood of the lamb. Now, fast forward to the cross. Jesus "gave up His spirit. At that moment the curtain of the temple was torn in two from top to bottom." Everything changed for the better that day! In spite of your failures, you can now come into God's presence, knowing your sins are covered by the blood of Jesus, and confidently ask for whatever you need. "Let us come boldly to the throne of our gracious God. There we will receive his mercy, and we will find grace to help us when we need it most" (Hebrews 4:16 NLT). Your acceptance with God is guaranteed when you approach Him saying, "I come in the name of Jesus and on the merits of His shed blood." It works like a credit system. "You are in Christ," so you have a perfect credit score! So even when you feel inadequate and undeserving, if you ask in faith believing, God will give it to you "for Christ's sake" (Ephesians 4:32).

September 17

"These things happened to them as examples... for us."
1 Corinthians 10:11 (NIV)

SAMSON AND JOSEPH (1)

Samson was a loser; Joseph was a winner. Samson had everything going for him. He was the product of a miracle birth, raised by godly parents, and given supernatural strength. Yet he failed miserably. Why? (1) He did not pray. The only time we read of Samson praying is when he was in trouble. Sound familiar? If you conduct a post-mortem on your biggest failures, somewhere in the wreckage you'll find that you've forsaken the place of prayer. You can't run your car on an empty tank, work on an empty stomach, or pay bills on an empty checking account. And you can't live a victorious Christian life without daily prayer. (2) He refused to live by God's Word. When confronted by his parents over marrying the wrong woman, Samson told them, "She pleaseth me well" (Judges 14:3). When you're led by sentiment rather than Scripture, you're heading for trouble. One of the best definitions of "disobedience" is "incomplete obedience." You can't pick which Scriptures you want to live by and turn a blind eye to the rest! (3) He had the wrong spirit. While Joseph extended forgiveness to those who'd harmed him, Samson prayed for revenge. Any time you give in to resentment you're allowing someone other than God to dictate your actions, and you end up suffering even more. (4) He was motivated by greed. Consorting with the Philistines, he placed a bet with thirty of them, saying, "If you lose, then you will give me thirty changes of raiment" (See Judges 14:13). You say, "What's the point?" If it could happen to Samson, it could happen to you!

September 18

"These things happened to them as examples . . . for us."
1 Corinthians 10:11 (NIV)

SAMSON AND JOSEPH (2)

While Samson had everything going for him, Joseph had everything going against him. Notice: (1) He was badly treated by the people of God. Joseph's brothers resented the vision God gave him and the favor that was upon his life, so they sold him into slavery. Who told you everybody would appreciate you? Not God! Jesus said, "If they hated you, it's because they hated me first" (See John 15:18). But Joseph maintained a forgiving spirit and not only ended up being reconciled with his family, but he fed them during the famine. (2) He was alone in a land where no one had knowledge of God. But like a lily in a mud marsh, he stayed clean and grew in faith. It's not the circumstances that surround you, but what's within you that determines your success. (3) He was exposed to temptation. Joseph was lonely, far from home, and subject to every impulse a red-blooded male can have. Potiphar's wife tried repeatedly to seduce him, but he said no. In his case, there's a good chance that he might have gotten away with it. But his reason for saying no was, "How then could I do such a wicked thing and sin against God?" (Genesis 39:9 NIV). Nothing meant more to Joseph than his relationship with the Lord. (4) His integrity came at a price. Based on false accusations by Potiphar's wife, Joseph went to prison for a crime he didn't commit. Did God fail him? No, the contacts needed to get him to the throne were waiting for him in prison. So be true to God and He will bless you.

September 19

"Father... Take this cup away from Me."
Mark 14:36 (NKJV)

FACING YOUR BIGGEST FEARS IN PRAYER

The next time you drink from the communion cup in church, stop and recall what was in the cup Jesus drank from in Gethsemane on the night before He was crucified. You can drink from the cup with assurance because He first drank from the cup in agony. On the eve of His death, He prayed: "My soul is exceedingly sorrowful, even to death... Father, all things are possible for You. Take this cup away from Me; nevertheless, not what I will, but what You will" (vv. 34-36 NKJV). Note the words, "exceedingly sorrowful." (If you think your sin is no big deal, perhaps those words will help to change your mind.) Christ drank from the cup of God's wrath so that you could drink from the cup of God's grace. Although He was sinless, He tasted the sins of both the most refined sinner and the most repulsive one. He had never felt God's fury; He didn't deserve to. He had never experienced isolation from His Father; the two had been one from before time began. He had never known physical death; He was an immortal being. Yet within a few hours God would unleash His sin-hating wrath on His sinlessly perfect Son. And as a man, Jesus was afraid. Deathly afraid. And what He did with His fear shows us what to do with ours. He prayed earnestly and persistently. He told His followers, "Sit here while I go and pray over there" (Matthew 26:36 NKJV). Jesus faced His ultimate fear with honest prayer and overcame it. And through prayer, you can overcome your fears too.

September 20

"Gentle words cause life and health."
Proverbs 15:4 (TLB)

SPEAK WORDS OF LIFE AND HEALTH

James writes, "Those who consider themselves religious and yet do not keep a tight rein on their tongues, deceive themselves, and their religion is worthless" (James 1:26 NIV). The poet wrote, "Oh I say the things that I never should, just want to be heard or I never would. Talk on and on and know it's wrong; the trouble is, my tongue's too long." So how can you control your tongue's negative propensity? Engage it positively. How? (1) Be an encourager! "Gentle words cause life and health." Your words can help a hopeless person keep on living and motivate a sick loved one to fight illness and become whole. Encouragers are God's frontline against defeat, despair, and depression! (2) Speak the truth in love. Saying what needs to be heard is often hard, but being a friend requires saying difficult things. "Wounds from a sincere friend are better than many kisses from an enemy" (Proverbs 27:6 NLT). Truth spoken in love can release people from their delusions, misperceptions, and inflexibility to live free, productive lives. (See John 8:32). (3) Ask God for the right words. "The lips of the righteous bring forth what is acceptable" (Proverbs 10:32 NAS). How do you know what words the hearer will accept? Let God be your guide. (4) Make your words life-giving. "The teaching of the wise is a fountain of life, turning a person from the snares of death" (Proverbs 13:14 NIV). The people you meet need words that turn them from spiritual death to eternal life. So today, speak words of life and health.

September 21

"But where sin increased, grace increased all the more."
Romans 5:20 (NIV)

GRACE AT HOME (1)

You need a lot of grace in marriage. Even in the best of relationships, things happen that cause misunderstanding and hurt. Speaking about his marriage, therapist Michael Sytsma says: "Before I was married, God said, 'Mike, you have some rough edges. To help you become more Christlike, I'm giving you Karen. That should do the trick.' So he brought Karen . . . into my life to identify all my shortcomings. My first response when she points out my flaws? Not gratitude! Instead, I strike back: 'How dare you point out those things? What's your problem?' Then I have the opportunity of either denying my feelings or owning them and maturing. And Karen can either harbor anger and resentment or offer grace and forgiveness. Imagine a marriage filled with grace: a spouse who extends joy, pleasure, sweetness, kind speech, and unmerited favor. My wife does that. I'm still working at it." Here is the first of four ways you can show grace to your spouse: (1) Try to look at it differently. Focus on the positive. If you think your spouse is stubborn, feeling loving toward them is hard. But if you exercise grace and choose to see them as persistent and tenacious, loving them becomes much easier. If they're disorganized, by grace you can choose to see that as a sign they are spontaneous, or creative, or the flexible type, or even over-extended. "You'll do best by filling your minds and meditating on things . . . noble . . . gracious—the best, not the worst; the beautiful, not the ugly; things to praise, not things to curse" (Philippians 4:8 MSG). People usually try to live up to the image you hold of them!

September 22

"If anyone is in Christ, he is a new creation."
2 Corinthians 5:17 (NKJV)

GRACE AT HOME (2)

Here are three more steps to treating your spouse with grace: (1) See them as God created them to be. Focusing on your partner's flaws doesn't help either of you. The Pharisees saw only the worst in the woman caught in adultery. Jesus didn't minimize her sin but chose to see what she could become through grace. "I don't condemn you. Go, and stop what you're doing" (See John 8:11). Grace enables you to see beyond your spouse's upsetting ways and work with God in helping them become the "new creature" He's called them to be. (2) Celebrate them. Too often we try to impose on our spouse our desired image of them. We resent them and insist they change, see it our way, and do things to our required standard. If they don't, we think they're inconsiderate, unloving, even un-Christian. Grace doesn't operate that way! It understands, accepts, forgives, and leaves changing others up to God. Try telling yourself, "Yes, that annoys me, but I wonder what God's trying to work out in my spouse." Then step back, love and accept them, and let God work on them. (3) Forgive them. Your spouse will irritate you at times because of what they are. We're all different. She thinks she's detailed; he thinks she's nit-picking. He thinks he's laid-back; she thinks he's lazy. We act out the image we hold of ourselves, and that'll change only when God changes it! Acknowledge your intolerance and forgive your partner's irritating behaviors—even before they do them. That's "pre-emptive forgiveness," the kind that denies resentment a toe-hold on your marriage.

September 23

"God has dealt to each one a measure of faith."
Romans 12:3 (NKJV)

USE YOUR "MEASURE OF FAITH"

The amount of faith God has given you is equal to the assignment He's given you. So whatever you're facing, tell yourself, "God has given me the faith to handle this." Nothing's more important than your faith. Jesus told Peter, "Satan has asked for you, that he may sift you as wheat. But I have prayed for you, that your faith should not fail (Luke 22:31-32 NKJV). Faith is more important than money, or career success, or reputation. Everything can be taken from you but if you have faith, you'll bounce back. Faith is like having a direct line to God. As the prayer of faith flows up, His power flows down. As a result, you are more than adequate for the challenge. Failure is never final, as long as your faith doesn't fail. That's why Satan will do everything he can to keep you from spending time each day in the Scriptures. "Faith cometh by hearing . . . the word of God" (Romans 10:17). Jesus said, "If you have faith as a mustard seed, you will say to this mountain, 'Move from here to there,' and it will move" (Matthew 17:20 NKJV). There are obstacles in your life that will only be removed by faith. And you don't need a truckload of it, just a mustard seed. Think: a tiny seed has the power to grow, overcome obstacles and become a mighty tree. It will press up through the ground, around rocks, braving storms, and withstanding other threats to its life. It's not so much the size of your faith, but the quality of it that determines your success. So today, use your "measure of faith."

September 24

"You do not know what manner of spirit you are of."
Luke 9:55 (NKJV)

A CALLOUS SPIRIT (1)

The disciples had a problem with their attitude, and Jesus "called them on it" six different times in two chapters. Let's look at each and see what we can learn. A callous spirit. Instead of believing Christ could feed the crowd with five loaves and two fishes, they said to Jesus, "Send the multitude away" (v. 12 NKJV). One of the dangers of succeeding in ministry is that you can end up loving crowds but not really caring for individuals. Or wanting contributors, but not wanting to spend time meeting people's individual needs. Years ago, a man decided to visit the churches of two well-known television ministers he liked. After hearing the first, he asked if he could say hello to him. But the minister's "handlers" said no, suggesting he call for an appointment. Disappointed, he went to hear the other minister, and was invited to lunch with him following the service. Feeling valued, he handed the minister a check for—four million dollars. (This is a true story.) You must always be approachable, available, and affirming. You must keep the personal touch. True, you can't personally minister to all who are sick and counsel all who are hurting. As a pastor, having quality time to prepare sermons and Bible studies must be a top priority. But Jesus was "touched with the feeling of our infirmities" (Hebrews 4:15) because He mixed and mingled with us. Only as you stay in touch with people's needs, can God use you to meet those needs in real time. The saying goes, "People don't care how much you know until they know how much you care." So, do you care?

September 25

"Peter ... not knowing what he said."
Luke 9:33 (NKJV)

AN IMPULSIVE SPIRIT (2)

On the Mount of Transfiguration, "Peter said to Jesus, 'Master, it is good for us to be here; and let us make three tabernacles: one for You, one for Moses, and one for Elijah'—not knowing what he said ... And a voice came out of the cloud, saying, 'This is My beloved Son. Hear Him!'" (vv. 33-35 NKJV). Another spirit Jesus identified among His disciples was an impulsive spirit. Note the words, "not knowing what he said." Peter's penchant for saying whatever came into his mind drew a strong rebuke from heaven: "This is My beloved Son—hear Him!" There's an important lesson here. Your need to appear wise and have all the answers can get you into trouble with people—and God! Generally speaking, you're not learning while you're talking. So learn to be quiet, observe what's going on, and listen for what God may want to say. When you don't know, don't speak. People respect you when you have the wisdom and humility to say, "I'm not sure, but if you give me time I'll pray about it, consider it more fully, and get back to you." Experts say the average person is now bombarded with thirty-five thousand messages a day: e-mails, text messages, billboards, television, radio, Twitter, Facebook, blogs, etc. It's "information overload." People don't need more information; they need answers that work! And God has those answers. Talk to Him first, then you'll have something to say to others that's worth listening to. "Everyone enjoys a fitting reply; it is wonderful to say the right thing at the right time!" (Proverbs 15:23 NLT).

September 26

"They came to Him . . . saying, 'Master, Master, we are perishing!'"
Luke 8:24 (NKJV)

A FEARFUL SPIRIT (3)

The Bible says: "He got into a boat with His disciples. And He said to them, 'Let us cross over to the other side of the lake.' And they launched out. But as they sailed, He fell asleep. And a windstorm came down . . . and they . . . were in jeopardy. And they . . . awoke Him, saying, 'Master, Master, we are perishing!' Then He arose and rebuked the wind and the raging of the water . . . But He said to them, 'Where is your faith?' And they were afraid, and marveled, saying to one another, 'Who can this be? For He commands even the winds and water, and they obey Him!'" (vv. 22-25 NKJV). Notice what is at work in this story: A fearful spirit. No matter how often God blesses us and answers our prayers, we still give in to fear the next time we face a crisis, especially when it's one we haven't faced before. Who told the disciples to get into the boat in the first place? Jesus. Understand this: faith doesn't exempt you from life's storms; it equips you to go through them. And when you are in the will of God, no storm, however severe, can take you under. Jesus knew the storm was coming before the disciples ever stepped into the boat. So why did He expose them to it? Because He was equipping them for the future, for the day when He'd no longer be around and they would face persecution, imprisonment, and even death. So the word for you today is, "Don't be afraid. The Lord is with you; you are going to make it to the other side."

September 27

"And You say, 'Who touched Me?'"
Luke 8:45 (NKJV)

AN UNDISCERNING SPIRIT (4)

One day a chronically ill woman who had hemorrhaged for twelve years pushed her way through the crowd and touched the hem of Jesus' garment. Immediately she was healed. "Jesus said, 'Who touched Me?' When all denied it, Peter and those with him said, 'Master, the multitudes throng and press You, and You say, 'Who touched Me?' But Jesus said, 'Somebody touched Me, for I perceived power going out from Me.' Now when the woman saw that she was not hidden, she came trembling; and falling down before Him, she declared to Him in the presence of all . . . how she was healed immediately. And He said to her, 'Daughter, be of good cheer; your faith has made you well. Go in peace'" (vv. 45-48 NKJV). What's at work in this story? An undiscerning spirit. Observe Peter's words, "Master, the multitudes throng and press You, and You say, 'Who touched Me?'" Understand this: Jesus can tell the difference between the indiscriminate touch of the crowd, and a touch of faith. Faith draws on His power and brings results! Notice this woman touched the "hem" of Jesus' garment. The last thing a dressmaker does when she makes a garment is to sew up the hem. So the hem represents "the finished work." The same back that bore the cross which takes away your sins, also bore the stripes which take away your sickness. "And by His stripes we are healed" (Isaiah 53:5 NKJV). What do you need today? Forgiveness of sins? Healing? Reach out in faith and touch Jesus, and you too will be made whole.

September 28

"A dispute arose among them as to which of them would be greatest."
Luke 9:46 (NKJV)

A SELF-SEEKING SPIRIT (5)

The Bible says: "Then a dispute arose among them as to which of them would be greatest. And Jesus, perceiving the thought of their heart, took a little child and set him by Him, and said to them, 'Whoever receives this little child in My name receives Me; and whoever receives Me receives Him who sent Me. For he who is least among you all will be great'" (vv. 46-48 NKJV). What's at work in this story? A self-seeking spirit. As long as your motive for serving is to make yourself look good, you'll never enjoy God's approval. And His "well done" is the only thing that counts. The ability to serve behind the scenes, and do it with joy, comes from the knowledge that ultimately your service will be recognized and rewarded by the only One whose opinion counts. Why did Jesus feature a child that day? For three reasons: (1) A child is teachable. When you're done learning, you're done! When you can't be told, God will have nothing more to tell you. "The heart of the discerning acquires knowledge, for the ears of the wise seek it out" (Proverbs 18:15 NIV). (2) A child is trusting. When you promise a child something, they believe you, act on it, and expect it to be so. "It is better to trust in the Lord than to put confidence in man" (Psalm 118:8 NKJV). (3) A child is tenderhearted. "Finally, all of you be . . . tenderhearted" (1 Peter 3:8 NKJV). The Holy Spirit is symbolized in Scripture as a gentle dove, so keep your heart tender and receptive to His dealings.

September 29

"You do not know what manner of spirit you are of."
Luke 9:55 (NKJV)

A JUDGMENTAL SPIRIT (6)

One day Jesus went into a Samaritan village and was not well received. So the disciples said: "'Lord, do You want us to command fire to come down from heaven and consume them, just as Elijah did?' But He turned and rebuked them, and said, 'You do not know what manner of spirit you are of. For the Son of Man did not come to destroy men's lives but to save them'" (vv. 54-56 NKJV). What's at work in this story? A judgmental spirit. A poll taken by the Barna Research Group reveals that today most nonbelievers view Christians as too judgmental. You can be sincere, but too severe. When you mix and mingle only with those who share your views and values, you can communicate with others in ways that attack, rather than attract. Let's be clear; never has it been more important to know the truth of God's Word and stand for it. But if you have the right doctrine and the wrong spirit, you'll drive more people away from Christ than you'll draw to Him. If Satan has his way, he will drive holiness out of our hearts and into our fists. Imagine—Christ's disciples wanting to incinerate those who didn't agree with them! They weren't even aware of the spirit that was at work within their own hearts. "Jesus said . . . 'You shall love your neighbor as yourself'" (Matthew 19:19 NKJV). That includes your non-Christian neighbor. You don't have to defend Jesus, or "sell" Him. All you have to do is introduce Him. The Psalmist says, "Taste and see that the Lord is good" (Psalm 34:8 NKJV).

September 30

"My future is in your hands."
Psalm 31:15 (NLT)

PEACE IN THE TIME OF TERROR!

September 11, 2001, Americans awoke to scenes of horror that would remain enduringly etched on the national memory. Its shock waves told the world that things would never be the same again. Sleepy eyes stared transfixed as television brought home the collapsing twin towers with their thousands of innocent occupants, the deadly attack on the Pentagon, and the cruel fate of an airliner and passengers hurtling into a rural Pennsylvania field. Unexpected, swift and violent, these attacks shook people to the core and exemplified a jarring new reality: the proliferation of universal terrorism. Fears of suicide bombers, chemical, and biological attack still reverberate through our world of high-tech, security-conscious cities, airports, trains, and bus terminals. King David faced the threat of conspiracy from both his enemies and his friends. Feeling abandoned, alone, and vulnerable, he cried out, "For I hear many whispering 'Terror on every side!'" (Psalm 31:13 NIV). King, warrior, and giant-slayer, David still felt the palpable terror of his situation. Frightened, he refocused his thoughts and heart to the source of real protection. "But, I am trusting you, O Lord" (v. 14 NLT). Afraid, but still trusting! And choosing trust restored his perspective. "My future is in your hands" (v. 15 NLT). His litany of fears gave way to faith and prayer. "How great is the goodness you have stored up ... You lavish it on those who come to you for protection" (v. 19 NLT). "You hide them in the shelter of your presence, safe from those who conspire against them" (v. 20 NLT). In Jesus, you'll find peace in the time of terror.

October 1

"What does the Lord require of you . . . to love kindness."
Micah 6:8 (NAS)

KINDNESS

Every day, we miss opportunities to be kind in order to save a few seconds. One author writes, "When I treat people as obstacles, or a means to getting things done, I become a smaller man. With each brusque comment . . . dismissive glance . . . curt reply I lose a little more of myself . . . my relationship with God suffers." Paul says, "The fruit of the Spirit is . . . kindness" (Galatians 5:22 NKJV), and you can't love God without being kind to those He loves. Consider Ruth and Naomi. When circumstances left them widowed, Ruth told her aging mother-in-law, "Don't ask me to leave you . . . May the Lord punish me . . . if I allow anything but death to separate us!" (Ruth 1:16-17 NLT). Consider Jonathan and David. When Saul tried to kill David, Jonathan stuck by him and "loved him as himself" (1 Samuel 18:3 NIV) although it meant sacrificing his chance to become king. Consider David and Mephibosheth. In an era when newly-appointed monarchs routinely banished those associated with former dynasties, David sought out Jonathan's son and said, "I will . . . show kindness to you for the sake of your father . . . and . . . restore to you . . . the land of your grandfather . . . you shall eat at my table regularly" (2 Samuel 9:7 NAS). Consider the Shunammite woman who noticed Elisha was always passing her house, so she built a little room so he could "turn in" when he was tired (2 Kings 4:9-10 NAS). You never regret kindness. Og Mandino says, "Treat everyone you meet as if they were going to be dead by midnight. Extend all the care, kindness, and understanding you can, with no thought of reward, and your life will never be the same."

October 2

"You ... harvest what you plant."
Galatians 6:7 (CEV)

DOING THE RIGHT THINGS

George Bernard Shaw said, "People are always blaming their circumstances for what they are. I don't believe in circumstances. The people who get ahead are those who get up and look for the circumstances they want, and if they can't find them, they make them." A farmer can plant anything he wants; the land doesn't care one way or the other. Suppose he plants both wheat and poisonous hemlock. The land will return poisonous hemlock as plentifully as it does wheat. Your mind is far more fertile, but the same principle applies. It doesn't care what kind of seeds you plant; success or failure, good or evil, anxiety or peace—what you sow returns to you. The Bible says, "If you follow your selfish desires, you will harvest destruction ... if you follow the Spirit, you will harvest eternal life" (v. 8 CEV). Success lies in your daily routine. So, get to know God better through His Word and prayer. Make up your mind to be of service to somebody every day. Tackle a problem bigger than you. Encourage everyone you meet. Take the first step toward overcoming a bad habit. Do something for somebody who can't repay you. Change your thinking from TGIF (thank goodness it's Friday!) to TGIT (thank goodness it's today!). Do three things that will take you outside your comfort zone. Be thankful for what you have. Ask for help when you need it. Give God the best part of your day. The Psalmist said, "This is the day the Lord has made ... rejoice and be glad in it" (Psalm 118: 24 NLT). The time to be happy is now, and the place to be happy is here.

October 3

"A double minded man is unstable in all his ways."
James 1:8 (KJV)

BE SINGLE MINDED (1)

The Bible says, "He that wavereth is like a wave of the sea driven with the wind and tossed. For let not that man think that he shall receive any thing of the Lord. A double minded man is unstable in all his ways" (vv. 6-8). Peter Marshall, chaplain to the Senate, prayed, "Give us clear vision that we may know where to stand, and what to stand for." A dream that isn't clear won't help you get anywhere. What do you want to accomplish? What do you want to contribute? Who do you want to become? In other words, what does success look like for you? If you don't define it, you won't be able to achieve it. Most people don't get what they want because they don't know what they want. They haven't defined their dream in clear and compelling detail. One author writes: "The indispensable first step to getting the things you want out of life is this: decide what you want! Instead of saying, 'I want to lose weight,' say, 'I will weigh one hundred and eighty-five pounds by June 1.' Instead of saying, 'I want to get out of debt,' say, 'I will pay off all credit card balances by December 31.' Instead of saying, 'I need to improve my leadership,' say, 'I will read one leadership book every month.' Being specific doesn't necessarily mean having every little detail thought out before you move forward. But your main goal should be clear. The rest will unfold as you move forward, making adjustments as you go." The question you need to answer is, "Am I single minded?"

October 4

"Fix your gaze directly before you."
Proverbs 4:25 (NIV)

BE SINGLE MINDED (2)

It doesn't take much effort to let your mind drift and dream. But it takes great effort to set your mind to the task of developing a clear goal, of having a clear and compelling dream. One leader says: "For me the whole process begins with questions I must ask myself. The dream is always rooted in the dreamer, in his or her experiences, circumstances, talents, and opportunities. I ask: 'What am I feeling—what are my emotions telling me? What am I sensing—what is my intuition telling me? What am I seeing—what is happening around me? What am I hearing—what are others saying? What am I thinking—what do my intellect and common sense say?' A clear picture may come to you all at once in lightning-bolt fashion, but for most people it doesn't work that way. Most people need to keep working at it, clarifying it, and redrawing it. If the process is difficult, that's no reason to give up. In fact, if it's too easy, maybe you're not dreaming big enough. Just keep working at it because a clear dream is worth fighting for." If you can get a clear sense of where you are, what you know, and what you want, you're well on your way to understanding and embracing the thing God put you on earth to do. Moses spent the first two-thirds of his life figuring out what God wanted him to do, trying to do things his own way, only to fail. But he had a heart for God, and a vision from God, and eventually he succeeded. And you will too!

October 5

"Ask, and you will receive, that your joy may be full."
John 16:24 (NKJV)

KEYS TO ANSWERED PRAYER

If your prayers are not being answered, ask yourself: (1) How is my relationship with the Lord? "If I regard iniquity in my heart, the Lord will not hear me" (Psalm 66:18). Anything that adversely affects your relationship with God also affects your prayers. Friendship gives you favor; intimacy gives you access. Jesus said, "If you abide in Me, and My words abide in you, you will ask what you desire, and it shall be done for you" (John 15:7 NKJV). (2) How strong is my faith? "Without faith it is impossible to please Him, for he who comes to God must believe that He is . . . a rewarder of those who diligently seek Him" (Hebrews 11:6 NKJV). Notice three words: (a) "Believe." God's deepest longing is to be believed, regardless of emotion or circumstance. (b) "Diligently." When you pray, put your heart and soul into it. Paul speaks of "laboring in prayer" (See Colossians 4:12). (c) "Him." God is not some "force out there," He's your heavenly Father Who "knows that you need all these things" (Matthew 6:32 NKJV). Your highest priority should not be getting your needs met, it should be building your relationship with God. (3) Am I showing patience? "Until God's time finally came—how God tested his patience!" (Psalm 105:19 TLB). Joseph was tested by the very promise God gave him. Can't you hear Satan whisper, "I thought the dream said you were supposed to be prime minister; what are you doing in prison?" But it only looks like a prison; in reality, it's the birthplace of destiny. Joseph saw God's promise fulfilled—in God's time. And you will too!

October 6

"Be patient in trouble, and prayerful always."
Romans 12:12 (TLB)

WHEN GOD PUTS YOU ON HOLD (1)

We've been dubbed "the microwave generation" for good reason—we charge through life like we're on fire! But God has His own timetable, and it can't be rushed. When He puts you on hold watch your words. Like a small rudder on a big ship, what you say determines your direction and helps stop the wrong thoughts from infiltrating your mind. Mel Weldon said, "My mind is a garden, my thoughts are the seeds; my harvest will be either flowers or weeds." Ask God to help you control your emotions. Paul says, "Be glad for all God is planning . . . Be patient in trouble . . . and prayerful always." Complaining magnifies the problem. Prayer turns negative energy into a powerful force for good. Look for the humor in it. Solomon said, "He who is of a merry heart has a continual feast" (Proverbs 15:15 NKJV). Laughter dispels tension, lightens the burden and fills your soul with joy. Appreciate the chance to learn. The Chinese view problems as prospects; in their culture the character/symbol for problems and opportunities is the same. Solomon said, "The diligent make use of everything" (Proverbs 12:27 NLT). Learn from your experience regardless of how hard it is, and remember, some of the world's greatest discoveries and breakthroughs resulted from crises. Love unconditionally. Problems are caused by people, and under pressure it's tempting to lash out. The bottom line is: we all make mistakes and nobody is beyond redemption! Aren't you glad about that? Learn to see people through God's eyes. "Overcome evil with good" (Romans 12:21) . . . be courteous, and maintain your dignity when you're under pressure (See Romans 12:10).

October 7

"By your patience possess your souls."
Luke 21:19 (NKJV)

WHEN GOD PUTS YOU ON HOLD (2)

Make peace your priority. Don't let your inner man be controlled by outside pressures. When you "go to war" everybody suffers but when "the peace that comes from Christ control[s] your thoughts" (Colossians 3:15 CEV), it restores your perspective and creates an atmosphere that's conducive to solutions. Look for a breakthrough from an unexpected source. When you "commit thy way unto the Lord" (Psalm 37:5), don't be surprised when the people and circumstances He sends into your life aren't what you expected. He spoke to Balaam through a donkey (See Numbers 22), and He used a burning bush to get Moses' attention (See Exodus 3). Don't be in such a hurry. Ever notice that the faster you go, the more behind you get? Jesus said, "By your patience possess your souls." As Henry Blackaby observes: "God's timing is ... best ... He may be withholding directions to cause you to seek Him more intently. Don't try to skip the relationship and get on with doing. God is more interested in a relationship with you than He is in what you can do for Him." Don't be too proud to ask for help. Solomon said, "With humility comes wisdom" (Proverbs 11:2 NLT). If the people you turn to aren't immediately available, be patient and don't give up. God designed us to work together, and somewhere up the road you will be called to help somebody by sharing what you're learning right now. "God ... comes alongside us when we go through hard times, and before you know it, he brings us alongside someone else ... so that we can be there for that person" (2 Corinthians 1:4 MSG).

October 8

*"When a storm strikes ... God will
keep safe all who obey him."*
Proverbs 10:25 (CEV)

YOUR STORM SHELTER (1)

Heart-rending scenes of nature's devastation are hard to forget. Victims caught in the path of hurricanes, floods, and earthquakes are tossed around like matchsticks. But those prepared in advance escape its destruction. There is no such thing as a storm-free life! The words "when (not if) a storm strikes," teach us that we all go through times of heartache and trouble. The question is: are you prepared? You can be. God can protect you in times of loss, sickness, divorce, unemployment, loneliness, and depression. You may not be able to predict life's storms or prevent them, but you can prepare for them and be protected in them by doing the following things: Locate your storm shelter. Mid-storm is no time to be caught in confusion seeking refuge for yourself and your family. You must know in Whom, and where your protection lies. The Bible says, "The name of the Lord is a fortified tower; the righteous run to it and are safe" (Proverbs 18:10 NIV). God's "name" speaks of His character, His reliability, and His faithfulness. A man or woman without God is forced to be their own god—what a fearful thought! But those who love God can say, "God is a safe place to hide, ready to help when we need him. We stand fearless ... courageous in sea storm and earthquake, before the rush and roar of oceans, the tremors that shift mountains" (Psalm 46:1-3 MSG). The old Irish preacher had his own take on the hymn. He'd say, "On Christ the solid rock I stand—all other rocks are sham-rocks!" Trust God! He's the only storm shelter you'll ever need.

October 9

"You have been . . . a shelter from the storm."
Isaiah 25:4 (NIV)

YOUR STORM SHELTER (2)

To be prepared for life's storms you must: (1) Know your storm manual. The hymnist wrote: "Standing on the promises that cannot fail, when the howling storms of doubt and fear assail, Standing on the living Word I shall prevail, standing on the promises of God." Emotion-based faith is like a broken crutch; it won't support you in life's storms. It's fair-weather Christianity and it doesn't work. God's Word stands sure; it's greater than surrounding conditions and will enable you to outlast any storm. "Let the message of Christ dwell among you richly" (Colossians 3:16 NIV). Keep a rich deposit of Scripture within you at all times so you can make a withdrawal when you need it. Withstanding life's storms depends on your willingness to "[hear] these words . . . and [put] them into practice" (Matthew 7:24 NIV). So, memorize the Scriptures; read them until, if you're cut, you bleed Scripture. Meditate on God's Word until it fills and shapes your consciousness. When the storm came, Job said, "I have treasured the words of His mouth more than my necessary food" (Job 23:12 NKJV). (2) Storm-proof yourself through prayer. Many of us treat prayer like a visit to the emergency room; until then we neglect it. Imagine where Daniel would have been if he'd held off praying until he was staring down the lion's throat? Not a smart move. Instead, in his time of crisis Daniel drew on faith built by a lifestyle of daily prayer. And in your crisis, you too can make withdrawals from your account—as long as you've been faithful to make regular deposits.

October 10

"I am with you and will watch over you wherever you go."
Genesis 28:15 (NIV)

YOUR STORM SHELTER (3)

To prepare for life's storms you must do the following: (1) Practice self-control. Storms are much harder on the undisciplined and self-indulgent. The illusion that life should be an easy, painless, air-cushioned ride makes you vulnerable to discouragement, disillusionment, and defeat in hard times. The truth is tough times don't last but tough people do! And tough people practice self-denial and self-control. It's their spiritual muscle for handling life's hardships. The Bible says, "The fruit of the Spirit is . . . self-control" (Galatians 5:22-23 NIV). God's Spirit will make you tough enough to control your greatest weakness—yourself—the thing that ultimately defeats you in the tough times. Paul lived by this principle. "I discipline my body and keep it under control" (1 Corinthians 9:27 ESV). Great athletes know that it's their conditioning, not the conditions, that determine their victory. (2) Depend on God, not people. "It is better to trust in the Lord than to put confidence in man" (Psalm 118:8 NKJV). Yes, others can help you at times, like a cast helps a broken leg. But once that leg is ready to bear its weight, you must discard the cast or your leg won't regain full strength. People can go so far; only God will go all the way with you. Paul writes: "No one stood with me, but all forsook me. May it not be charged against them. But the Lord stood with me and strengthened me . . . The Lord will deliver me from every evil work and preserve me for His heavenly kingdom. To Him be glory forever and ever. Amen!" (2 Timothy 4:16-18 NKJV).

October 11

"Let him ... rely upon his God"
Isaiah 50:10 (NKJV)

INSTEAD OF WORRYING, TRUST GOD

One morning a man received four long-distance calls before he could even get out of bed. Everybody had problems they wanted solved "right now." He told his wife to forget about breakfast, only to discover his car wouldn't start. So he called a taxi. When he got in the taxi he yelled, "Let's go!" The driver asked, "Where do you want me to take you?" He shouted, "I don't care, I've got problems everywhere!" Do you feel like that today? Have you done all you know to do, but the situation hasn't improved? "Who among you fears the Lord? Who obeys the voice of his Servant? Who walks in darkness and has no light? Let him trust in the name of the Lord and rely upon his God." Note the word "name." God values His good name because it represents His power, His character, and His faithfulness. So when you pray for anything in His name, you're trusting His power, His character, and His faithfulness. It's like standing on a rock! We spend so much of our lives worrying about yesterday and tomorrow, yet one is buried and the other is unborn. There's not a thing we can do about either—except let them steal today right out of our hands. The Psalmist said, "This is the day which the Lord hath made; we will rejoice and be glad in it" (Psalm 118:24). Seize this day with its blessings and challenges and live every moment of it. Don't long for "someday." "God is ... a very present help" (Psalm 46:1). Just hand your worries to Him and let Him take care of them for you.

October 12

"Underneath are the everlasting arms."
Deuteronomy 33:27 (NKJV)

GOD OF THE BOTTOM

Addressing the nation of Israel for the last time, Moses told them, "There is no one like the God of Israel. He rides across the heavens to help you . . . The eternal God is your refuge, and his everlasting arms are under you" (vv. 26-27 NLT). As you read the Bible you discover that God did a lot of spectacular things for His people on mountaintops. On Mount Moriah He met with Abraham and Isaac, revealing Himself as "Jehovah Jireh" which means "the Lord will provide." On Mount Horeb, He spoke to Moses through a burning bush and changed the nation of Israel's destiny. On Mount Sinai, He gave the Ten Commandments. On Mount Carmel, He sent down fire from heaven, consuming the prophets of Baal and turning the hearts of His people back to Him. But suddenly Moses made a shift in the middle of telling about this great God of high places. It is as though he was thinking, "I can't leave these people with the thought that God is only on top; that He's with us only when everything is going right." So he continued, "The eternal God is your refuge, and underneath are the everlasting arms." The Hebrew word for "underneath" means "bottom." So it could be translated, "God's arms are underneath you when you're on the bottom." No matter how deep the valley you have to walk, God's presence is deeper. It may feel like you are down today, but you cannot go so low that He is not there. Underneath you are His everlasting arms. The truth is He's not just the God of the top; He's also the God of the bottom.

October 13

*"They looked to Him and were radiant, and
their faces were not ashamed."*
Psalm 34:5 (NKJV)

I AM NOT ASHAMED (1)

The Psalmist wrote, "They looked to Him and were radiant, and their faces were not ashamed." As a follower of Christ, that should be your testimony. Because you have placed your trust in Him you are able to say, "I am not ashamed" of: (1) His birth. Mary was His mother, but God was His Father. He was tainted with neither inherited sin nor practiced sin, hence He meets all of God's requirements to be our Savior. (2) His miracles. He never demanded money in exchange for a miracle. Not one supernatural act was performed for selfish or ostentatious purposes, but only to meet people's needs. (3) His preaching. Even His enemies had to admit, "No man ever spoke like this Man!" (John 7:46 NKJV). Other men's words inform us; His words transform us. (4) His claims. He said, "He that hath seen me hath seen the Father" (John 14:9). You see the fullness of God expressed in the person of Jesus Christ. (5) His death. He bore your shame. You were morally and spiritually bankrupt. But He satisfied all of God's claims against you at the cross, writing "paid in full" across your account. (6) His resurrection. "Lifted up was He to die, it is finished was His cry. Now in heaven exalted high, Hallelujah, what a Savior." And His promise is, "Because I live, you will live also" (John 14:19 NKJV). (7) His mediator-ship. Picture this: when you fail, He stands before God on your behalf, offering His blood as atonement for your sin. If you saw Him now, you would say, "I am not ashamed of Jesus."

October 14

"I am not ashamed of the gospel."
Romans 1:16 (KJV)

I AM NOT ASHAMED (2)

As a follower of Christ you can also say, "I am not ashamed of the gospel, because it is the power of God that brings salvation to everyone that believes." Our gospel is not education or sophistication, but salvation. It's not reformation or rehabilitation, but redemption from the penalty and the power of sin. The Bible says, "If any man be in Christ, he is a new creature: old things are passed away; behold, all things are become new" (2 Corinthians 5:17). This is not the old car with a new set of plugs, points and a carburetor; it's a brand-new model. Notice the words, "To everyone that believes." By placing your trust in Christ, you are forgiven from all sin, clothed in Christ's righteousness, made fully acceptable in God's sight, and qualified for heaven. You ask, "How long does a prayer for salvation have to be?" The thief on the cross prayed only nine words: "Lord, remember me when You come into Your kingdom" (Luke 23:42 NKJV). The publican in the temple prayed only seven words: "God be merciful to me a sinner" (Luke 18:13). When Peter was sinking in the Sea of Galilee he only had time for three words: "Lord, save me" (Matthew 14:30). And the good news is—Christ saved them all. You ask, "How do I receive this life-changing power?" By faith! "For it is with your heart that you believe and are justified, and it is with your mouth that you profess your faith and are saved. As Scripture says, 'Anyone who believes in him will never be put to shame'" (Romans 10:10-11 NIV).

October 15

"Let me not be ashamed of my hope."
Psalm 119:116 (KJV)

I AM NOT ASHAMED (3)

The Psalmist wrote, "Uphold me according unto thy word, that I may live: and let me not be ashamed of my hope." What is our hope? It's found in the second coming of our Lord Jesus Christ. Paul spells it out: "We believe that Jesus died and rose again, and so we believe that God will bring with Jesus those who have fallen asleep in him... For the Lord himself will come down from heaven, with a loud command, with a voice of the archangel and with the trumpet call of God, and the dead in Christ will rise first. After that, we who are still alive and are left will be caught up together with them in the clouds to meet the Lord in the air" (1 Thessalonians 4:14-17 NIV). Jesus said, "For a time is coming when all who are in their graves will hear his voice and come out—those who have done... good will rise to live, and those who have done... evil will rise to be condemned" (John 5:28-29 NIV). In that day the Lord's Prayer will finally be answered: "Thy kingdom come. Thy will be done in earth, as it is in heaven" (Matthew 6:10). The hymnist wrote, "O Lord, 'tis for Thee, for Thy coming we wait. The sky, not the grave, is our goal. O trump of the angel! O voice of the Lord! Blessed rest, blessed hope of my soul." Jesus has not changed His mind; He's coming again. Coming for whom? For a prepared people, to take them to a prepared place, where they will dwell with Him forever. Are you planning to be there?

October 16

"How can they hear, unless someone tells them?"
Romans 10:14 (CEV)

REACH OUTSIDE YOUR COMFORT ZONE (1)

One author writes: "While visiting my parents I needed a haircut, so I went to where my mom goes. As the owner, Jim, trimmed my hair, we started talking about spiritual things. The more we talked . . . the more he cut. I ended up with very short hair but our conversation about Jesus was worth it. Later when I suggested to my mom that she invite Jim and his wife to church, she said, 'No way they'd be interested . . . they lead a pretty wildlife. I don't know two people further from God.' Nevertheless . . . the next time she went to the salon she shot up a silent prayer: 'God, I don't think these people are interested in You. So if You want me to say anything . . . make something happen.' Just then Jim's wife said . . . 'I understand you're in a group that discusses spiritual things. We'd like to come.' Pam and Jim . . . eventually prayed with my folks and gave their lives to Christ—all because of a conversation that developed over a series of haircuts. This kind of reaction rarely happens. Most Christians spend virtually all their time with other Christians . . . But when it comes to important matters . . . people listen to people they trust . . . especially about spiritual matters. Paul says, 'How can people have faith in the Lord . . . if they have never heard about him? And . . . unless someone tells them?' If people are going to be reached for Christ, for the most part, it'll happen through friends, not strangers. So, cultivate a relationship with somebody who works at a restaurant you frequent, or the people at your health club. Have the neighbors over for dinner . . . follow Christ's example and befriend people who don't know God."

October 17

"How can they hear, unless someone tells them?"
Romans 10:14 (CEV)

REACH OUTSIDE YOUR COMFORT ZONE (2)

John Ortberg says: "(1) Never rule anybody out. Jesus reached out to tax collectors, lepers, sinners, and Gentiles, and they shocked the religious establishment by saying yes… Maybe there's somebody in your world who's so far from God you've written them off… a relative who ridicules your faith… an acquaintance who's resisted for years… somebody so steeped in sin you think there's no hope? Never say no for another person… you don't know when their heart will soften or how God's Spirit will work." (2) Put yourself in the other person's shoes. Ortberg continues: "Blocks from my parents' home… is the largest Buddhist temple in America. I checked it out and received amazing insight into how intimidating it is to go into a place of worship as a stranger not knowing the customs. When you invite someone to church, they're much more likely to go if you go together. Then have coffee together and talk about what took place." (3) Be the hands and feet of Jesus. Jewish law prohibited lepers from having contact with non-lepers. But when a leper approached Jesus, He reached out and touched the man who hadn't been touched in years (See Mark 1:40-45). Was Jesus infected by his leprosy? No, He infected the leper with the gospel, because Jesus was more contagious with God's power than the leper was with his disease. Be a contagious Christian who infects others with God's love. Look at your hands. How often do you extend them to someone far from God? His kingdom has been spread the same way for two thousand years—by believers who reach out and bring people to Christ!

October 18

"I will pour out water to quench your thirst."
Isaiah 44:3 (NLT)

ARE YOU RUNNING ON EMPTY?

Julie Coleman writes: "I was headed for a writer's conference in Philadelphia when I realized I'd better think about stopping for gas... Normally I'm fussy about where I stop... but as I drove the lonely stretch of road, I began to feel desperate... any minute... I'd be stranded in 100-plus degrees and I didn't even have a water bottle... I drove several long miles till I came to a tiny crossroads. Four houses....and a gas station! It looked like it could be called 'Joe's Gas Station and Storm Door Company'... I'd probably have turned up my nose at it in another circumstance. But at that moment [it] was the best thing I'd seen! Funny how our circumstances can dictate how we feel!" Running from his enemies, David prayed, "My soul thirsts for you... in a dry... land where there is no water... Teach me to walk in the way I should" (See Psalm 143:6-8). Would his prayer have been different if David had been living in luxury surrounded by servants? Not knowing where his next meal was coming from and sleeping outside every night changed his perspective. When life goes well, we become self-sufficient and forget God. Spiritually speaking, we run on empty until a spark ignites an outburst. If your car's on empty whose fault is it? The gas station hasn't moved! You chose to drive by without stopping! When you're running on empty you end up hurting those closest to you, then dealing with the guilt that comes after a flare-up. God said, "I will pour out water to quench your thirst." So today pick up your Bible and refuel your soul!

October 19

"Stir up the gift of God . . . in you."
2 Timothy 1:6 (NKJV)

START STIRRING . . . AND DON'T STOP (1)

God gave you your talent, but it's your job to develop it. And it's not that complicated because your gift usually relates to something that excites you. Think about it. God made you; He hardwired the desires of your heart. Knowing that helps you to understand why the things you find rewarding involve your innate talents and abilities. One author says: "It's natural for a hunting dog to hunt. Coop him up and he'll lie around with no enthusiasm. But when he realizes he's going hunting, he comes alive. That's because God designed hunting dogs that way. They have that passion inside them . . . They don't have to get themselves worked up . . . or say, 'Let me go listen to a sermon or motivational message so I can work up some zest and zeal.' No, when those dogs know they're going hunting they're naturally excited . . . And when we're doing what we know we're called to do, enthusiasm and excitement exude from us naturally. We may not jump up and down . . . but deep within, we know 'This is what I was called to do. This is why I was born.' On the other hand, if you're doing something that's not natural, it's a struggle. If you try, train, practice and push and you still can't get a skill down, recognize that it may not be in your nature. Of course, we must persevere . . . push through and learn hard things . . . but in general, life shouldn't be a constant struggle." When you're fulfilling your purpose, one of the most noticeable results is how rewarding it feels to "stir up the gift of God . . . in you" by utilizing your natural abilities.

October 20

"A gift is as a precious stone in the eyes of him that hath it: whithersoever it turneth, it prospereth."
Proverbs 17:8 (KJV)

START STIRRING . . . AND DON'T STOP (2)

Paul speaks of "the gift of God" in you (2 Timothy 1:6-7). It isn't something you learn; it's something He gives you and nobody else can activate it for you. You 'stir' it up by developing and using it. Solomon said, "A gift is as a precious stone in the eyes of him that hath it: whithersoever it turneth, it prospereth." Your gift will enrich many different areas in your life, not all of which are financial. While money is the wrong reason to devote your life to something, developing your God-given gift is rewarding on multiple levels. Unfortunately, many people are jealous of other people's gifts. Don't waste time on jealousy; it's a gift-robber, an energy-drainer, and besides, you should be so busy stirring up your own gift that you've no time for envy. When Louis Armstrong auditioned for music school, he was asked to sing scales. But he could only sing two notes properly, so they wrote him off. Armstrong cried when he was rejected, but later told his friends, "There's music in me and they can't keep it out." Consequently, he went on to become one of the world's most successful and beloved musicians, selling more records than others who were more talented. We're all born originals, but many of us settle for becoming carbon copies. Think, if you become like everybody else and join the rat race, even if you do win, that just makes you a big rat! Your gift will make room for you (See Proverbs 18:16). So go ahead and fill the slot God designed for you.

October 21

"What is your name?"
Genesis 32:27 (NIV)

WALKING IN YOUR GOD-GIVEN IDENTITY

As they wrestled together, the angel of the Lord asked Jacob, "What is your name?" He answered, "Jacob." Then the angel said, "Your name will no longer be Jacob, which means deceiver, but Israel, which means 'a prince with God', because you have struggled … and have overcome" (See Genesis 32:27-28). God forced Jacob to look at his true identity. He wrestled him into a revelation of who he was—not who others said he was. His parents gave him his name and others called him by it, so he believed that's who he'd always be. But God had a different plan for him. Hear this: you are not who others say you are. Why should they name you? Determine who you are before God. Let Him determine the level of your success. Why should others be allowed to live at their highest potential but not you? You are more than your past, more than your education or résumé, more than the color of your skin, more than your bank account, and more than your circumstances. Tell those who talk down to you and devalue you, "You're confusing me with somebody else. God says I am a prince. And if I'm a prince, then I have the right to be treated like one!" You ask, "But is that true?" Yes, the Bible says that when you walk with God you are part of a royal priesthood (See 1 Peter 2:9). You are an overcomer (See 1 John 2:13-14). You are the head and not the tail, above and not beneath (See Deuteronomy 28:13-14). Dry your tears, lift your head, square your shoulders and begin walking in your God-given identity.

October 22

"Do not fear therefore; you are of more value than many sparrows."
Luke 12:7 (NKJV)

SPARROWS (1)

In teaching us how to live, Jesus used sparrows to illustrate His point. For the next few days, let's look at them. A worthless sparrow. "Are not five sparrows sold for two copper coins? And not one of them is forgotten before God . . . Do not fear therefore; you are of more value than many sparrows" (vv. 6-7 NKJV). In Christ's day they didn't sell hamburgers, they sold sparrows on a stick that had been roasted over a fire. You could buy two of them for one copper coin. But you could get five for two copper coins; the vendor threw in the fifth one for free. That meant it was worthless. What was Christ's point? You are valuable in God's eyes! Do you feel like if you weren't around nobody would miss you; like your life means nothing? You'd be surprised how many people, even high-profile ones, struggle with a sense of inferiority and inadequacy. When God called Jeremiah to be a prophet, he explained to God that he was afraid of people. So God said, "Do not be afraid of their faces, for I am with you to deliver you" (Jeremiah 1:8 NKJV). When you feel worthless you conclude that others feel the same way about you, so you begin to approach them fearfully, or aggressively, or even resentfully. What's the answer? Remembering your worth in God's eyes! There is no rejection in His love, only complete acceptance. You're connected! You have a friend in high places. Jesus said, "I have called you friends" (John 15:15). Will everybody accept you? No, but when you base your worth on God's love and acceptance, you're free to enjoy life.

October 23

"I am like ... a sparrow alone on the housetop."
Psalm 102:6-7 (NKJV)

SPARROWS (2)

A lonely sparrow. The Psalmist wrote, "I am like ... a sparrow alone on the housetop." Has your nest been torn apart by a storm? Have you lost your mate? Jesus can relate. His disciples didn't "get Him." They argued over who would be the greatest. They failed to pray with Him in His most difficult moments. On the cross He cried out, "My God, my God, why hast thou forsaken me?" (Matthew 27:46) We smile at the story of the single lady who hung a pair of trousers on her bedpost, then sent God a letter: "Father in heaven, help me if you can. I've hung a pair of trousers here, please fill them with a man." Seriously, loneliness can be devastating to your self-worth. Young people wonder if they will ever find the right person to marry. Older people fear ending life all alone. The God who knew that Adam was incomplete not only created Eve for him, but actually introduced them and brought them together. And He can do the same for you. If you are widowed, divorced, or never married and want to find a mate, don't be anxious. God says, "I know ... where you dwell" (Revelation 2:13 NKJV). God knows your name, your address, and every detail about you. And better yet, He cares! And one more thought: sometimes loneliness is not the absence of affection but the absence of direction; not the absence of people but the absence of purpose. So begin to reach out to others. Find a need no one is meeting, pour your life into it and watch how things begin to improve for you.

October 24

*"The sparrow has found a home . . .
a place near your altar."*
Psalm 84:3 (NIV)

SPARROWS (3)

A lost sparrow. The hit TV series, *Lost*, was about a plane crashing on a remote island and the survivors rebuilding their lives amidst the wreckage. The secret of the show's success was that we could all relate to it. We've lost marriages, businesses, homes, self-worth, security, and a lot of other things. But Jesus came to "seek and to save that which was lost" (Luke 19:10). Unlike us, Jesus didn't see people as "good" or "bad," but as "lost." He knew they'd lost their way, lost their values, lost their relationships, lost their ability to cope, lost their faith, and in some cases lost their reason to live. And He sought them out like the woman at the well with five divorces and a live-in boyfriend; like the man who lay at the Pool of Bethesda for thirty-eight years, chronically ill, noticed by no one; like Mary who wept at the tomb of the One she loved most. If you're lost today, you can have a personal audience with the Lord. "The sparrow has found a home . . . where she may lay her young—even Your altars, O Lord of Hosts . . . Blessed are those who dwell in Your house; they will still be praising You" (Psalm 84:3-4 NKJV). Today you can "come home" to God! You can build your nest and raise your family in the shelter of His protection. You can feel safe with Him. As you bow in worship, He will lift you up and make you feel valuable again. He will deliver you from the fear of rejection and loneliness. You can't hide from God, but you can hide in Him.

October 25

"Not one of them falls to the ground apart from your Father's will."
Matthew 10:29 (NKJV)

SPARROWS (4)

A fallen sparrow. Jesus said, "Are not two sparrows sold for a copper coin? And not one of them falls to the ground apart from your Father's will." Great news: God knows when you fall, and His will is to lift you up again. Perhaps you were flying high, then you made a mistake. You were sabotaged by a secret struggle you couldn't share with anyone. Or your trust was devastated by someone you loved. As a result, you are afraid to begin again. Afraid you can't overcome your past and rise again to fulfill your destiny. Regardless of how many times you've failed, God still loves you. Have you been attacked in a specific area of your life and it's become an area of repeated failure? Have you asked yourself, "What is this battle about?" Hear this: the battle is not over your past, it's over your future! That's why you are a target. And the God Who gave Peter and Jonah a second chance, will lift you from the ashes of failure and remake your life into something beautiful. God saw you when you fell, so there's no reason to try and hide from Him. Like the shepherd who went looking for his one lost sheep, God is looking for you today. Not to condemn you but to restore you. Self-exaltation leads to pride, which God hates. But self-loathing leads to paralysis. There's only one unpardonable sin, so you can go to God with confidence knowing He will give you a fresh start. And this time He will empower you to be strong and succeed.

October 26

"Your heavenly Father feeds them."
Matthew 6:26 (NKJV)

SPARROWS (5)

A needy sparrow. Jesus said: "Look at the birds. They don't plant or harvest or store food in barns, for your heavenly Father feeds them. And aren't you far more valuable to him than they are? Can all your worries add a single moment to your life? And why worry about your clothing? Look at the lilies of the field and how they grow. They don't work or make their clothing, yet Solomon in all his glory was not dressed as beautifully as they are. And if God cares so wonderfully for wildflowers that are here today and thrown into the fire tomorrow, he will certainly care for you. Why do you have so little faith? . . . These things dominate the thoughts of unbelievers, but your heavenly Father already knows all your needs. Seek the Kingdom of God above all else, and live righteously, and he will give you everything you need" (vv. 26-33 NLT). If you need some more scriptural promises to stand on, here they are: "Fear the Lord, you his godly people, for those who fear him will have all they need" (Psalm 34:9 NLT). "Blessed is the man who fears the Lord, who delights greatly in His commandments. His descendants will be mighty on earth; the generation of the upright will be blessed. Wealth and riches will be in his house . . . He will not be afraid of evil tidings; his heart is steadfast, trusting in the Lord" (Psalm 112:1-7 NKJV). God recorded these promises in His Word so that you could read them over and over, and in reading them, rise above worry and live your life with joy and confidence.

October 27

"Is your life full of difficulties and temptations? Then be happy."
James 1:2 (TLB)

DEALING WITH ADVERSITY (1)

Lori Schneider is one of very few women to climb Mt. Everest—yet another step on a climb she started ten years earlier when she was diagnosed with multiple sclerosis. Terrified but determined to achieve her goal, she quit her job and devoted herself to climbing. Nine years later she'd conquered the peaks on six of the earth's continents! "Lori sees MS not as a negative, but a positive," her father said. "She accepted it as a challenge." Unfurling a banner in honor of the first World MS Day, she called her dad on a satellite phone: "I'm here on the summit! I made it!" A dream sixteen years in the making realized! Now her goal is to show others who face challenges that even the highest mountain can be climbed one step at a time. In *Staying the Course*, BJ Gallagher writes: "Our journey... is about progress, not perfection. It's not about doing one thing 100 percent better—it's doing 100 things 1 percent better each day. Progress is evolutionary, not revolutionary... most days we measure in inches, not miles. What matters most is showing up for your life whether you feel like it or not. Ask yourself, 'What two or three little things can I do today that would move me forward?' You'll be amazed how much distance you can cover taking it in increments. Little things add up; inches turn to miles. We string together our efforts like so many pearls, and before long... you have a whole strand!"

October 28

"God led you through the wilderness...
to prove your character."
Deuteronomy 8:2 (NLT)

DEALING WITH ADVERSITY (2)

God led the children of Israel through the wilderness "to prove [their] character, and . . . find out whether or not [they] would obey his commandments." They could choose to perish there or trust Him to bring them safely to the Promised Land. One author writes: "How many times have you changed courses in life, rather than pass the test and get through the tough stuff to the promises of God? He wants to know if you are worthy of the blessing that awaits you on the other side of the Jordan. Do you have the courage to face the challenges, or will you go back and settle for second best? If you're facing a challenge that stands between you and your promise . . . look at Joshua 1:9 and Daniel 10:19 for courage. Ask God to give you the courage to face whatever hurdles stand in the way of your claiming what God has prepared for you." The landscape along Florida's Everglades is dotted with wiry, primitive-looking trees known as Caribbean Pines. They thrive in a rugged environment, can withstand prolonged periods of drought and fire, and hold their own against the fiercest hurricanes. In fact, if you plant them in a cultivated setting, they usually shrivel and die. Joni Eareckson Tada says: "Like Caribbean Pines, our souls usually don't thrive during good times. Our hearts grow complacent, our need of God becomes less urgent, our hope of heaven dims, and our prayer life dries up . . . in a beautiful setting with our needs met and every resource at our fingertips . . . our soul shrivels . . . We need an occasional blast of storm or fiery trial if our faith is to mature."

October 29

"The works that I do [you] will do also."
John 14:12 (NKJV)

FIND A MENTOR. BECOME A MENTOR.

Jesus was the perfect mentor. He told His disciples, "The works that I do [you] will do also." If you want to reach the fullness of your God-given potential, ask God for the right mentors. You will always go further with a good mentor coaching and pushing you. Some mentors are given for a short season, others for a lifetime, so you must know the difference. How do you recognize a mentor? There are eight ways. The credo of the true mentor is this: (1) I am willing to spend the time it takes to build a close relationship with the learner. (2) I commit myself to believing in the potential of the learner; to telling them the exciting future I see ahead for him or her; to visualizing and verbalizing the possibilities for his or her life. (3) I am willing to be vulnerable and transparent before the learner. I'm willing to share not only my strengths and successes, but also my weaknesses, failures, brokenness, and sins. (4) I am willing to be honest yet affirming in confronting the learner's errors, faults, and areas of immaturity. (5) I am committed to standing by the learner through trials—even trials that are self-inflicted as a result of ignorance or error. (6) I am committed to helping the learner set goals for his or her spiritual life, career, or ministry, and to helping the learner dream his or her dream. (7) I am willing to objectively evaluate the learner's progress toward his or her goal. (8) Above all, I am committed to faithfully living out everything I teach.

October 30

"His sheep follow him because they know his voice."
John 10:4 (NIV)

KNOWING GOD'S VOICE

Here are seven occasions when knowing God's voice is all-important: (1) Hearing from God before you entertain the ideas of others. Why? Because their ideas are not His commands. Don't make commitments and end up bound by promises you can't keep. You must love others but be led only by God's Spirit. (2) Hearing from God before you listen to the complaints of others. Why? Because you are not responsible for their happiness. Your need to "fix" others in order to feel good about yourself is called "co-dependency." Give them to God! (3) Hearing from God before you consider the needs of others. Why? Because their needs are driving them; only the plan of God should be leading you. (4) Hearing from God before you respond to the requests of others. Why? Because you must discern what's behind their requests. Check the soil before you sow your seed. (5) Hearing from God before you share your dream with others. Why? Because it's not enough to have a dream, you must have a team. You need people to help you, cheer you on, and lift you to a higher level. The right people motivate you to grow stronger, think better, work harder, and risk more. They compel you to continue! (6) Hearing from God before you seek the approval of others. Why? Because people with an agenda will flatter and manipulate you. Hearing God's voice will keep you from falling into their trap. (7) Hearing from God before you make significant changes. Why? Because it's not your job to decide what God wants you to do, but to discover it and do it.

October 31

"They . . . compare themselves with themselves."
2 Corinthians 10:12 (NIV)

STOP COMPARING YOURSELF TO OTHERS

One definition of success is "gaining wealth and fame." But how much wealth do you need to be successful? How much fame? Should you pick an arbitrary target? Should you compare yourself to others? What if you have decided to devote yourself to raising children of character, or serving your church and your community? Does that mean you are less successful? No. Success is doing the best you can, with what you have, wherever you are in life. The Bible warns, "When they measure themselves by themselves and compare themselves with themselves, they are not wise." When you play the comparison game you are like the two cows that saw the milk truck go by with a sign, "Pasteurized, homogenized, Vitamin A added." One cow said to the other, "Makes you feel sort of inadequate, doesn't it?" God will help you be all that you can be, but He will never help you be someone else. When you focus your attention on who you aren't by comparing yourself with someone else, you lose sight of who you need to become. Ever heard of the eighteen/forty/sixty rule? When you're eighteen, you worry about what everybody's thinking about you. When you're forty, you realize that it doesn't really matter what they think about you. When you're sixty, it dawns on you that most of them weren't thinking about you at all! Paul's life changed dramatically with one question: "Lord, what do You want me to do?" (Acts 9:6 NKJV). Only when you ask that question, will you discover who you are and what God's called you to be.

November 1

"They called the name of that place Baal Perazim."
1 Chronicles 14:11 (NKJV)

DO YOU NEED A BREAKTHROUGH?

The Bible says, "The Philistines . . . made a raid on the Valley of Rephaim. And David inquired of God saying, 'Shall I go up against the Philistines? Will You deliver them into my hand?' The Lord said to him, 'Go up, for I will deliver them into your hand.' So they went up to Baal Perazim, and David defeated them there. Then David said, 'God has broken through my enemies by my hand like a breakthrough of water.' Therefore they called the name of that place Baal Perazim [which means "breaking through"] (vv. 9-11 NKJV). To get a breakthrough in your life you must do what David did: (1) He reminded himself that "the Lord had made him king" (See v. 2 NKJV). You must remember Who called you, and Whose spirit lives within you. God called David, and He's called you too. When you know that, you won't let the Enemy put you down or push you around. (2) He inquired of the Lord, "Shall I go up against the Philistines?" (v. 10 NKJV). Have you talked it over with the Lord? God doesn't respond to your need—He responds to your obedience. When you've obeyed Him—you'll win. (3) He gave God the credit: "God has broken through my enemies" (v. 11 NKJV). Sometimes God will do it for you, other times He will do it through you. That's why you must hear from Him before you make a move. You can't do God's part, and He won't do yours. It's not just a matter of "doing something," it's a matter of doing what God tells you! When you do, you'll get a breakthrough.

November 2

"It is sin to know what you ought to do and then not do it."
James 4:17 (NLT)

DECISION, DISCIPLINE, AND DETERMINATION

Brian Tracy says, "There are so many good things you can do, that your ability to decide may be the critical determinant of what you accomplish. If you're like most people, you're overwhelmed with too much to do and too little time. Mark Twain once joked that if first thing every morning you eat a frog, you'll go through the rest of the day knowing that's the worst that can happen! Your 'frog' is the most important task ... the one you're likely to procrastinate on ... the one that can have the greatest positive impact ... Treat it as a personal challenge ... resist the temptation to start with the easier task. If you 'eat' it first, it'll give you energy and momentum for the rest. Success is determined by the habits you develop. Setting priorities, overcoming procrastination, and getting on with the most important task is a mental and physical skill learnable through practice and repetition until it becomes a permanent part of your behavior. Once it becomes a habit, it's automatic and easy to do. When you complete a task of any size or importance, you get a surge of energy. It triggers the release of endorphins that give you a natural 'high.' The 'rush' that follows makes you feel more positive, personable, creative and confident." What you put off until tomorrow, you'll put off again tomorrow. Plus, it's "sin to know what you ought to do and ... not do it." Success requires decision, discipline, and determination. Make the decision, discipline yourself until it becomes automatic, and stay determined until it becomes part of who you are.

November 3

"I will make you fishers of men."
Matthew 4:19 (NKJV)

FISHING OR FIGHTING

We read, "Jesus ... saw ... Simon ... and Andrew ... casting a net into the sea; for they were fishermen. Then He said to them, 'Follow Me, and I will make you fishers of men!'" (vv. 18-19 NKJV). To follow Christ, you must learn how to fish for men and women, and then do it! Max Lucado grew up fishing. He said, "We set out ... dreaming of ... sun. But ... next morning the sky was gray, the lake a mountain of white-topped waves ... there was no way we could fish ... Next day ... it was ice! We tried to be cheerful ... but I began to notice ... Mark had a few personality flaws ... Dad was touchy ... Nothing like being cooped up with someone to see his real nature! When we awoke the next morning to sleet ... we were flat-out grumpy ... Mark became even more of a jerk ... Dad couldn't do anything right, and when he announced we were going home, nobody objected ... When energy intended for outside is used inside ... instead of casting nets, we cast stones. Instead of helping hands we point accusing fingers. Instead of being fishers of the lost, we become critics of the saved. Rather than helping the hurting, we hurt the helpers. The result? Split churches. Poor testimonies. Broken hearts. Legalistic wars. But when those who are called to fish, fish—they flourish ... Nothing unites soldiers like a common task. Leave them inside and they'll invent things to complain about. The bunks will be too hard, food too cold, leadership too tough. Place those same soldiers in the trench and let them duck a few bullets, and a boring barracks will seem like a haven ... The next time outside challenges tempt you to stay inside ... get out! When those who are called to fish don't fish, they fight!"

November 4

"Do not be afraid of their faces, for I am with you."
Jeremiah 1:8 (NKJV)

ARE YOU FEELING INSECURE? (1)

Jeremiah writes: "Then the word of the Lord came to me, saying: 'Before I formed you in the womb I knew you; before you were born I sanctified you [set you apart]; I ordained you a prophet to the nations.' Then said I: 'Ah, Lord God! Behold, I cannot speak, for I am a youth.' But the Lord said to me: 'Do not say, "I am a youth," for you shall go to all to whom I send you, and whatever I command you, you shall speak. Do not be afraid of their faces, for I am with you to deliver you,' says the Lord. Then the Lord put forth His hand and touched my mouth, and … said: 'Behold, I have put My words in your mouth. See, I have this day set you over the nations and over the kingdoms, to root out and to pull down, to destroy and to throw down, to build and to plant … I am ready to perform My word'" (vv. 4-12 NKJV). Does the job you've been called to do seem too big for you? On your own it is, but not when you include God! You're not working alone—God is with you. Whether it's to pull down or build up, the One who called you will equip you, empower you, and give you success. He didn't make a mistake when He picked you. You say, "If only I had the education, talent and experience of so-and-so." If God wanted them, He'd have chosen them, but He chose you. Just be yourself, trust God, and everything will go well for you.

November 5

"Get yourself ready! Stand up and say to them whatever I command you."
Jeremiah 1:17 (NIV)

ARE YOU FEELING INSECURE? (2)

Are you embarrassed about your beginnings? Jeremiah was. He begins his book by listing the good people and the bad people in his background. Well, guess what? We all came from a less-than-perfect gene pool! We're all a mixed bag. So what should you do? Learn from those who did it the wrong way and follow those who did it the right way. Discover God's purpose for you on the earth and fulfill it. Keep the torch burning brightly, then hand it off to the next runner. Endeavor to finish strong and hear your "well done, good and faithful servant." And watch what you say! The words you speak not only influence others, they influence you too. When Jeremiah told God that he wasn't the right age, God said, "Don't say that!" When he complained that he was not a gifted speaker, God said, "Don't say that either!" When he saw the size of the opposition his knees buckled, but God said, "'Get yourself ready! Stand up and say to them whatever I command you. Do not be terrified by them, or I will terrify you before them. Today I have made you a fortified city, an iron pillar and a bronze wall to stand against the whole land—against the kings of Judah, its officials, its priests and the people of the land. They will fight against you but will not overcome you, for I am with you and will rescue you,' declares the Lord" (vv. 17-19 NIV). And God didn't promise just to be with Jeremiah, He's promised to be with you.

November 6

"The Lord ... said to me, 'I have put my words in your mouth.'"
Jeremiah 1:9 (NIV)

ARE YOU FEELING INSECURE? (3)

The people God calls usually start out feeling ill-equipped and insecure. Indeed, if you jumped up and said, "No problem, Lord, I can handle that," He wouldn't call you at all. You say, "But I've made so many mistakes." Everybody falls; the winners are just the ones who get back up again. "The Lord ... delights in him; though he may stumble, he will not fall, for the Lord upholds him with his hand" (Psalm 37:23-24 NIV). When Jeremiah told God that he had neither the competence or confidence needed to do the job, God said to him what He says to us. (1) You are not going in your own authority. "You must go to everyone I send you to" (Jeremiah 1:7 NIV). Who's sending you, sponsoring you, and sustaining you? God! What more do you need? (2) The message is not yours. "You must ... say whatever I command you" (v. 7 NIV). Don't agonize, compromise, rationalize, or apologize. Just say what God told you to say and He will do the rest: "For I am watching to see that my word is fulfilled!" (v. 12 NIV). (3) When God touches you, you're qualified. "Then the Lord reached out his hand and touched my mouth and said to me, 'I have put my words in your mouth'" (v. 9 NIV). Be yourself; you can't be anybody else! You're not who others say you are; you're who God says you are! You can do what God says you can do. Just get in agreement with Him.

November 7

"Problems and trials... are good for us."
Romans 5:3 (TLB)

WHAT YOU LEARN IN TOUGH TIMES

We all want "the crown of life" the Lord promised (James 1:12 NKJV)—but we don't want the "problems and trials" that develop "strength of character in us" (Romans 5:4 NLT). But it can't be done. Here's what you learn in tough times: (1) Enjoyment. "Count it all joy when you fall into... trials" (James 1:2 NKJV). It's when you pass God's test that He fills you with His joy. So pull some of the groans out of your prayers and throw in a few hallelujahs. Remember, pain is inevitable—misery is optional! (2) Enlargement. The Psalmist wrote, "Thou hast enlarged me when I was in distress" (Psalm 4:1). Most of the things we know best, we learned the hard way. Our greatest progress comes from our greatest pain; hence God doesn't save us from it but strengthens us in it. (3) Enlightenment. The Bible says, "Unto the upright there arises light in the darkness" (Psalm 112:4 NKJV). We don't realize how little we know until we walk through life's dark places and God turns on the light. (4) Endurance. James writes, "See how the farmer waits for the land to yield its valuable crop, patiently waiting for the autumn and spring rains. You too, be patient and stand firm" (James 5:7-8 NIV). You can't shorten the seasons or hurry the harvest, so be patient. And pay attention. While you're waiting, God is working. Bruce Wilkinson says, "Tests of faith are trials and hardships that invite you to surrender something of great value to God, even when you have every right not to."

November 8

"Your word is truth."
John 17:17 (NIV)

WHY YOU CAN DEPEND ON GOD'S WORD (1)

When your "back is against the wall," where can you turn to find strength? Awash in a sea of moral and ethical questions, where can you go to find a reliable compass? One author says, "There can be no more reliable authority than God's Word. This timeless, trustworthy source holds the key that unlocks life's mysteries. It alone provides us with the shelter we need in times of storm. Why does [it] qualify as our final authority? (1) God's Word is truth. Jesus said as He prayed to the Father, 'Your word is truth.' Real truth you can rely on . . . that'll never shrivel up . . . turn sour . . . backfire or mislead . . . That's what the Bible's about . . . [it] provides us with the constant and the needed support. (2) God's Book is God's voice. Paul writes, 'You received the word of God . . . not as the word of men, but as . . . the word of God, which . . . effectively works in you who believe' (1Thessalonians 2:13 NKJV). Think of it this way . . . If the Lord were to return to earth and speak . . . His message would tie in exactly with what you see in Scripture—His opinion, counsel, commands, desires, and warnings. When you rely on God's voice you have a sure foundation . . . truth that can be trusted . . . power that imparts new life and releases grace by which you can grow in faith and commitment. (3) God's Word endures. There are only two eternal things on earth today . . . people and God's Word. Everything else will ultimately be burned up . . . stuff we place on the shelf, things we put frames around, trophies and whatnots we shine and love to show off . . . all headed for the final bonfire (See 2 Peter 3:7, 10-12) . . . God's Book 'endures forever' (1 Peter 1:25 NIV)."

November 9

"The word of God which ... effectively works in you."
1 Thessalonians 2:13 (NKJV)

WHY YOU CAN DEPEND ON GOD'S WORD (2)

Observe two things: (1) God's Word is inspired. Chuck Swindoll writes, "We've no problem with the Giver of truth ... but wasn't the truth corrupted when He relayed it through sinful men? This is the perfect moment to get acquainted with revelation, inspiration, and illumination. Revelation occurred when God gave His truth, inspiration when writers received and recorded it, and illumination when we understand and apply it. Your confidence in the Bible is directly related to your confidence in its inspiration. How can we be sure it's error-free and trustworthy? Paul provides help answering this question: 'All Scripture is inspired by God ... for teaching ... showing people what is wrong in their lives ... correcting faults, and for teaching how to live right' (2 Timothy 3:16 NCV). When God revealed His truth to human writers, He 'breathed out' His Word. When we dictate a letter, we 'breathe out a message' and someone else types it. So did the writers simply take dictation? If you know much about the Bible you realize ... Peter doesn't sound like John. John doesn't sound like David. Somehow each writer's personality was preserved without corrupting the text ... That rules out the idea of dictation. Peter says, 'No ... Scripture ever came from the prophet's own understanding, or ... human initiative ... [They] were moved by the Holy Spirit, and ... spoke from God' (2 Peter 1:20-21 NLT). That answers that question! (2) It'll hold you up. When you go through chaotic experiences God's Word gives you stability. No other counsel will get you through the long haul. No other truth will help you stand firm in storms of doubt and uncertainty. No other reality will give you the strength you need each day."

November 10

"Daniel purposed in his heart."
Daniel 1:8 (KJV)

COMPLACENT OR COMMITTED?

The Bible says, "Daniel purposed in his heart that he would not defile himself with . . . the king's meat." Daniel had settled the issue before the challenge arose. Joseph had also decided his values; therefore, he was able to say no to Potiphar's wife. The three Hebrew children already knew what they were going to do, fiery furnace or not: "Our God . . . is able to deliver us . . . and He will . . . But if not . . . we do not serve your gods" (Daniel 3:17-18 NKJV). What do you believe about God? If you think He might fail you, you'll never totally commit yourself to Him. Commitment grows! You can't make big commitments until you've first made small ones. The three Hebrew children first said no to the king's food; later they were able to say no to worshiping his idols. You don't get that kind of faith suddenly. Most of us can look back over the years and identify a point at which our lives changed significantly. Because of a readiness within us, we made a choice that would affect us from that point forward. But before you can make a real commitment to anything you must overcome three problems: (1) The security problem. Insecure people fear taking risks. They have a "Plan B" in case God doesn't come through for them; they depend on themselves rather than on Him. (2) The success problem. When you've had some success, you want to guard it. You want people to continue thinking well of you, so you start living defensively. (3) The satisfaction problem. The lukewarm Laodicean church said, "I am . . . increased with goods, and have need of nothing" (Revelation 3:17). Ask yourself, "Am I complacent or committed?"

November 11

"My times are in Your hand."
Psalm 31:15 (NKJV)

LEARN TO WAIT

The Psalmist writes, "I trust in You, O Lord; I say, 'You are my God.' My times are in Your hand" (vv. 14-15 NKJV). As you walk with God, you'll find that you spend more time waiting than you do receiving. And when you receive what you're waiting for, then you'll begin waiting for something else! So if you don't learn to wait with joy, you'll live in frustration. Paul writes, "Let us not be weary in well doing: for in due season we shall reap, if we faint not" (Galatians 6:9). "Due season" is when God knows the time is right, not when you think it is. God has a set time for accomplishing things in your life, so you might as well settle down and wait because that's when it will happen, and not before. God knows what you need, when you need it, and how to get it to you. You ask, "And what am I supposed to do while I'm waiting?" Trust Him! One Bible teacher writes, "God has taught me to keep living the life I now have while I'm waiting for the things that are in my heart to come to pass. We become so intent on trying to give birth to the next thing, that we neither enjoy nor take care of the things at hand. I had a vision from God ten years before I began to see it fulfilled. During those years I believe I missed a lot of joy by trying to give birth outside of God's timing. Learn to enjoy where you are, while you are waiting to get to where you want to be."

November 12

"When I was a child ... When I became a man."
1 Corinthians 13:11 (NIV)

GETTING THEM FROM CHILDHOOD TO ADULTHOOD (1)

Do you sometimes wonder if your teenager is ever going to reach maturity? Welcome to the toughest phase of parenting! A teenager can go from optimism to pessimism, excitement to boredom, self-confidence to self-doubt, happiness to despair, sociability to reclusiveness, tranquility to volatility, cooperation to opposition—in a head-spinning second! And when you ask them, "What's wrong?" they say, "Nothing," or, "I don't know." And the truth is, they don't! Bombarded by changing biochemistry, your child is navigating between the worlds of childhood and adulthood, needing your understanding and patience. For them the odyssey of adolescence can feel freakish, embarrassing, and perplexing. Children know the roles and rules of their world, adults know theirs. Children are expected to act like children, and adults like adults. But teenagers have traits of both worlds yet belong in neither. When they're in childmode, they're forbidden to be childish. "Will you ever grow up?" we ask. When they're in adult-mode, they're denied adult privileges. "Of course you can't ... You're just a kid!" The worlds of adults and children are relatively distinct, stable, predictable places. But it's not so in the fuzzy realm of your teen. They alternate between two worlds, never certain whether they're fish or fowl, adult or child. So they gravitate toward peers who share but also don't understand their experiences. What do they need? Parents who understand and assure them, "When I was a child, I talked ... thought ... reasoned like a child. When I became a man [or woman], I put the ways of childhood behind me."

November 13

"Be alert and of sober mind."
1 Peter 4:7 (NIV)

GETTING THEM FROM CHILDHOOD TO ADULTHOOD (2)

Going from childhood to adulthood is a transition that requires a lot of wisdom and love. Your teen will feel and behave child-like sometimes, and adult-like other times. Your job is to realize that whatever their status, they will become a man (woman) and they will remain adult! Navigating through their child-adult struggles elevates your teen's stress levels, sometimes making them feel out of control. To help them become a mature adult: (1) Be rational, not reactive. Your role requires you to be "clear minded and self-controlled." Be the grownup; you cannot help your child to become an adult if you're not one. (2) Be their parent, not their buddy. They need someone "in charge" to shepherd them toward maturity. If you abdicate your role because you're afraid of your child's anger, rejection or unhappiness, you abandon them to their own confused ways. You are the calm God put in their storm—the lighthouse to guide them. In the short term they may consider your values, rules, lifestyle, and morals outdated. Expect no less; that's par for the course in parenting. Hold this line! Forget becoming "cool" by lowering your standards; that's a no-win alternative to good parenting. They'll challenge you if you're not cool and they'll challenge you if you are. (Nothing is as "uncool" to a teen as a parent trying to be "cool"!) Be yourself and maintain biblical standards; they need you to have character. Yes, they'll fight you now, but if you remain resolute, loving, and consistent, they'll follow in your footsteps.

November 14

*"Get ready to cross the Jordan River into
the land I am about to give."*
Joshua 1:2 (NIV)

GET READY TO MOVE (1)

God said to Joshua, "Moses my servant is dead. Now then... get ready to cross the Jordan River into the land I am about to give [you]... I will give you every place where you set your foot, as I promised Moses. Your territory will extend from the desert to Lebanon, and from the great river, the Euphrates... to the Mediterranean Sea in the west. No one will be able to stand against you all the days of your life. As I was with Moses, so I will be with you; I will never leave you nor forsake you. Be strong and courageous, because you will lead these people to inherit the land I swore to their ancestors to give them" (vv. 2-6 NIV). Are you standing today at the crossroads of change, contemplating a new season or assignment, and feeling anxious about it? If so, observe two things in this story: (1) When his time came to lead, Joshua was ready. Until then, he faithfully served Moses and found fulfillment in the number-two slot. He didn't push and he didn't play politics; he just prepared himself. And when he was ready God promoted him. (2) He went further than his mentor did. Moses' leadership ended where the Promised Land began. Under Joshua's leadership, Israel would move into it and become a great nation. Every day he had spent in the wilderness equipped him for this moment. God never wastes experience. Everything you've been through, including the things you didn't understand, are preparation for what God has in store for you.

November 15

"I will give you every place where you set your foot, as I promised."
Joshua 1:3 (NIV)

GET READY TO MOVE (2)

Can you imagine how Joshua felt stepping into Moses' shoes? He needed assurance, so God told him: (1) "I will give you every place where you set your foot." In other words, just step out in faith and claim it. It's yours if you're willing to walk toward it and take possession. Would it be easy? Would they get there overnight? No, but their confidence came from the words, "as I promised." The song goes: "Standing on the promises that cannot fail; when the howling winds of doubt and fear assail. Standing on the living word I shall prevail; standing on the promises of God." (2) "No one will be able to stand against you all the days of your life" (v. 5 NIV). Will you face criticism? Yes. Will you come under attack? Yes. There were thirty-one kings, seven nations, and giants the size of telephone poles waiting for the Israelites in the Promised Land. But every battle you fight is just an opportunity for God to show Himself strong on your behalf. (3) "As I was with Moses, so I will be with you" (v. 5 NIV). If you're anxious about the future, recall God's faithfulness to you in the past. At the end of his life Joshua wrote: "Now I am about to go the way of all the earth. You know with all your heart and soul that not one of all the good promises the Lord your God gave you has failed. Every promise has been fulfilled" (Joshua 23:14 NIV). And the God who came through for Joshua, will come through for you.

November 16

GET READY TO MOVE (3)

If you've ever packed up and moved to another house, you may remember saying, "This is the last time I'm moving!" Now you know how Joshua felt moving almost two million people into a new homeland. And they did it on foot. So God told Joshua two things: (1) "Be strong and very courageous" (Joshua 1:7 NKJV). Why? Because his enemies were going to attack him and his own people were going to make endless demands on him. Where do you find courage? In these words: "The Lord is the stronghold of my life—of whom shall I be afraid?" That word "stronghold" means you are held in the safety of God's strong arms. That means nothing can get to you, without first coming through Him. Victor Hugo wrote, "Have courage for the great sorrows of life, and patience for the small ones. And when you have laboriously accomplished your daily task, go to sleep in peace. God is awake." (2) "I will never leave you nor forsake you" (Joshua 1:5 NIV). Who, but God, could make and keep such a promise? Did He keep His Word to them? Yes! "So the Lord gave Israel all the land he had sworn to give their ancestors, and they took possession of it and settled there. The Lord gave them rest on every side, just as he had sworn to their ancestors. Not one of their enemies withstood them; the Lord gave all their enemies into their hands. Not one of all the Lord's good promises to Israel failed; everyone was fulfilled" (Joshua 21:43-45 NIV). And their God—is your God!

November 17

"[God] . . . will not . . . leave you without support."
Hebrews 13:5 (AMPC)

LIVING SINGLE

Colleen Alden writes, "I'm single . . . The kind of companionship I ache for . . . I don't have. This feeling drives me to seek God . . . Why am I single when I long to love and be loved? . . . Though it's pointless to use our limited understanding to critique God's plans, it's helpful to catch glimpses of what He's creating in me: Courage: to go home every night to someone who believes in me might make facing the scary parts of life easier . . . Singleness forces me to lean on God . . . to face an uncertain future without fear. Psalm 27:1 NIV says, 'The Lord is the stronghold of my life—of whom shall I be afraid?' He's my protector, provider and Savior whether I've a husband or not. Faith: Paul says, 'Be satisfied with your present circumstances . . . God . . . will not . . . leave you without support.' Do I believe He knows best even when it hurts, and I don't understand? When we've tasted loneliness past what we think we can bear . . . cry out to Jesus. He's 'close to the brokenhearted and saves those who are crushed in spirit' (Psalm 34:18 NIV). He knows what it is to long for something . . . He's longed for the affection of his loved ones for centuries. Authenticity: once in a while a man sparks my interest . . . Then a funny thing happens. The more interested I become, the more I become someone else . . . The old fears kick in. Am I pretty enough? Thin enough? Charming and talkative enough? God made me who I am, and years of being single have allowed me to learn who this woman is . . . I'd rather be single than be with someone who wants me to be someone else."

November 18

"Love never fails."
1 Corinthians 13:8 (NIV)

RELEASE LOVE

Forming a negative opinion based on appearance takes less than twenty seconds. As Thelma Wells says, "It's easy to do when someone doesn't look, sound, shake hands, or think like you. However, John says, 'Whoever does not love his brother and sister . . . cannot love God' (1 John 4:20 NIV). You cannot love God if you harbor bad feeling towards others. We're more than flesh—we're spiritual beings—and our God-given gifts, character, values, intellect, and passions are the foundation of who we are, not our height, weight, mannerisms, hair color and age. When we realize God loves us even though He doesn't like some of our attitudes and actions, it becomes easier to love others. When we realize our negative feelings towards others get in the in the way of our love for God, it becomes easier to love. And when we're in communion with our Creator asking Him to give us His eyes and heart . . . it becomes easier to love. Jesus said, 'If you only love the lovable, do you expect a pat on the back? [Even] run-of-the-mill sinners do that' (Luke 6:31 MSG). It may never be easy to love certain people, but when you make the tough choice to love them anyway, the rewards are always worth it." The Bible says, "Love never fails," and when you refuse to love you miss out on God's best. One Bible teacher says: "Don't miss out on any of it . . . God is love, and when you release love, you release God, and He becomes responsible for the outcome. Release love every moment into every situation, every prayer and every thought . . . It will strengthen . . . and cast out fear . . . it's the one solution that always works."

November 19

"Jesus wept. Then the Jews said, 'See how he loved him!'"
John 11:35-36 (NIV)

SHOWING HONEST EMOTION

Some of us are like a closed book; people never get to know what's on the inside of us. Jesus was not afraid to be vulnerable. He wept openly at the grave of His friend Lazarus. So, can you show honest emotion? Do you talk of the trophies you have won but not the tears you have shed? When you speak only of your success but fail to share what you went through to achieve it, you leave people feeling like they'll never be able to rise as high as you have. Is that what you want? Jesus was infuriated when the strong took advantage of the weak; it's why He threw the moneychangers out of the temple. Yet He wept over the people of Jerusalem because He knew what the consequences of their rejecting Him would be. Now we're not talking about displays of uncontrolled temper or dissolving into tears each time trouble comes. But unless you have the ability to show an appropriate level of empathy and transparency, you will have no credibility. The Bible says, "For everything there is a season, a time for every activity under heaven . . . A time to cry and a time to laugh. A time to grieve and a time to dance" (Ecclesiastes 3:1,4 NLT). If you are able to be tough but not tender, people may admire your achievements and comply with your instructions, but they will keep you at a distance—and you will be lonely. But it's a self-imposed loneliness brought on by your unwillingness to open up and let them in. Jesus showed honest emotion; you must too.

November 20

STOP WAITING FOR PERFECT CONDITIONS (1)

Too many of us stand on the dock waiting. We want the ship in place, the gangplank perfectly positioned, the weather right, and an engraved invitation before we're willing to launch out. It will never happen! Dreams don't move toward us; we have to move toward them. One author writes, "It's time to quit waiting for perfection, inspiration, permission, reassurance, someone to change, the right person to come along, the kids to leave home, the new administration to take over, an absence of risk, someone to discover you, a clear set of instructions, more self-confidence, or the pain to go away. Instead of saying, 'We've never done it before,' say, 'We have the opportunity to be first.' Instead of saying, 'We don't have the resources,' say, 'Necessity fuels invention.' Instead of saying, 'There's not enough time,' say, 'We'll change how we work.' Instead of saying, 'We've already tried that,' say, 'We learned from experience.' Instead of saying, 'We don't have the expertise,' say, 'Let's network with those who do.' Instead of saying, 'Our vendors and customers won't go for it,' say, 'Let's show them the opportunities.' Instead of saying, 'We don't have enough money,' say, 'Maybe there's something we can cut.' Instead of saying, 'We're understaffed,' say, 'We're a lean, hungry team.' Instead of saying, 'It'll never get any better,' say, 'We'll try one more time.' Instead of saying, 'Let somebody else deal with it,' say, 'I'm ready to learn something new.' Instead of saying, 'It's not my job,' say, 'I'll be glad to take the responsibility.' Instead of saying, 'I can't,' say, 'By God's grace I can!'"

November 21

"Faith is confidence in what we hope for."
Hebrews 11:1 (NIV)

STOP WAITING FOR PERFECT CONDITIONS (2)

Successful people do not spend the majority of their time thinking about what must be done. Instead, they spend twice as much time reflecting on what they have already accomplished, and on how they are capable of accomplishing what they set out to do. Football coach John Wooden said, "Things turn out best, for the people who make the best of the way things turn out." Pursuing a God-given dream is a bumpy ride, as every leader in the Bible found out. And only those who think right succeed. The greatest gap between successful people and unsuccessful people is the thinking gap. This is especially so when it comes to failure. Successful people see failure as a regular part of success, and they get over it. Jonah Salk, the developer of the polio vaccine, said: "As I look upon the experience of an experimentalist, everything that you do is, in a sense, succeeding. It's telling you what not to do, as well as what to do. Not infrequently, I go into the laboratory, and people would say something didn't work. And I say, 'Great, we've made a great discovery!' If you thought it was going to work, and it didn't work, that tells you as much as if it did. So my attitude is not one of pitfalls; my attitude is one of challenges and 'what is nature telling me?'" Such tenacity only comes from right thinking, and it is the hallmark of all successful people. They keep trying, keep learning, and keep moving forward. They win the battle in their minds, and then it overflows into what they do.

November 22

"He kept his eyes on the one who is invisible."
Hebrews 11:27 (NLT)

STOP WAITING FOR PERFECT CONDITIONS (3)

There is a strong relationship between our movement toward our dreams and the resources we need becoming available to us. Too often we want to see the resources or have them in hand before we start moving forward. When we do that, we have neither the resources nor the movement. We need to be like the snail that started climbing up the apple tree one cold day in February. As he inched his way upward, a worm stuck his head out from a crevice in the tree and said, "You're wasting your energy. There isn't a single apple up there." The snail kept on climbing, and replied, "No, but there will be by the time I get up there!" Over and over in Scripture, God sent people out with what seemed like little or inadequate resources. But when they got to where God wanted them to be, the resources needed to get the job done were in place waiting for them. Vision doesn't follow resources, it's the other way around. First, we have a dream, then we have to move forward. Then—and only then—do people and resources follow, and the plan God has given to us begins to fall into place. A wise man once said, "Effort only releases its reward after a person refuses to quit." People who succeed "see" what others don't. It's what keeps them moving forward. "It was by faith that Moses left the land of Egypt, not fearing the king's anger. He kept right on going because he kept his eyes on the one who is invisible."

November 23

"Faith . . . if it is not accompanied by action, is dead."
James 2:17 (NIV)

STOP WAITING FOR PERFECT CONDITIONS (4)

There's a wonderful story behind the success of Mark Victor Hansen and Jack Canfield's Chicken Soup for the Soul books. At first, they had a very difficult time getting anyone to publish the book and an equally hard time getting anybody to buy it. Then one day they got a piece of advice from a teacher called Scolastico, who told them, "If you would go every day to a very large tree and take five swings at it with a very sharp axe, eventually, no matter how large the tree, it would have to come down." So Hansen and Canfield developed what they call "the rule of five." Every day they did five specific things that would move them closer to their dream of selling books. They write: "Every day it meant having five radio interviews, or sending out five copies to editors who might review the book, or calling five network marketing companies and asking them to buy the book as a motivational tool for their sales people, or giving a seminar to at least five people and selling the book in the back of the room . . . We wrote press releases, we called in to talk shows (some at 3:00 a.m.) . . . we even got gas stations, bakeries and restaurants to sell the book. It was a lot of effort—a minimum of five things a day, every day, day in and day out —for over two years." As a result, Chicken Soup for the Soul has sold 112 million copies in forty-one languages. With tenacious faith, you too will begin to make progress toward your dream.

November 24

"He gives more grace."
James 4:6 (NKJV)

THE GRACE TO HANDLE IT

Nancy and Ed Huizinga were at church rehearsing for the Christmas program when their home burned down. It wasn't their first tragedy that year. Three months earlier when a friend, a widow with two teenagers, died of cancer, the Huizingas took her kids into their family. So when the house was destroyed it wasn't just their home they lost, it was the home of two kids who'd already lost their parents. The following week, as they sifted through the ashes, they found a slip of paper that survived the fire. On it they read these words: "Contentment: Realizing God has already provided everything we need for our present happiness." God gives you "more grace" when you walk through fiery trials. One Bible teacher says, "Our perspective changes when we catch a glimpse of the purpose of Christ. Take that away, and it's nothing more than a bitter, terrible experience. Suffering comes in many forms, but His grace is always there to carry us beyond it. I've endured a sufficient number of trials to say without hesitation that only Christ's perspective can replace resentment with rejoicing. Jesus is the central piece of suffering's puzzle. If we fit Him into place, the rest begins to make sense." Donna VanLiere writes, "When life blindsides us... and the diagnosis, abuse, foreclosure, broken marriage, death, or financial collapse brings us to our knees... grace says there's more love after infidelity, more joy after the diagnosis, and more life after financial ruin... grace is real... an indomitable gift with power to change your life. But it comes with one condition—like any gift, you have to reach out and take it."

November 25

"Jesus went . . . to a place called Gethsemane."
Matthew 26:36 (NIV)

ARE YOU IN GETHSEMANE?

The word Gethsemane means "crushed olives." And from crushed olives comes oil that heals, illuminates, and nourishes. We all have our Gethsemane. To understand and embrace yours, look at the night Christ spent there before going to the cross. "Jesus went with his disciples to a place called Gethsemane, and he said to them . . . 'My soul is overwhelmed with sorrow to the point of death. Stay here and keep watch [pray] with me.' Going a little farther, he fell with his face to the ground and prayed, 'My Father, if it is possible, may this cup be taken from me. Yet not as I will, but as you will'" (vv.36-39 NIV). Notice: (1) Gethsemane is where your prayers are not answered as you'd like them to be. God understands how you feel and He has a better plan in mind. (2) Gethsemane is where those closest to you cannot help. Like Christ's disciples, they will pray with you for a while but then grow tired and give up. At this point, you pray alone. You go on alone. (3) Gethsemane is where you feel the full weight of God's will. The Old Testament prophets spoke of "the burden of the Word of the Lord." Luke tells us that in Gethsemane, Jesus was "full of pain" and that "his sweat was like drops of blood falling to the ground" (See Luke 22:44). We used to sing in church, "All that I have, all that I am, all I shall ever be; cannot repay the love debt I owe; I surrender to Thee!" If you're finding it easier to sing than to surrender, you're in Gethsemane!

November 26

"Oh, the joys of those who are kind to the poor!"
Psalm 41:1 (NLT)

THE BLESSINGS OF THE COMPASSIONATE HEART (1)

Even in a bad economy most of us are still better off than others, and better off than we have ever been. We may lack the latest, the biggest, the finest and the fastest, but we seldom lack the necessary, right? Now God doesn't "guilt-trip" us, but He does want us to "Consider [remember, be mindful of] the poor." The Bible says, "He who shuts his ear to the cry of the poor will also cry himself and not be answered" (Proverbs 21:13 NAS). Could this be a key to your prayers getting answered? To be comfortably provided for is a blessing, but you must not forget those in need. What is God's attitude toward the poor? And what does He expect of us? "If anyone is poor among your fellow Israelites … do not be hardhearted or tightfisted toward them … and give him nothing … you will be found guilty of sin" (Deuteronomy 15:7-9 NIV). Helping others is an obligation, not an option. In Scripture the tithe took care of God's work and God's servants, but it was also to be shared with "the foreigner, the fatherless and the widow, so that they may eat … and be satisfied" (Deuteronomy 26:12 NIV). God said, "If any of your fellow Israelites become poor … unable to support themselves … help them as you would a foreigner and stranger, so they can continue to live among you" (Leviticus 25:35 NIV). The truth is, we've been called to feed, shelter and clothe the needy (See Isaiah 58:5-12). God is compassionate and generous to the poor, and He promises us His blessing for following His example.

November 27

"Those who give to the poor will lack nothing."
Proverbs 28:27 (NIV)

THE BLESSINGS OF THE COMPASSIONATE HEART (2)

When it comes to charitable giving some folks say, "That's Old Testament doctrine. What's the New Testament teaching?" Glad you asked! Jesus launched His ministry saying, "The Spirit of the Lord is on me, because he has anointed me to proclaim good news to the poor" (Luke 4:18 NIV). And it didn't stop with Jesus. The New Testament church carried out Christ's mission of mercy on a daily basis. "All the believers... shared everything they had. They sold their property and possessions and shared the money with those in need." As a result, they experienced "great joy" (Acts 2:44-46 NLT). You say, "Won't that leave me financially strapped?" No. Because of their compassion and generosity, "There was not a needy person among them" (Acts 4:34 NAS). The giver and receiver were both blessed. The rules of God's Kingdom are, "Give freely and become more wealthy; be stingy and lose everything. The generous will prosper; those who refresh others will themselves be refreshed" (Proverbs 11:24-25 NLT). It seems counterintuitive, especially when you are struggling financially, but God promises that the generous will prosper. Your giving initiates God's giving back to you. So look for someone in need, give, and watch it come back to you. The Bible says, "The Lord blesses everyone who freely gives food to the poor" (Proverbs 22:9 CEV). "Those who give to the poor will lack nothing." Try it. Next time God nudges you to show compassion and give, do it. Then when you have a need, pray, "Lord, I have honored You, now I believe You will honor me."

November 28

"They gave themselves . . . to the Lord, and then . . . to us."
2 Corinthians 8:5 (NIV)

THE BLESSINGS OF THE COMPASSIONATE HEART (3)

Have you ever encountered a homeless person, given them some money, watched them shuffle away and wondered, "Have I just paid for their next drink or drug, or rewarded laziness?" In some cases, you may be right, in other cases wrong. So what should you do? In Second Corinthians chapter eight, God gives us a plan we can understand and follow. The Macedonian church did it this way: (1) Both the well-off and the needy participated. They all gave, even those in "extreme poverty welled up in rich generosity . . . [and] gave as much as they were able, and even beyond their ability" (vv. 2-3 NIV). (2) They gave gladly, not under pressure. "Entirely on their own, they urgently pleaded with us for the privilege of sharing" (vv.3-4 NIV). (3) Their giving flowed from their devotion to Christ. "They gave themselves first to the Lord and then to us" (v.5). They didn't give to impress others, or for a tax deduction, or to get the preacher off their backs, or because they "felt bad" for the needy. No, it was a natural response to being in love with Jesus. (4) The church leaders received, oversaw and distributed their collective giving. They didn't give naively, trusting the integrity of the unknown and unproven. Their leaders handled and distributed their gifts openly, consistently, and with accountability. They knew the finances were handled honestly "in the eyes of the Lord but also in the eyes of man" (v. 21 NIV). Bottom line: you can give without loving, but you can't love without giving to those God loves.

November 29

"The time has come, he said."
Mark 1:15 (NIV)

WAIT AND PREPARE YOURSELF

The Bible says, "After John was put in prison, Jesus went into Galilee, proclaiming . . . 'The time has come . . . The kingdom of God has come near'" (vv.14-15 NIV). The average preacher takes three years to prepare for a ministry that will last thirty years or so. Jesus did the reverse. He took thirty years to prepare for a ministry that would last just over three. What's the point? The quality of your preparation determines the quality of your performance. The world's greatest pianists invest hundreds of hours into practice before a concert. That's because they know those grueling hours of preparation will allow them to give their best performance. World champion boxers don't become champions in the ring; they are merely recognized in the ring. Their "becoming" is a result of their daily routine. Something important is happening at each stage of your development. For example, God can introduce you to someone today who will play a major role in your life twenty or thirty years from now. If you're in a hurry you may not stop long enough to connect with them. Think what a loss that would be. Waiting also reveals the weakness in your plans. Haven't you looked back and said, "Thank You, Lord, for saving me from that!" Each chapter and season of life has a benefit and a product, if only you will look for it. Before Christ launched His ministry, we read: "Jesus increased in wisdom and stature, and in favour with God and man" (Luke 2:52). Jesus understood the value of timing and training. He was willing to wait and prepare Himself. You must too.

November 30

"Who are you to judge someone else's servant?"
Romans 14:4 (NIV)

STOP JUDGING OTHERS

It is always a lot easier to stand on the sidelines and take potshots than to get involved and try to help. The Bible repeatedly warns us not to criticize, compare, or condemn one another. When you judge what someone else is doing in sincere faith, you are on dangerous ground with God. "What right do you have to [judge] someone else's servants? Only their Lord can decide if they are doing right" (CEV). Since you are not their "lord," you need to exercise wisdom and restraint. Refuse to stand in judgment on those whose opinions differ from yours. Here Paul weighs in: "Why, then . . . criticize your brother's actions, why . . . try to make him look small? We shall all be judged one day, not by each other's standards or even by our own, but by the judgment of God" (vv. 10-11 PHPS). Whenever you take it upon yourself to analyze, scrutinize, and categorize one of God's children, four things happen. (1) You upset their Father. (2) You display your ego and insecurity. (3) You set the standard by which you yourself will be judged. (4) You alienate people. When you get a reputation for being critical, people will avoid you like a plague. They know that if you criticize others, you will criticize them too. The Bible says, "Help others with encouraging words; don't drag them down by finding fault" (v. 19 MSG). Someone said, "The largest room in the world is room for improvement." If you doubt that, look at the disciples Christ picked and promoted—then look in the mirror.

December 1

"Cast me not off in the time of old age."
Psalm 71:9 (KJV)

YOUR GOLDEN YEARS (1)

Sometimes we joke about getting older and say things like, "I'm thirty-nine, and holding," meaning we don't want to turn forty and be considered "old." As long as you have a dream in your heart you will never be old. The Psalmist said, "I have been young, and now am old; yet have I not seen the righteous forsaken, nor his seed begging bread" (Psalm 37:25). The main fear about aging is ending up lonely, needy, and unwanted. As the cost of living goes up and pensions go down, it's wonderful to be able to say, "My God shall supply all [my] needs" (Philippians 4:19 NKJV). Your golden years can be the greatest years of your life. All the things you wanted to do when you didn't have time are now available to you. "I wish I had more time to read." Now you can. "I wish I had more time to spend in prayer." Now you can. So many things: travel, ministry, grandchildren, hobbies, visiting friends; now you have time to enjoy them. Job 5:26 speaks of going to the grave in a full age. Judges 8:32 speaks of a good old age. Genesis 25 speaks of old men and women, full of years. You can die—full of years! That word "full" means filled to the brim and running over. How good is that? Senior citizen, God has a word for you today: "Even to your old age . . . even to gray hairs I will carry you!" (Isaiah 46:4 NKJV). Do you remember the commercial for Maxwell House coffee, "Good to the last drop"? Make that your life's motto!

December 2

"When I am old . . . Thou shalt increase my greatness, and comfort me on every side."
Psalm 71:18, 21 (KJV)

YOUR GOLDEN YEARS (2)

When do the golden years begin? With your first gray hairs? When somebody says you remind them of their father instead of their brother? If you can still sleep—dream. If you can still work—plan. Take on new projects, make new friends, learn new skills, venture into a new ministry, take a short-term mission trip, volunteer for a worthy cause. Your golden years are not to be wasted; they are to be invested. With God, there is no generation gap. "Then shall the virgin rejoice in the dance, both young men and old together" (Jeremiah 31:13). The Psalmist said, "When I am old . . . Thou shalt increase my greatness, and comfort me on every side." They say young people aren't interested in older people. Don't you believe it! Young people are looking for those with wisdom and experience. They trust them when it comes to counsel and guidance, and you can be such a person. Don't be like the old man who said, "It's not hard to tell when your youth has been spent, 'coz your get-up-and-go has got up and went." Get up and go after it! Caleb was climbing mountains and slaying giants in his last years. And Caleb's God is your God! At a hundred and twenty, Moses' eyes were not dim and his strength had not gone (See Deuteronomy 34:7). And Moses' God is your God! At seventy, Paul announced, "I am eager to come to . . . Rome . . . to preach the Good News" (Romans 1:15 NLT). And Paul's God is your God! Keep the torch burning brightly, then hand it off to the next runner before you go.

December 3

"Even to your old age... will I carry you."
Isaiah 46:4 (KJV)

YOUR GOLDEN YEARS (3)

Growing old graciously should be one of your life's goals. You don't need to fear aging or try to gloss over your uneasiness about approaching it or attempt to cover up your anxiety. The story's told of a lady buying a new hat. When she tried one on, her friend said, "My, that hat makes you look ten years younger." Quickly she put it back on the shelf and said, "I don't want that one. I'd hate to look ten years older every time I took it off!" Mother Nature and Father Time may have brought you backaches, baldness, and bifocals, but you don't have to act old. And you don't have to think old. Instead of trying to add years to your life, try adding life to your years. Instead of resenting the fact that you are getting old, think how much you would resent being denied the privilege. When asked how he felt about turning eighty, President Dwight D. Eisenhower replied, "It sure does beat the alternative!" If you are still alive, God kept you around for a reason. Find out what it is, then pour every day and every ounce of energy you've left into it. You can be "old" at twenty-five and "young" at eighty-five. You are only old when you feel old; or feel like you know all there is to know; or find yourself saying, "I'm too old to do that;" or think that tomorrow holds no promise; or take no interest in the activities of youth; or would rather talk than listen; or long for the "good old days," feeling they were the best.

December 4

"Three times a day he got down on his knees and prayed."
Daniel 6:10 (NIV)

YOUR HABITS DETERMINE YOUR FUTURE

Your habits either work for you or against you. Take any habit you practice, multiply it by 365 days, then multiply it by seventy or eighty years and you can write your own obituary. Simply stated, great people have great habits. One billionaire says, "I arrive at my office at seven a.m. It is a habit." A best-selling author says, "I get up at the same time every day. I start writing at eight a.m. and quit at four each afternoon. I do it every day. It is a habit." Jesus was a creature of habit. "And he came to Nazareth, where he had been brought up: and, as his [habit] was, he went into the synagogue on the sabbath day" (Luke 4:16). Daniel prayed three times a day. His prayer life was so predictable that his enemies used it to trap him. When measured by the same standard, how is your prayer life? Habit is a gift from God. It's said that if you can do something consistently for twenty-one days you have proven that you can do it for twenty-one years. Will you slip at times? Sure, you're only human. But once you have tasted success it's hard to be satisfied with less. Jesus said, "If you continue in My word, then you are truly My disciples" (John 8:31 NAS). Note the word "continue;" it's the secret of true greatness. Your success can be found in your daily routine. If you're serious about changing your life you must stop practicing bad habits and start instituting good ones.

December 5

"We walk by faith, not by sight."
2 Corinthians 5:7 (KJV)

STEP OUT IN FAITH AND DO IT!

It's not that you don't know this, it's that you keep forgetting it and need to be reminded of it: God can use you! Yes, the same God who worked through Moses and Esther, Deborah and Paul, works today through imperfect people like you. He can give you victory in the place of defeat and turn last year's humiliation into this year's celebration. All the great achievers in the Bible had one thing in common: they were just ordinary folks who took risks in obedience to God, believed Him, and ended up doing amazing things. Can you imagine trying to fill Moses' shoes? God had used him to dry up the Red Sea, wipe out the Egyptian army, receive the Ten Commandments on Mount Sinai, and feed millions of Israelites every day in the wilderness. How would you like to follow someone like that? The thought of it must have shaken Joshua to his core. But God reassured him: "No man shall be able to stand before you ... as I was with Moses, so I will be with you" (Joshua 1:5 NKJV). Once he heard those words, he had the confidence needed to pick up where Moses left off. The Bible says, "We walk by faith, not by sight." The devil doesn't mind you speaking words of faith as long as you don't take steps of faith. So trust God. When He says something to you it's always for a good reason. When He tells you to do something, He will give you the strength and resources to do it. What's God asking you to do? Step out in faith and do it!

December 6

"By faith the harlot Rahab did not perish."
Hebrews 11:31 (NKJV)

RAHAB (1)

For the next few days let's look at the story of Rahab the harlot. She lived in a doomed civilization. God told Abraham, "I give to you and your descendants... all the land of Canaan" (Genesis 17:8 NKJV). Since Rahab lived on the "wall" of Jericho, in a sense she lived on the "brink of doom." So do we. Today, leaders are scrambling to stop the spread of nuclear weapons because, in the wrong hands, they have the power to destroy the world. The Bible speaks of a rider on a red horse with a weapon of such destructive potential, it could remove peace from the earth (See Revelation 6:4). Could that be a nuclear device? Peter writes, "But the day of the Lord will come as a thief in the night, in which the heavens will pass away with a great noise, and the elements will melt with fervent heat; both the earth and the works that are in it will be burned up. Therefore, since all these things will be dissolved, what manner of persons ought you to be in holy conduct and godliness, looking for and hastening the coming of the day of God?" (2 Peter 3:10-12 NKJV). Should we be frightened? No, the death throes of this old order are just the birth pangs of a new one. "Nevertheless we, according to His promise, look for new heavens and a new earth in which righteousness dwells. Therefore, beloved, looking forward to these things, be diligent to be found by Him in peace, without spot and blameless" (vv. 13-14 NKJV). What God has in store for His redeemed people—is awesome!

December 7

"'I know the plans I have for you,' says the Lord. 'They are plans for good.'"
Jeremiah 29:11 (NLT)

RAHAB (2)

While everybody else was preparing to fight, she was preparing to surrender. Somehow Rahab had heard about the things God had done for Israel; how He'd turned the Red Sea to a red carpet, converted rocks into drinking fountains, made breakfast for them every morning in the wilderness, and dried up the waters of the Jordan River. Rahab may not have been wise when it came to her body, but she was wiser than everybody else in town when it came to her soul. She wasn't about to fight God, for she knew it's a fight you can't win. For her the path to victory was—surrender! And that is the right path for you too. If only you'll stop trying to "run the show" and turn your life over to Christ, He will take you to places of blessing you've always dreamed of, longed for, but didn't know how to get to. God had a great future for Rahab. He planned to make her a progenitor to King David, and also our blessed Lord Jesus. How's that for recycling? And God, who loves both the down-'n'-outer and the up-'n'-outer, will do the same for you regardless of the spiritual condition you may be in today. Read this: "For I know the plans I have for you," says the Lord. "They are plans for good and not for disaster, to give you a future and a hope. In those days when you pray, I will listen. If you look for me wholeheartedly, you will find me . . . I will end your captivity and restore your fortunes" (vv. 11-14 NLT).

December 8

"You were redeemed from the empty way of life ... with the precious blood of Christ."
1 Peter 1:18-19 (NIV)

RAHAB (3)

What she trusted in stood when what everybody else trusted in fell. What did Rahab trust in? Her morality? No, the Bible says she was a harlot. Her nationality? No, she was a Gentile, and therefore excluded from the blessings of Abraham. So what did she trust in? A scarlet cord! What a beautiful picture of the power and protection afforded us by Christ's shed blood. "You know that it was not with perishable things such as silver or gold that you were redeemed from the empty way of life handed down to you from your ancestors, but with the precious blood of Christ, a lamb without blemish or defect." Notice what the blood of Jesus has rescued you from: "The empty way of life." Do you remember when you had no interest in church because your soul was at war with God; the God who brokered peace between you and Himself? "And you, who once were alienated and enemies in your mind by wicked works, yet now He has reconciled" (Colossians 1:21 NKJV). How did it happen? "Having made peace through the blood of His cross" (v. 20 NKJV). You say, "But I still fall far short of God's standards." We all do. And God has made provision for that: "If we confess our sins, He is faithful and just to forgive us our sins and to cleanse us from all unrighteousness" (1 John 1:9 NKJV). When Joshua's troops saw the scarlet cord flying from the window of Rahab's home it meant she was accepted by God. And Christ's blood does that for you.

December 9

"If any of them go outside your house ... their blood will be on their own heads."
Joshua 2:19 (NIV)

RAHAB (4)

She was safe as long as she stayed in the house. Before conquering Jericho, Joshua sent two spies in on a reconnaissance mission. That's when they met Rahab and she befriended them. As a result, they gave her a scarlet cord to hang from her window, identifying her house as "off limits" to the invading army. But notice the instructions that were given to her: "If any of them go outside your house into the street, their blood will be on their own heads." There's a lesson here: if you're a procrastinator the lesson is, "Get into the household of faith while you still have time!" If you're drifting away from God the message is, "Don't leave the house." When it comes to the importance of staying under God's protection, here are two great Bible illustrations: (1) "You shall take a bunch of hyssop, dip it in the blood that is in the basin, and strike the lintel and the two doorposts with the blood ... And none of you shall go out of the door of his house until morning" (Exodus 12:22 NKJV). (2) "Paul said to the centurion and the soldiers, 'Unless these men stay in the ship, you cannot be saved'" (Acts 27:31 NKJV). Are you getting the message? Stay in church. Stay in God's Word. Stay in the place of prayer. Stay in the company of those who can build you up spiritually. The hour is too late and the attack is too great. "He who dwells in the secret place of the Most High shall abide under the shadow of the Almighty" (Psalm 91:1 NKJV).

December 10

"You shall go to all to whom I send you."
Jeremiah 1:7 (NKJV)

YOU'RE QUALIFIED! (1)

Jeremiah told God, "I cannot speak, for I am a youth" (v. 6 NKJV). Sound familiar? Have you been saying, "I don't have what it takes?" God told Jeremiah, "Do not say, 'I am a youth,' for you shall go to all to whom I send you, and whatever I command you, you shall speak. Do not be afraid of their faces, for I am with you" (vv. 7-8 NKJV). After an actor auditions for a part, the director conducts what are known as "callbacks." At that point the actor either gets the part or it goes to somebody else. But when an actor is experienced and well-known, sometimes the director will offer them the part without an audition. Understand this: God doesn't do auditions and callbacks! That's because He's already designed a role for you that nobody else could fill. Even if others were to study you endlessly, they still couldn't be you. When God says, "I know you by name and you have found favor with me" (Exodus 33:12 NIV), be careful about responding to any other call except the one that comes from Him. Since God designed you with all the built-in qualifications you need, you don't have to compromise your convictions, manipulate, drop names or do special favors. The part is yours! And don't be jealous or intimidated by anybody else no matter how talented they are. In God's eyes there are no other contenders; you're it! You're the only one who can fill the slot because He created it with you in mind. When you feel insecure and unqualified, remind yourself of that.

December 11

"If you're content to . . . be yourself, your life will count."
Matthew 23:12 (MSG)

YOU'RE QUALIFIED! (2)

Do you remember Rosa Parks, the black woman who refused to surrender her seat to a white man and move to the back of the bus? There was more at stake that day than just a ride home from work. By simply being herself, Rosa suddenly moved to center stage. She wasn't playing games. She was the real thing, and God shone a light on her soul that day that changed history. That's how it works. When God's light shines on your efforts, little becomes much. Jesus said, "If you're content to . . . be yourself, your life will count." Now, since God is the only One who knows when your time will come, you must be prepared. "How do I do that?" you ask. The Bible answers: "Be content with who you are . . . don't put on airs. God's . . . hand is on you; he'll promote you at the right time" (1 Peter 5:6-7 MSG). Allow the Holy Spirit to be your agent and advance man. Don't get ahead of Him. Just be faithful; when the time is right God will shine His spotlight on the next stage and assign you an even bigger role. And when the moment comes for you to stride confidently into the spotlight and fulfill your God-given role, try to remember that there's no room for self-importance and pretense. This moment calls for: (1) stripping away all lesser roles you've acted out and settled for; (2) discovering who you are and what your life is really about; (3) depending totally on God to help you give the most authentic performance of your career.

December 12

"Except the Lord build the house, they labour in vain that build it."
Psalm 127:1 (KJV)

YOU'RE QUALIFIED! (3)

In God's Kingdom, center stage is not for those who think they've got their act together and deserve public recognition. Nor is it limited to those in leadership and public ministry. It's a call to action, to you, whoever and wherever you are today. When you trust God's timing, He grooms you for bigger and better parts. But there are some things you must and must not do: (1) Don't try to make it on your own. Popular wisdom says, "Fake it till you make it," and you'll be tempted to debut in your own strength. Don't do it! If you do, you will get in the way of a much greater production. The Bible says, "Except the Lord build the house, they labour in vain that build it." Trust God, and when your moment comes, He will give you your cue. (2) Leave the shadows. Are you ready to transform "acting" into an authentic performance that reveals the real you? Fear of rejection is powerful. It takes courage to be yourself. But you gain strength from the struggle and power from the pain when you are willing to risk moving from the shadows into the light. (3) Confront your inner critic. We are all subject to the little voice within that says, "You'll never be smart enough, rich enough, pretty enough or good enough to stand in the spotlight." But when God raises you up, nobody can put you down. So remind your inner critic of God's promise: "You shall go to all to whom I send you, and whatever I command you, you shall speak" (Jeremiah 1:7 NKJV).

December 13

"Troublemakers listen to troublemakers."
Proverbs 17:4 (CEV)

GOSSIP

The moment somebody begins to gossip stop them and ask, "Why do I need to know this? Have you talked to the person you're talking about?" Wise up; people who gossip can't be trusted! The Bible says that when you listen to gossip you are a troublemaker. "Troublemakers listen to troublemakers." And Jude adds, "These are the people who divide you, people whose thoughts are only of this world" (Jude v.19 NCV). Those are serious charges. And the internet has only made the problem worse because now you can spread gossip faster and wider and remain anonymous while you are doing it. Paul speaks about those who "devour one another . . . [and your whole fellowship]" (Galatians 5:15 AMPC). He says they should be avoided and disciplined. When was the last time you saw that happen in church? Solomon said, "A gossip reveals secrets; therefore do not associate with a babbler" (Proverbs 20:19 NRSV). In other words, "keep clear of them." The quickest way to end gossip is to confront those who are spreading it. The church is not a "tell all" television show where we expose people and hang out their dirty linen for all the world to see. Quite the opposite. "Fire goes out for lack of fuel, and tensions disappear when gossip stops" (Proverbs 26:20 TLB). Jesus taught us how to deal with personal difficulties when they arise: (1) "Work it out between the two of you." (2) "If he (she) won't listen, take one or two others along." (3) "If he (she) still won't listen, tell the church [leadership]" (Matthew 18:15-17 MSG). That's Christ's way, and it must be our way too.

December 14

"The Lord ... will never leave you nor forsake you."
Deuteronomy 31:6 (NIV)

OVERCOMING THE FEAR OF LONELINESS (1)

To overcome the fear of loneliness you must: (1) Understand who you are. Let scientists argue about whether or not there was a "big bang." If there was, you were not the result of it! Nor did you descend from an amoeba in a pond. You are "fearfully and wonderfully made" (Psalm 139:14). Made "in his own image" (Genesis 1:27). God didn't assign your creation to His most powerful angels. You're a hands-on, made-to-order, one-of-a-kind product. As a redeemed child of God, you are His "handiwork, created in Christ Jesus to do good works" (Ephesians 2:10 NIV). Believe that and stand on it—regardless of your feelings or your social status. (2) Understand who God is. He calls Himself your "Heavenly Father," not just your creator and designer. Your creator and designer refer to what He does; your Father refers to who He is. "He will be called Wonderful Counselor, Mighty God, Everlasting Father, Prince of Peace" (Isaiah 9:6 NIV). These aren't His roles, they're His proper names. They are capitalized in Scripture because they are what you are to call Him! When Jesus taught us to pray, He didn't begin with "O, omnipotent, omnipresent, omniscient God." Yes, He's all of those but when it comes to us, He wants to be recognized and called "Father" (Matthew 6:9). That's how He thinks about us and wants us to think and to feel about Him. "Father" is meant to convey warmth, security, acceptance, concern, compassion, protection, assurance, provision, etc. He's your Father—when you grasp the truth of that you will begin to overcome the fear of loneliness.

December 15

"Nothing can ever separate [me] from God's love."
Romans 8:38 (NLT)

OVERCOMING THE FEAR OF LONELINESS (2)

Overcoming the fear of loneliness requires understanding God's commitment to you. His fatherhood isn't based upon mood, sentiment, or emotion; it's based on His unchanging character and reputation. Everything He is, and claims to be, stands or falls apart, depending on His faithfulness to you. "For the sake of his great name the Lord will not reject his people, because the Lord was pleased to make you his own" (1Samuel 12:22 NIV). Notice two things in this Scripture: concern for His good name and the pleasure He takes in being your Father, are why He will never turn His back on you. Your problems don't mean that God is judging or disowning you. Satan would love to convince you of that. He will tell you that you've failed God, or that God has failed you in order to make you feel unworthy, hopeless, disowned by God, and abandoned. No, generations of believers have sung through their soul's dark night, "Great is thy faithfulness, O God, my father." In your circumstances and suffering, "God's loyal love couldn't have run out, his merciful love couldn't have dried up. They're created new every morning. How great your faithfulness!" (Lamentations 3:22-23 MSG). Suffering and adversity don't cancel His faithfulness, He's "the same yesterday, today, and forever" (Hebrews 13:8 NKJV). He can't love you once, and not love you always. "After you suffer for a short time, God, who gives all grace, will make everything right. He will make you strong and support you and keep you from falling" (1 Peter 5:10 NCV). Today declare, "Nothing can ever separate me from God's love."

December 16

"Then David got up."
2 Samuel 12:20 (NIV)

GET UP AND GO ON WITH YOUR LIFE

David committed adultery with another man's wife, got her pregnant, then arranged to have her husband put to death in an attempt to cover it up. Then he married her and thought everything would be okay. But the child became critically ill. Desperately wanting to save the baby's life, David "fasted and spent the nights lying in sackcloth on the ground. The elders of his household stood beside him to get him up from the ground, but he refused, and he would not eat any food" (vv.16-17 NIV). In spite of all his praying, the child died. Why did God let this happen? Was it because the child deserved better parents? Or because the Bible says that to depart and be with the Lord is "far better" (See Philippians 1:23)? We don't have a clear answer. But this much we know; when you have repented of your sin and experienced God's forgiveness, you must get up and go on with your life. And that's what David did. "Then David got up from the ground . . . washed, put on lotions and changed his clothes . . . went into the house of the Lord and worshiped. Then he went to his own house, and . . . they served him food, and he ate" (v. 20 NIV). We discover three important things in this story: (1) Until you are willing to make things right with God and those you've hurt, you can't go forward with confidence. (2) Until you process your emotions in a healthy way, whether guilt or grief, you will remain stuck and forfeit the joy of what God has for you next. (3) When you've done these two things, get up and get on with your life.

December 17

"We do not know what to do, but we are looking to you for help."
2 Chronicles 20:12 (NLT)

DEALING WITH UNCERTAINTY (1)

As a leader you'll be called upon to make decisions regarding relationships, money, time, values, opportunities, and disputes. And your decisions will show up on the bottom line. There, in the clear light of day, your leadership will be judged. And there's something else you need to know; in that realm it takes longer to recognize your brilliance or stupidity, because you're forced to lead for long periods of time without the benefit of knowing if you made the right call. By the time your crop starts coming in, it's too late to change your agricultural procedure. You have to wait until the next season of planting. When it comes to leadership, uncertainty is a permanent part of all progress; it never goes away! Furthermore, uncertainty isn't an indication of poor leadership, it just underscores the need for it; it's the environment in which good leadership is most often discovered. As a leader you may think you should always know what to do but in reality, there will be few occasions when you are absolutely certain. It's why King Jehoshaphat prayed, "We do not know what to do, but we are looking to you for help." Since you'll constantly be called on to make decisions with limited information, your goal should not be to eliminate uncertainty, but to develop the ability to trust God and be courageous and clear in spite of it. It's not your job to remove uncertainty; it's your job to inspire clarity, faith and progress in the midst of it. When you can do that, you are learning to be a leader.

December 18

"The Lord your God will be with you wherever you go."
Joshua 1:9 (NIV)

DEALING WITH UNCERTAINTY (2)

When Moses passed the torch to Joshua, a lot of things had changed. For forty years Joshua had been taught to navigate and survive in a wilderness, but now it was time to enter the Promised Land. And what worked in the wilderness didn't necessarily work in the Promised Land. Can't you hear Joshua's thoughts? "I know a lot about wandering, but not much about warfare." So God told him, "Be strong and courageous... for the Lord your God will be with you wherever you go." Why would God tell Joshua to be strong and courageous? Because he must have felt anxious! Everything about his new situation reeked of uncertainty. The only thing Joshua knew for sure was that God had said, "Go." So, "Joshua commanded the... people, saying... 'Prepare... yourselves, for within three days you are to cross this Jordan... [and] possess the land" (vv.10-11 NAS). Can't you imagine the people's thoughts? Question: "But Joshua, how are we going to get across the river?" Answer: "I'm not sure, but in three days be ready to go." Question: "But Joshua, what are we going to do when we get to the other side?" Answer: "I'll tell you when we arrive. Just be ready to move out." Are you getting the picture? As a leader you will always be uncertain as to many things, especially when you go into new territory. But you can never afford to be unclear or in doubt as to your calling, your vision, and your ultimate victory. And where does such confidence come from? God's promise, "I am with you."

December 19

*"I will instruct you ... in the way you
should go; I will guide you."*
Psalm 32:8 (NKJV)

DEALING WITH UNCERTAINTY (3)

Dr. John Maxwell points out that in order to thrive in uncertain territory you must be able to do the following things: (1) Understand your certainty quotient. Think back to your last big decision that turned out right. How certain were you? Eighty percent? Fifty percent? If your best decisions are usually made at the 75 percent mark, that's your "certainty quotient." When you reach that point, it's time to stop debating and start moving. (2) Express your uncertainty with confidence. Never look at successful people and assume that single-handedly and with no hesitation, they fearlessly navigated the currents of uncertainty. No, they just understood that with each step, answers would be given. So instead of pretending to know more than you do, begin to encourage a culture of transparency that fosters the free exchange of ideas. When you don't know, just say, "I don't know, but I'll try to find out." (3) Consult others. King Solomon wrote more about seeking counsel than any other writer in the Bible. Do kings need good input? Yes, absolutely! And only those with the humility to acknowledge it ever prosper. (4) Measure your success by the scoreboard, not the playbook. Every good coach goes into the game with a plan, but he is willing to change it in order to win. Pencil in your plans but write your vision in ink! Good leaders, like good coaches, are often forced to abandon or amend some of their plans in order to deliver on the vision. The ones who do are the ones who reach their destination.

December 20

"We have seen his glory."
John 1:14 (NIV)

I MET THE MASTER FACE TO FACE

The Bible says, "The Word became flesh and made his dwelling among us. We have seen his glory, the glory of the one and only Son, who came . . . full of grace and truth." To know the Lord Jesus Christ personally is to love Him, to love Him is to serve Him, and to serve Him is to experience life's highest joy and fulfillment. An unknown author wrote the following poem about Jesus. If you know Him as your Lord and Savior it will resonate in your heart. If you don't, it's our prayer you will want to accept Him today as your Lord and Savior: "I walked life's way with an easy tread, had followed where comforts and pleasures led; until one day in a quiet place, I met the Master face to face. With station and rank and wealth for my goal, much thought for my body but none for my soul; I entered to win in life's mad race, when I met the Master face to face. I met Him, and knew Him, and blushed to see that His eyes full of sorrow were fixed on me. And I faltered and fell at His feet that day, while my castles melted and vanished away. Melted and vanished, and in their place, nought else did I see but the Master's face; And I cried aloud, 'O, make me meet, to follow the steps of Thy wounded feet.' My thought is now for the souls of men; I have lost my life to find it again; e'er since one day in a quiet place, I met the Master face to face."

December 21

"Work . . . as though you were working for the Lord."
Colossians 3:23 (NLT)

LEARN TO RESPECT AUTHORITY

Can you imagine a nation without a leader, a workplace without a boss, or an army without a general? It would be chaotic. Structure creates order; without it no progress can be made. That's why you don't park your car in the bedroom or sleep in the garage. Learn to respect those in authority over you. Honor those who have lived longer than you because they possess a wealth of knowledge. Listen to them and grow. Until you learn to take orders you will never be qualified to give them. Jesus understood this. He was the Son of God. He knew more than any other human being, yet He honored the authority of the government in power. When the Pharisees asked Him His opinion on paying taxes He answered, "Render to Caesar the things that are Caesar's, and to God the things that are God's" (Mark 12:17 NKJV). Are you speaking words of doubt about your own organization? Are you belittling those in authority over you? Stop it now! True, they are not perfect. (Perhaps that's why they can tolerate you.) If you rebel against every instruction you are given, don't complain when those around you rebel against your words and opinions. The law of reciprocity states that if you want to be treated with respect, you must respect others. That includes those you don't agree with, or even like. Jesus did. Pray, "Father, I know that respect for authority is taught in Your Word. So remind me today that my success depends upon my attitude toward those You've placed in leadership over me. As I honor them, I believe You will honor me."

December 22

"There is no condemnation for those who belong to Christ Jesus."
Romans 8:1 (NLT)

STOP CONDEMNING YOURSELF!

The word for you today is—stop condemning yourself! God says, "I, even I, am he that blotteth out thy transgressions for mine own sake, and will not remember thy sins" (Isaiah 43:25). When God says He forgets your sin and you insist on remembering it, it's like saying your standards are higher than His. That's akin to idolatry! The Bible says, "God for Christ's sake hath forgiven you" (Ephesians 4:32). In the Old Testament when someone sinned, they brought a lamb to the priest, and he would shed its blood on the altar as payment for their sin. Once that was done the record was expunged and the issue was settled. You say, "But I don't feel forgiven." Forgiveness comes by faith, not feelings. As long as you live by feelings, Satan has a weapon he can use against you at every turn. You say, "But what I did was so wrong." As long as you have not committed the unpardonable sin, whatever you have done is—pardonable. You say, "But Satan keeps bringing it up." That's because he is called the "accuser" (Revelation 12:10). But notice how you overcome Satan, the accuser: "They overcame him by the blood of the Lamb, and by the word of their testimony" (v. 11). Next time Satan accuses you, say, "I'm glad you brought that up." Then tell him what the blood of Jesus has accomplished on your behalf. If you do that he will flee. Learn from your failure, grow stronger through it, use it to bless others, move on with your life and stop condemning yourself!

December 23

"The smell of fire was not on them."
Daniel 3:27 (NKJV)

TOTAL DELIVERANCE

Deliverance is when God brings you out of a fiery trial that was meant to destroy you. Total deliverance is when, like the three Hebrew children, He brings you out without even the smell of smoke on you. You see, it's possible to be delivered but still be "damaged." You can hear it in what a person says. They speak only of the past because they stopped living at a certain point. They survived the trauma, but because they haven't dealt with it the right way, they constantly refer back to it. When they talk, part of them is still "in the fire." Now we are not talking about some "quick fix," or a "one size fits all" form of healing. Your temperament, your faith level, and the depth of your pain at the time are all determining factors in how long it takes to recover and become whole. But this much is clear: whatever was binding the three Hebrew children when they went into the fiery furnace, wasn't binding them when they came out of it. And that's what God wants to do for you too. Does that mean you're not supposed to talk about what you've been through? No, but don't talk like a victim, talk like a victor! David said: "He also brought me up out of a horrible pit (the past) ... and set my feet upon a rock (the present) ... He has put a new song in my mouth—praise to our God; many will see it and fear, and will trust in the Lord" (the future) (Psalm 40:2-3 NKJV). Your experience may be old, but your song will be new.

Christmas Eve - December 24

"The virgin will . . . give birth to a son."
Matthew 1:23 (NIV)

THE VIRGIN BIRTH

Heaven announced the birth of Jesus in these words: "The virgin will . . . give birth to a son, and . . . call him Immanuel (which means 'God with us')." Isn't it ironic that the first people to question the miracle of the virgin birth were religious leaders? The Pharisees said to Jesus, "We are not illegitimate children" (John 8:41 NIV). Their insinuation was clear and cruel. After all, Jesus couldn't point to Joseph and say, "He's My father." Understand this, Jesus had to be man in order to die, and He had to be God in order to save. You were the child of an earthly father, so you were "born in sin." But Jesus was the child of a heavenly Father, so He broke the genetic cycle of sin before He was born. In the Old Testament a sacrificial lamb had to be without blemish (birth defect) or spot (something picked up along the way). Since Jesus had neither inherited sin nor practiced sin, He qualifies as "the Lamb of God, which taketh away the sin of the world" (John 1:29). The virgin birth is true because: (a) The angel of the Lord announced it (See Matthew. 1:20). (b) Mary's husband-to-be accepted it (See Matthew 1:24). (c) Elizabeth, her cousin, received it by divine revelation (See Luke 1:41-42). (d) The story was written by a well-respected medical doctor who knew the character of all concerned: "Since I myself have carefully investigated everything from the beginning, I too decided to write an orderly account for you . . . that you may know the certainty of the things you have been taught" (Luke 1:3-4 NIV).

Christmas Day - December 25

"Now I can die in peace ... I have seen the Savior."
See Luke 2:29-30

SIMEON

The Bible says: "There was a man named Simeon who lived in Jerusalem. He was a righteous man and very devout ... and he eagerly expected the Messiah to come ... The Holy Spirit had revealed to him that he would not die until he had seen the Lord's Messiah. That day the Spirit led him to the Temple. So when Mary and Joseph came to present the baby Jesus to the Lord as the law required, Simeon was there. He took the child in his arms and praised God, saying, 'Lord, now I can die in peace ... I have seen the Savior'" (See Luke 2:25-34 NLT). The story of Simeon teaches us three important truths: (1) No matter how long it takes, if you seek the Lord you will find Him. Or better yet, He will find you and reveal Himself to you. (2) God, not you, chooses the time and the manner in which He will come to you. Simeon didn't live to see Christ's amazing three and a half years of ministry; he only saw a newborn baby in Mary's arms. But he saw God, and that was enough for him. (3) Even though he was "very devout," Simeon realized that he was ready to die only when he met the Lord and embraced Him. Some of us don't want to die until we've seen the world; Simeon didn't want to die until he had seen the Redeemer of the world. So the question you must answer is—have you met the Lord? Is He your personal Savior? Only when you have the right answer, are you ready to die.

December 26

"Now there were ... shepherds."
Luke 2:8 (NKJV)

GET DOWN ON YOUR KNEES

The Christmas story goes like this: "Now there were ... shepherds ... keeping watch over their flock by night. And behold, an angel of the Lord stood before them ... the angel said to them, 'Do not be afraid, for behold, I bring you good tidings of great joy which will be to all people. For there is born to you this day in the city of David a Savior, who is Christ the Lord. And this will be the sign to you: You will find a Babe wrapped in swaddling cloths, lying in a manger" (vv. 8–12 NKJV). Have you ever wondered why the angel talked to shepherds, a job considered to be the lowest on the social totem pole? Think about it. If he'd talked to church leaders, they'd have had to consult their doctrinal textbooks and denominational boards. If he'd appeared to celebrities, they'd have had to check and see who was watching. If he'd appeared to chief executives, they'd have had to consult their Day-Timers and spreadsheets. So he gave the greatest news story in history to those with no axe to grind, no reputation to protect, and no ladder to climb; people with humble hearts and open minds; people with simple, child-like faith. Getting the idea? Outside Bethlehem there is a church marking Jesus' birthplace. Behind the altar is a cave with a symbolic star embedded in the floor. You can enter the cave, but with one requirement: you must kneel. The door is too low to get in standing up! God still operates that way—you will find Him among the commonplace. But to experience Him, you must get down on your knees.

December 27

"Hezekiah ... spread it before the Lord."
2 Kings 19:14 (NKJV)

HOW TO HANDLE BAD NEWS (1)

The Bible says: "Hezekiah received the letter from the hand of the messengers and read it; and Hezekiah went up to the house of the Lord and spread it before the Lord. Then Hezekiah prayed before the Lord, and said: "O Lord God of Israel, the One who dwells between the cherubim, You are God, You alone ... have made heaven and earth. Incline Your ear, O Lord, and hear; open Your eyes, O Lord, and see ... save us ... that all the kingdoms of the earth may know that You are the Lord God, You alone" (vv. 14-19 NKJV). Hezekiah was in a hopeless situation. An army of 185,000 soldiers was amassed against him, planning to destroy him. But in answer to prayer, God sent an angel to wipe every one of them out. Sometimes bad news comes in the form of a letter, an e-mail, or a telephone call. It can come as the sound of screeching tires and broken glass, a lump in your breast, a court date, or a pink slip at work. Bad news knows no class lines, gender, or age. It comes to us all. So what should you do when you have a problem you can't resolve and can't escape? Do what Hezekiah did. Take it to the Lord in prayer. Spread it out before Him. But go to Him first, not last. When you do that, you honor Him as "Lord" of the situation and He will respond to you. God's promise is: "He shall call upon me, and I will answer him: I will be with him in trouble; I will deliver him, and honour him" (Psalm 91:15).

December 28

"Hezekiah ... spread it before the Lord."
2 Kings 19:14 (NKJV)

HOW TO HANDLE BAD NEWS (2)

When bad news comes don't allow it to panic you and cause you to act in haste. Stop, think rationally, and get the facts before you arrive at a conclusion or make a decision. Prayerfully ask, "Lord, what can I do about this situation?" If you can do it for yourself, God won't do it for you. The poet said, "His part we cannot do, our part He will not do." Faced with a well-armed, vastly superior force there was nothing Hezekiah could do to save himself. So he went to the house of God and spread out his need before the Lord. That's always a wise move. When you respond in faith, a crisis becomes an opportunity for God to demonstrate what He can do on your behalf. The truth is, when you've nothing left but God—you've got enough! Enough to handle the situation, enough to get through it, and enough to bounce back. Ask yourself, "Is this problem really mine?" Yes, we're supposed to bear one another's burdens (See Galatians 6:2). But you're not supposed to let everybody dump their problems on you. Sometimes in our eagerness to rescue others we get in God's way when He's dealing with them. And stop listening to round-the-clock news. If you do, you'll begin to "awfulize" and think, "Things are bad everywhere, so I guess I can't expect any better." What has God said about you, and your situation? God doesn't respond to your need; He responds to your faith! So get into the Scriptures and discover what God has to say, then stand on it.

December 29

"He ... was strengthened in faith."
Romans 4:20 (NKJV)

TRUST GOD'S WORD, NOT YOUR FEELINGS

Have you read the story of Isaac blessing his two sons when he was old, almost blind, and nearing death (See Genesis 27)? When Jacob, the younger son, wanted his older brother Esau's part of the family inheritance, which was twice as much, his mother Rebekah helped him steal it. Here's how she did it. Esau was hairy and Jacob had smooth skin. So Rebekah wrapped Jacob's arms and neck in goat hair and gave him some of Esau's clothes to wear. When Jacob went into his aging father pretending to be Esau, his father asked him to come near so that he could feel him. His father told him that he sounded like Jacob, but he felt like Esau, so he decided to trust what he felt over what he heard. As a result, he gave the birthright that was destined for his firstborn, Esau, to his second-born son, Jacob. Bottom line: he was deceived by what he felt. Now we know God was at work in all this. But the point here is, you can't always trust your feelings because they don't always line up with God's Word and they can deceive you. You say, "I got my feelings hurt so I haven't spoken to my family in over a year." Get over it! Learn to forgive. Refuse to remain offended. Practice love. If you let feelings rule your life, they will mess you up. Feelings are like spoiled children. The more you indulge them the more they will control you. You shouldn't suppress your feelings or deny them, but you must not be led by them.

December 30

"Forget not all His benefits."
Psalm 103:2 (NKJV)

KEEP YOUR SENSE OF GRATITUDE

Author Philip Yancey writes, "On my first visit to Yellowstone National Park flocks of tourists surrounded the geyser, Old Faithful, cameras trained like weapons, while a big digital clock predicted the next eruption. We were in the dining room of the inn overlooking the geyser when the clock showed one minute to go. So along with every other diner, we rushed to the window to see the big event. We 'oohed' and 'aahed' and clicked our cameras; some even applauded. But glancing back I noticed that not a single waiter or busboy even bothered to look up. Old Faithful had become so familiar that it had lost its power to impress them." So here's the question: why do we lose our sense of gratitude and begin to overlook God's goodness? For three reasons: (1) Problems. If you close one eye and hold a penny close enough to your other eye, you can actually block out the light of the sun. Getting the point? (2) Pressures. Sometimes the perks we thought would bring us pleasure end up wearing us down. (3) People. When they disappoint us we turn sour and forget all that God has done for us. What's the solution? "The [unfailing] love of the Lord never ends... Great is his faithfulness; his mercies begin afresh each morning" (Lamentations 3:22-23 NLT). God's mercies begin each morning, and your gratitude should too. Indeed, your days should be saturated in it. Continual gratitude comes from looking beyond your blessings to their unfailing source, the Lord. His love, His faithfulness and His mercy are already at work when your eyes open each day.

New Year's Eve - December 31

"Forgive one another if any of you has a grievance against someone."
Colossians 3:13 (NIV)

START THE NEW YEAR RIGHT

To start the New Year right you must let go of any old grudges that are weighing you down. Philip Yancey describes forgiveness as an unnatural act and says, "You don't find dolphins forgiving sharks for eating their playmates. It's a dog-eat-dog world . . . not a dog-forgive-dog world." Grudges come naturally when you've been hurt, whereas forgiving requires God's enabling grace. Jesus said, "If you do not forgive . . . your Father will not forgive your sin" (Matthew 6:15 NIV). Humanly speaking, there's not one single reason God should forgive your sins, yet the offenses He pardons you for every day far outweigh anything you'll ever be asked to forgive others for. By forgiving, you change the whole dynamic. You open the door of a prison where you are both prisoner and jailer, setting yourself and the other person free. Grudges not only isolate you from people who were once friends, they actually shorten your life by producing deadly enzymes that contribute to a host of physical ailments. One man told his counselor, "I wish my brother could come to my wedding, but we haven't spoken in years." The counselor asked, "How come?" Pausing, the man replied, "It sounds ridiculous now, but I don't even remember." Drifting apart is the natural result of an unforgiving spirit; forgiveness reverses the trend by restoring and healing broken relationships. It's a medical fact that forgiveness adds years to your life. As a rule, when you talk to people who've passed the eighty-year mark you find they are at peace with themselves—because they've learned to forgive and let go.

ACKNOWLEDGEMENTS

January 10	Maxwell, John C. Put Your Dream to the Test. (Nashville, Tenn.: Thomas Nelson, 2009). 148, 149.
January 16	Meyer, Joyce. New Day, New You. 366 Devotions for Enjoying Everyday Life. (Brentwood, Tenn. Faith Words, 2007).
January 26	Meyer, Joyce. New Day, New You. 366 Devotions for Enjoying Everyday Life. (Brentwood, Tenn. Faith Words, 2007).
January 30	Maxwell, Put Your Dream to the Test. 146.
February 1	Gordon, Jon. 3 Ways to Deal with Layoffs: "How to Make a Bad Situation Better." www.jongordon.com Posted February 8, 2009.
February 6	Lucado, Max. Fearless. (Nashville, TN Thomas Nelson, 2009). 74-75.
February 7	Gordon, Jon. "5 Things to Do Instead of Complain." www.jongordon.com. Posted March 1, 2010.
February 9	Words of Encouragement: Dick Mills www.cfaithdevotional.com Posted February 2, 2010. Walker, Jon. Growing With Purpose. (Zondervan, 2009). 64.
February 10	Walker, Jon. Dear Friend, I got you note. www.gracecreates.com. Posted April 14, 2010.
February 15	Ortberg, John. The Me I Want to Be. (Zondervan, 2010).
February 17	Hamlin, Rick. "On the Journey: Fear Not." www.guideposts.com. Posted February 9, 2009. Eareckson, Joni. Pearls of Great Price. (Zondervan Grand Rapids, Mich.) 2006.
February 18	Cooke, Phil. Jolt! (Thomas Nelson, Nashville TN 2011). Pg 102.
February 23	Meyer, Joyce. The Power of Simple Prayer. (FaithWords. Brentwood, TN 2007). 2, 6.
February 28	Scannell, Christy. "I Stayed." www.christianitytoday.com. Posted June 18, 2009.

March 1	Merritt, James. How to Impact and Influence Others. (Harvest House, Eugene, OR 2002). 36-37.
March 2	Merritt, James. How to Impact and Influence Others. (Harvest House, Eugene, OR 2002). 35-37.
March 15	Cooke, Phil. Jolt! (Nashville, TN: Thomas Nelson, 2011). 166, 167.
March 16	Armstrong, Kristin, Strength For the Climb: A Daily Devotional. FaithWords, Brentwood, TN 2007). 50, 52.
March 20	Blackaby, Henry T. & Richard Blackaby. Experiencing God Day-by-Day. (Nashville, Tenn.: Broadman & Holman, 1998). Jakes, T. D. Woman, Thou Art Loosed! (New York: Berkley Trade, 2004). Ortberg, John. Love Beyond Reason. (Grand Rapids, Mich.: Zondervan, 1998). Stanley, Andy. The Next Generation Leader. (Portland, Ore.: Multnomah, 2003).
March 31	Gregoire, Sheila Wray. "Parenting with Trust and Faith." ParentLife. (May, 2002).
April 1	Maxwell, John C. Put Your Dream to the Test. (Nashville, Tenn.: Thomas Nelson, 2009). 145.
April 2	Sanders, J. Oswald. A Spiritual Clinic. (Chicago, Ill.: Moody Press, 1958).
April 4	MacDonald, Gordon. Ordering Your Private World. (Nashville, Tenn.: Thomas Nelson, 1984).
April 6	Maxwell, Put Your Dream to the Test. (Nashville, Tenn. Thomas Nelson 2009). 199-200.
April 9	Walker, Jon. "A Better Place to Be." Posted January 16, 2009. www.gracecreates.com.
April 15	Shorb, Dr. Ann. A Light for My Path Weekly Devotional. (Accessed December 3, 2008). www.ccesonline.com. Jakes, T.D. 365 Days to Healing, Blessings, and Freedom. (Destiny Image, Inc. Shippensburg, PA 2009). 174.
April 24	Meyer, Joyce. The Power of Simple Prayer. (FaithWords, Brentwood TN 2007). 3.
April 26	Meyer, Joyce. The Power of Simple Prayer. . (FaithWords, Brentwood TN 2007).. 7-9.
April 28	Shorb, Dr. Ann. "The New Cookbook." Posted February 23, 2009. A Light for My Path Weekly Devotional. www.ccesonline.com.
May 7	Maxwell, John C. *Leadership Gold*. (Nashville, Tenn.: Thomas Nelson, 2008). 3-4.
May 8	Maxwell, John C. Leadership Gold. (Nashville, Tenn.: Thomas Nelson, 2008). 5-9

May 9	Maxwell, John C. Leadership Gold. (Nashville, Tenn.: Thomas Nelson, 2008). 13,14
May 12	Jakes, T.D. Power for Living. (Shippensburg, Pa. Destiny Image, 2009), 18-23.
May 30	Lucado, Max. Fearless. (Nashville, TN: Thomas Nelson, 2009). 69- 70.
May 31	Lucado, Max. Fearless. (Nashville, TN: Thomas Nelson, 2009). 72-73.
June 3	Miller, Kevin. "Is This Gossip?" Posted September 30, 2009. www.buildingchurchleaders.com. "Story about Gossip." Posted May 24, 2007. www.words4mind.blogspot.com.
June 4	Gordon, Jon. "The Power to Change." Posted October 12, 2009. www.jongordon.com. Mason, John L. Let Go of Whatever Makes You Stop. (Tulsa, OK: Insight International, 1994).
June 6	McMillan, Dr. Otis T. "Be Given to Hospitality." Accessed October 17, 2009. www.sermoncentral.com.
June 7	Eaton, Kate. "All Aboard!" Chicago Tribune. September 4, 1944, Section 17. 1, 5.
June 12	Armstrong, Kristin. Work in Progress. (Brentwood, TN: FaithWords, 2009). 183-188.
June 13	Savelle, Jerry. "Rejoice! For This is the Will of God Concerning You." Posted April 12, 2010.
June 20	Hybels, Bill. Who You Are When No One's Looking. (Westmont, IL: Intervarsity Press, 1987).
June 21	Lucado, Max. *Fearless*. (Nashville, TN: Thomas Nelson, 2009). 25-26.
June 24	Kristin. Work in Progress. (Brentwood, TN: FaithWords, 2009). 33-39.
June 27	Goleman, Daniel. Emotional Intelligence. (Random House Publishing Group – 10th anniversary edition September 2005).
June 30	Armstrong, Kristin. *Strength for the Climb: A Daily Devotional*. (Brentwood, TN: FaithWords, 2007). 92, 98, 392.
July 4	Walker, Jon. "When Regret Enters Sorrow." Accessed September 22, 2009. www.info@gracecreates.com. Walker, Jon. "Regretting Our Way Towards God." Accessed September 21, 2009. www.info@gracecreates.com.
July 5	Armstrong, Kristin. *Strength for the Climb: A Daily Devotional*. (Brentwood, TN: FaithWords, 2007). 343.

July 6	Jakes, T.D. *God's Leading Lady.* (New York: Putnam. 2002). 138-139, 142
July 8	Jakes, T.D. *Strength for Every Moment.* (Shippensburg, PA: Destiny Image, 2009). 15-31.
July 17	Lucado, Max. Fearless. (Nashville, TN: Thomas Nelson, 2009).
July 23	Lucado, Max. Fearless. (Nashville, TN: Thomas Nelson, 2009). 81.
July 24	Lucado, Max. Fearless. (Nashville, TN: Thomas Nelson, 2009). 82
July 30	Blanke, Gail. "Throw Out 50 Things: Clear the Clutter, Find Your Life." AARP Magazine. (May 2010). 43. Gordon, Jon. "Eliminate Clutter Inside and Out." Posted March 29, 2010. www.jongordon.com.
July 31	Gillmor, Verla. "Facing Failure." Accessed March 29, 2010. www.kyria.com.
August 9	Davis, Ellen F. Getting Involved with God: Rediscovering the Old Testament. (Cambridge, Mass.: Cowley Publications, 2001). 102, 103.
August 10	Davis, Ellen F. Getting Involved with God: Rediscovering the Old Testament. (Cambridge, Mass.: Cowley Publications, 2001). 102, 103.
August 13	Gordon, Jon. "How to Stay Positive When the Boss Isn't." Posted March 8, 2010. www.jongordon.com.
August 15	Franklin, Jentezen. Fear Fighters. (Lake Mary, FL: Charisma House, 2009). 111-119.
August 20	Gordon, Jon. "20 Ways to Get Mentally Tough." Accessed June 21, 2010. www.jongordon.com.
August 23	Maxwell, John C. Put Your Dream to the Test. (Nashville, TN: Thomas Nelson, 2009). 15.
August 26	Pitt, Frederick William (1859-1943). "Maker of the Universe."
August 29	Armstrong, Kristin. Work in Progress. (Brentwood, TN: FaithWords, 2009). 26-39.
August 30	Osteen, Joel. Become a Better You. (New York: The Free Press, 2007). 9-10.
September 5	Ortberg, John. The Me I Want to Be. (Grand Rapids, MI: Zondervan, 2010). 237, 241.
September 6	Lucado, Max. Fearless. (Nashville, TN: Thomas Nelson, 2009). 88.
September 8	Ortberg, John. The Me I Want to Be. (Grand Rapids, MI: Zondervan, 2010). 236.

September 9	Ortberg, John. The Me I Want to Be. (Grand Rapids, MI: Zondervan, 2010). 236-237.
September 11	Armstrong, Kristin. Work in Progress. (Brentwood, TN: FaithWords, 2009). 118-121.
September 12	Armstrong, Kristin. Work in Progress. (Brentwood, TN: FaithWords, 2009).
September 13	Ortberg, John. The Me I Want to Be. (Grand Rapids, MI: Zondervan, 2010). Pg. 224-225. Zinsser, William. On Writing Well: An Informal Guide to Writing Nonfiction. (New York: HarperCollins, 1980). 176.
September 19	Lucado, Max. Fearless. (Nashville, TN: Thomas Nelson, 2009). 83, 165-171.
September 23	Franklin, Jentezen. Fear Fighters. (Lake Mary, FL: Charisma House, 2009). 12-14.
October 1	Swindoll, Charles R. A Life Well Lived. (Nashville, TN: Thomas Nelson, 2009). 36-39.
October 2	Nightingale, Earl. "The Strangest Secret." Accessed June 5, 2008. www.simpletruthsnews.com. Mason, John. The Impossible Is Possible. (Bloomington, MN: Bethany House, 2003). 72-73.
October 3	Maxwell, John C. Put Your Dream to the Test. (Nashville, TN: Thomas Nelson, 2009). 30-31.
October 4	Maxwell, John C. Put Your Dream to the Test. (Nashville, TN: Thomas Nelson, 2009). 32-34.
October 6	Davis, Paul. "Patience: The Power of Patience—12 Tips to Patiently Possess Your Soul." Accessed April 10, 2009. www.ezinarticles.com.
October 7	Davis, Paul. "Patience: The Power of Patience—12 Tips to Patiently Possess Your Soul." Accessed April 10, 2009. www.ezinarticles.com.
October 12	Franklin, Jentezen. Fear Fighters. (Lake Mary, FL: Charisma House, 2009). 10-11.
October 16 & 17	Ortberg, John. "Start Spreading the News." Accessed July 2, 2010. www.kyria.com.
October 18	Coleman, Julie. "Perspective." Accessed June 9, 2008. www.crosswalkmail.com. Becoming: The Devotional Bible for Women. (Nashville, TN: Thomas Nelson, 2007). 405.
October 19	Osteen, Joel. Become a Better You. (New York: Free Press, 2007). 73-75.
October 20	Munroe, Myles. "Stir Up Your Gifts." Accessed July 2, 2010. www.gillistriplett.com.

October 27	Secondary Author: Anderson, Mac. "The Power of Staying the Course." Accessed June 6, 2009. www.simpletruths.com. Miller, Evan. "On Top of the World." Accessed June 4, 2009. www.guideposts.com. Mason, John. The Impossible Is Possible. (Bloomington, MN: Bethany House, 2003).. 56-57.
October 28	Blackaby, Henry, et al. Encounters with God Daily Bible. (Nashville, TN: Thomas Nelson, 2008). 290. Tada, Joni Eareckson. Pearls of Great Price: 366 Daily Devotional Readings. (Grand Rapids, MI: Zondervan, 2006).
October 29	Davis, Ron Lee. Mentoring: The Strategy of the Master. (Nashville, TN: Thomas Nelson, 1991).
October 31	Maxwell, John C. Put Your Dream to the Test. (Nashville, TN: Thomas Nelson, 2009). 17-18.
November 2	Tracy, Brian. "Eat That Frog!" Accessed March 18, 2008. news@simpletruthsnews.com.
November 3	Lucado, Max. In the Eye of the Storm. (Nashville, TN: Word Publishing, 1991).
November 7	Rogers, Adrian. "Learning to Endure. Accessed May 19, 2008. www.oneplace.com.
November 8	Swindoll, Charles R. "Why We Have Confidence in the Bible." Accessed May 19, 2008.
November 9	Swindoll, Charles R. "Why We Have Confidence in the Bible." Accessed May 19, 2008. www.oneplace.com.
November 11	Secondary Author: Meyer, Joyce. New Day, New You: 366 Devotions for Enjoying Everyday Life. (Brentwood, TN: FaithWords, 2007).
November 17	Alden, Colleen. "Lessons from Longing: Three ways I've grown during my single years." January 2005. www.todayschristianwoman.com.
November 18	Wells, Thelma. "Tough Love." Accessed May 14, 2010. www.kyria.com.

OTHER SOURCES

Canfield, Jack. The Success Principles: How to Get from Where You Are to Where You Want to Be. (New York: Collins Living, 2006). 104-105.

Franklin, Jentezen. Fear Fighters. (Lake Mary, Fla.: Charisma House, 2009). 21-65.

Hicks, Roy and Margaret. Ready or Not, Here Comes Trouble! (Tulsa, Okla.: Harrison House, 1980).

Lucado, Max. A Gentle Thunder. (Nashville, Tenn.: Word Publishing, 1995).

Lucado, Max. Just Like Jesus Devotional. (Nashville, Tenn.: W. Publishing Group, 2002). 121-122; 143-149; 165-167.

Maxwell, John. The Winning Attitude. (Nashville, Tenn.: Thomas Nelson, 1996).

Sala, Harold. Guidelines for Finding Your Way. (Uhrichville, Ohio: Barbour Publishing, 2003).. 338.

Swindoll, Charles R. Hope Again. (Nashville, Tenn.: Word Publishing, 1996). 20-22.

VanLiere, Donna. "When the Wheels Come Off." www.thehighcalling.org. Posted May 26, 2009.

Warren, Rick. The Purpose Driven Life. (Grand Rapids, Mich.: Zondervan, 2004).

Lightning Source UK Ltd.
Milton Keynes UK
UKHW020957051022
409889UK00027B/626